National Book Critics Circle Award Winner

***New York Times* Bestseller**

A *New York Times* Notable Book of the Year

A *Washington Post* Notable Nonfiction Book of the Year

A *Boston Globe* Best Book of 2016

A *Chicago Review of Books* Best Nonfiction Book of 2016

A *Globe and Mail* Best Book of the Year

A *Dallas Morning News* Top 10 of 2016

More Praise for ***White Rage***

"An extraordinarily timely and urgent call to confront the legacy of structural racism bequeathed by white anger and resentment, and to show its continuing threat to the promise of American democracy." —***The New York Times Book Review*, Editors' Choice**

"Anderson convincingly shows that African Americans' economic and social progress has historically, and sometimes ferociously, been reversed . . . *White Rage* is a sobering primer on the myriad ways African American resilience and triumph over enslavement, Jim Crow and intolerance have been relentlessly defied by the very institutions entrusted to uphold our democracy." —***The Washington Post***

"[Anderson] writes with grace and precision, smoothly condensing two centuries into this compact but powerful book. From the growth of Jim Crow segregation to the massive resistance to the Brown v. Board school desegregation decision to the current attempt to impose new voting restrictions, Anderson convincingly rebuts the narrative of our complicated, often ugly history. Much of what she details is horrible, but she writes with hope, too, ending with a call to 'take our country forward into the future, a better future.'" —***The Boston Globe***

"Anderson has shown, with her well-sourced (she has several hundred detailed footnotes) and readable book, why the fights over race and access to the perquisites of American citizenship grind on . . . *White Rage* lends perspective and insight for those of us who are willing to confront, study and learn from the present situation in this country." —***St. Louis Post-Dispatch***

"In every episode of *White Rage* Anderson amplifies and elongates this initial claim [white America's seething resistance to African Americans' sociopolitical advancements] into a striking argument about the nation's failure to recognize African Americans as full members of the citizenry. Though stretching a stand-alone essay into an extended study doesn't work very often, *White Rage* operates efficiently and elegantly, offering readers new intelligence about American experience. Following Anderson, one gains insight by accrual." —**LitHub**

"It's shocking, beautifully written, and, with white supremacy knocking on the White House door, more important than ever. Some books are great, some books are essential. *White Rage* is the latter." —**Ed Yong, *The Millions***

"Powerful . . . Like a meticulous prosecutor assembling her case, Anderson lays out a profoundly upsetting vision of an America driven to waves of reactionary white anger whenever it's confronted with black achievement." —***Bookforum***

"Bracing . . . It might all seem very conspiratorial and cloak-and-dagger, were it not also true. Reading through all the frightfully inventive ways in which America makes racial inequality a matter of law (and order) has a dizzying effect: like watching a quick-cut montage of social injustice spanning nearly half a millennium." —***The Globe and Mail***

"For readers who want to understand the sense of grievance and pain that many African Americans feel today, *White Rage* offers a clearly written and well-thought-out overview of an aspect of U.S. history with which the country is still struggling to come to terms." —***Foreign Affairs***

"Prescient . . . Provides necessary perspective on the racial conflagrations in the U.S." —***Kirkus Reviews***

"Anderson's mosaic of white outrage deserves contemplation by anyone interested in understanding U.S. race relations, past and present." —***Library Journal***

"[An] engaging, thought-provoking work . . . Anderson's clear, ardent prose detailing the undermining of America's stated ideals and democratic norms is required reading for anyone interested in the state of American social discourse." —***Booklist***

"Few historians write with the grace, clarity, and intellectual verve Carol Anderson summons in this book. We are tethered to history, and with *White Rage*, Anderson adeptly highlights both that past and the tenacious grip race holds on the present. There is a handful of writers whose work I consider indispensable. Professor Anderson is high up on that list." —**William Jelani Cobb, author of *The Substance of Hope***

"*White Rage* is a harrowing account of our national history during the century and a half since the Civil War—even more troubling for what it exposes about our present, our deep and abiding racial divide. This is necessary reading for anyone interested in understanding—and perfecting—our union." —**Natasha Trethewey, winner of the Pulitzer Prize for *Native Guard* and two-term poet laureate of the United States**

"To overcome our racial history, Americans must first learn our racial history—as it truly and painfully happened. This powerful book is the place to start." —**David Von Drehle, author of *Rise to Greatness: Abraham Lincoln and America's Most Perilous Year***

BY THE SAME AUTHOR

Bourgeois Radicals: The NAACP and the Struggle for Colonial Liberation, 1941–1960

Eyes off the Prize: The United Nations and the African American Struggle for Human Rights, 1944–1955

WHITE RAGE

The Unspoken Truth of Our Racial Divide

Carol Anderson

B L O O M S B U R Y
NEW YORK • LONDON • OXFORD • NEW DELHI • SYDNEY

Bloomsbury USA
An imprint of Bloomsbury Publishing Plc

1385 Broadway
New York, NY
10018
USA

50 Bedford Square
London
WC1B 3DP
UK

www.bloomsbury.com

First published 2016
This paperback edition 2017

ISBN: HB: 978-1-63286-412-3
ePub: 978-1-63286-414-7
PB: 978-1-63286-413-0

Library of Congress Cataloging-in-Publication Data is available.

18 20 19 17

Typeset by RefineCatch Limited, Bungay, Suffolk
Printed and bound in the U.S.A. by Berryville Graphics Inc., Berryville, Virginia

To Those Who Aspired and Paid the Price

Contents

Prologue

Kindling

Although I first wrote about "white rage" in a *Washington Post* op-ed following the killing of Michael Brown and the subsequent uprising in Ferguson, Missouri, the concept started to germinate much earlier.[1] It was in the wake of another death at the hands of police: that of Amadou Diallo, a West African immigrant, who, stepping out of his apartment building in New York City, was mowed down in a hail of NYPD bullets on February 4, 1999.[2]

Though the killing was horrific enough—forty-one bullets were fired, nineteen of which hit their target—what left me truly stunned was the clinical, antiseptic policy rationale espoused by New York City mayor Rudy Giuliani. On the news show *Nightline*, the mayor, virtually ignoring Diallo's death, glibly and confidently spouted one statistic after the next to demonstrate how the NYPD was the "most restrained and best behaved police department you could imagine." He touted policies that had reduced crime in New York and dismissed African Americans' concerns about racial profiling, stop-and-frisk, and police brutality as unfounded. If the NYPD weren't in those poorer neighborhoods, he asserted, the police would be accused of caring only about the affluent. Giuliani then countered that the real issue was the "community's racism against the police" and unwillingness to take responsibility for the issues plaguing their neighborhoods.[3]

But restrained and behaved police don't fire forty-one bullets at an unarmed man. Moreover, New York's aggressive law enforcement policy appeared to expend most of its energy on the groups bringing the smallest yield of criminal activity. In 1999, blacks and Hispanics, who made up 50 percent of New York City's population, accounted for 84 percent of those stopped and frisked by the NYPD; while the majority of illegal drugs and weapons were found on the relatively small number of whites detained by police.[4]

There obviously was so much more going on here with Amadou Diallo's death than was actually being discussed throughout the media, more than Giuliani was letting on, and more than even the outraged discussions in the beauty shops and barbershops managed to pinpoint.[5] Only I didn't know what to call it, what to name the unsettling and disturbing performance by Giuliani that I had just witnessed.

Fifteen years later, I experienced that same feeling, although the circumstances this time were somewhat different. In August 2014, Ferguson, Missouri, went up in flames, and commentators throughout the print and digital media served up variations of the same story: African Americans, angered by the police killing of an unarmed black teen, were taking out their frustration in unproductive and predictable ways—rampaging, burning, and looting.

Framing the discussion—dominating it, in fact—was an overwhelming focus on black rage. Op-eds and news commentators debated whether Michael Brown was surrendering to or assaulting a police officer when six bullets took him down. They wrangled over whether Brown was really an innocent eighteen-year-old college student or a "thug" who had just committed a strong-arm robbery. The operative question seemed to be whether African Americans were justified in their rage, even if that rage manifested itself in the most destructive, nonsensical ways. Again and again, across America's ideological spectrum, from Fox News to MSNBC, the issue was framed in terms of black rage, which, it seemed to me, entirely missed the point.

I had previously lived in Missouri and had seen the subtle but powerful ways that public policy had systematically undercut democracy in the state. When, for example, the *Brown v. Board of Education* (1954) decision came down, the state immediately declared that all its schools would be integrated, only to announce that it would leave it up to the local districts to implement the Supreme Court decision. Movement was glacial. It took another generation of black parents fighting all the way up to the U.S. Supreme Court in search of some relief.[6] In the final analysis, however, Missouri's schools remained separate and unequal. Thus, in the twenty-first century, Michael Brown's school district had been on probation for fifteen years, annually accruing only 10 out of 140 points on the state's accreditation scale.[7] It was the same with policing, housing, voting, and employment, all of which carried the undercurrents of racial inequality—even after the end of slavery, the triumphs of the Civil Rights Movement, and the election of Barack Obama to the presidency.[8] The policies in Missouri were articulated as coolly and analytically as were Giuliani's in New York.

That led to an epiphany: What was really at work here was *white* rage. With so much attention focused on the flames, everyone had ignored the logs, the kindling. In some ways, it is easy to see why. White rage is not about visible violence, but rather it works its way through the courts, the legislatures, and a range of government bureaucracies. It wreaks havoc subtly, almost imperceptibly. Too imperceptibly, certainly, for a nation consistently drawn to the spectacular—to what it can *see*. It's not the Klan. White rage doesn't have to wear sheets, burn crosses, or take to the streets. Working the halls of power, it can achieve its ends far more effectively, far more destructively. In my *Washington Post* op-ed, therefore, I set out to make white rage visible, to blow graphite onto that hidden fingerprint and trace its historic movements over the past 150 years.

The trigger for white rage, inevitably, is black advancement. It is not the mere presence of black people that is the problem; rather, it is blackness with ambition, with drive, with purpose, with aspirations, and with demands for full and equal citizenship. It is blackness that refuses to accept subjugation, to give up. A formidable array of policy assaults and legal contortions has consistently punished black resilience, black resolve.[9]

And all the while, white rage manages to maintain not only the upper hand but also, apparently, the moral high ground. It's Giuliani chastising black people to fix the problems in their own neighborhoods instead of always scapegoating the police. It's the endless narratives about a culture of black poverty that devalues education, hard work, family, and ambition. It's a mantra told so often that some African Americans themselves have come to believe it. Few even think anymore to question the stories, the "studies" of black fathers abandoning their children, of rampant drug use in black neighborhoods, of African American children hating education because school is "acting white"—all of which have been disproved but remain foundational in American lore.[10]

The truth is that enslaved Africans plotted and worked—hard—with some even fighting in the Union army for their freedom and citizenship. After the Civil War, they took what little they had and built schools, worked the land to establish their economic independence, and searched desperately to bring their families, separated by slavery, back together. That drive, initiative, and resolve, however, was met with the Black Codes, with army troops throwing them off their promised forty acres, and then with a slew of Supreme Court decisions eviscerating the Thirteenth, Fourteenth, and Fifteenth Amendments.

The truth is that when World War I provided the opportunity in the North for blacks to get jobs with unheard-of pay scales and, better yet, the chance for their children to finally have good schools, African Americans fled the oppressive conditions in the South. White authorities stopped the trains, arresting people whose only crime was leaving the state. They banned a nationally distributed newspaper, jailed people for carrying poetry, and instituted another form of slavery under the ruse of federal law. Not the First Amendment, the right to travel, nor even the basic laws of capitalism were any match.

The truth is that opposition to black advancement is not just a Southern phenomenon. In the North, it has been just as intense, just as determined, and in some ways just as destructive. When, during the Great Migration, African Americans moved into the cities, ready to work hard for decent housing and good schools, they were locked down in uninhabitable slums. To try to break out of that squalor with a college degree or in a highly respected profession only intensified the response: Perjured testimony was transmuted into truth; a future Nuremberg judge ran roughshod over state law; and even the bitterest newspaper rivals saw fit to join together when it came to upholding a lie.

The truth is that when the *Brown v. Board of Education* decision came down in 1954 and black children finally had a chance at a decent education, white authorities didn't see children striving for quality schools and an opportunity to fully contribute to society; they saw only a threat and acted accordingly, shutting down schools, diverting public money into private coffers, leaving millions of citizens in educational rot, willing even to undermine national security in the midst of a major crisis—all to ensure that blacks did not advance.

The truth is that the hard-fought victories of the Civil Rights Movement caused a reaction that stripped *Brown* of its power, severed the jugular of the Voting Rights Act, closed off access to higher education, poured crack cocaine into the inner cities, and locked up more black men proportionally than even apartheid-era South Africa.

The truth is that, despite all this, a black man was elected president of the United States: the ultimate advancement, and thus the ultimate affront. Perhaps not surprisingly, voting rights were severely curtailed, the federal government was shut down, and more than once the Office of the President was shockingly, openly, and publicly disrespected by other elected officials. And as the judicial system in state after state turned free those who had decided a neighborhood's "safety" meant killing first and asking questions later, a very real warning was sent that black lives don't matter.

The truth is, white rage has undermined democracy, warped the Constitution, weakened the nation's ability to compete economically, squandered billions of dollars on baseless incarceration, rendered an entire region sick, poor, and woefully undereducated, and left cities nothing less than decimated. All this havoc has been wreaked simply because African Americans wanted to work, get an education, live in decent communities, raise their families, and vote. Because they were unwilling to take no for an answer.

Thus, these seemingly isolated episodes reaching back to the nineteenth century and carrying forward to the twenty-first, once fitted together like pieces in a mosaic, reveal a portrait of a nation: one that is the unspoken truth of our racial divide.

One

Reconstructing Reconstruction

James Madison called it America's "original sin."[1] Chattel slavery. Its horrors, Thomas Jefferson prophesied, would bring down a wrath of biblical proportions.[2] "Indeed," Jefferson wrote, "I tremble for my country when I reflect that God is just: that his justice cannot sleep forever."[3]

In 1861, the day of reckoning came. The Southern states' determination to establish "their independent slave republic" led to four years of war, 1.5 million casualties, including at least 620,000 deaths, and 20 percent of Southern white males wiped off the face of the earth.[4]

In his second inaugural address, in 1865, Abraham Lincoln agonized that the carnage of this war was God's punishment for "all the wealth piled by the bondsman's 250 years of unrequited toil."[5] Over time the road to atonement revealed itself: In addition to civil war, there would be the Emancipation Proclamation, three separate constitutional amendments—one that abolished slavery, another that defined citizenship, and the other that protected the right to vote—and, finally, the Freedmen's Bureau, with its mandate to provide land and education. Redemption for the country's "sin," therefore, would require not just the end of slavery but also the recognition of full citizenship for African Americans, the right to vote, an economic basis to ensure freedom, and high-quality schools to break the generational chains of enforced ignorance and subjugation.

America was at the crossroads between its slaveholding past and the possibility of a truly inclusive, vibrant democracy. The four-year war, played out on battlefield after battlefield on an unimaginable scale, had left the United States reeling. Beyond the enormous loss of life to contend with, more than one million disabled ex-soldiers were adrift, not to mention the widows seeking support from a rickety and virtually nonexistent veterans' pension system.[6] The mangled sinews of commerce only added to the despair, with railroad tracks torn apart; fields fallow, hardened, and barren; and bridges that had once defied the physics of uncrossable rivers now destroyed. And then this: Millions of black people who had been treated as no more than mere property were now demanding their full rights of citizenship. To face these challenges and make this nation anew required a special brand of political leadership.

Could the slaughter of more than six hundred thousand men, the reduction of cities to smoldering rubble, and casualties totaling nearly 5 percent of the U.S. population provoke America's come-to-Jesus moment? Could white Americans override "the continuing repugnance, even dread" of living among black people as equals, as citizens and not property?[7] In the process of rebuilding after the Civil War, would political leaders have the clarity, humanity, and resolve to move the United States away from the racialized policies that had brought the nation to the edge of apocalypse?

Initially, it appeared so. Even before the war ended, in late 1863 and early 1864, Representative James M. Ashley (R-OH) and Senator John Henderson (D-MO) introduced in Congress a constitutional amendment abolishing slavery. The Thirteenth Amendment was, in important ways, revolutionary. Immediately, it moved responsibility for enforcement and protection of civil rights from the states to the federal government and sent a strong, powerful signal that citizens were first and foremost U.S. citizens. The Thirteenth Amendment was also a corrective and an antidote for a Constitution whose slave-owning drafters, like Thomas Jefferson, were overwhelmingly concerned with states' rights. Finally, the amendment sought to give real meaning to "we hold these truths to be self-evident" by banning not just government-sponsored but also private agreements that exposed blacks to extralegal violence and widespread discrimination in housing, education, and employment.[8] As then-congressman James A. Garfield remarked, the Thirteenth Amendment was designed to do significantly more than "confer the bare privilege of not being chained."[9]

That momentum toward real freedom and democracy, however, soon enough hit a wall—one that would be more than any statesman was equipped to overcome. Indeed, for all the saintedness of his legacy as the Great Emancipator, Lincoln himself had neither the clarity, the humanity, nor the resolve necessary to fix what was so fundamentally broken. Nor did his successor. And as Reconstruction wore on, the U.S. Supreme Court also stepped in to halt the progress that so many had hoped and worked for.

Lincoln had shown his hand early in the war. Heavily influenced by two of his intellectual heroes—Thomas Jefferson, who advocated expulsion of blacks from the United States in order to save the nation; and Kentuckian Henry Clay, who had established the American Colonization Society, which had moved thousands of free blacks into what is now Liberia—Lincoln soon laid out his own resettlement plans. He had selected Chiriquí, a resource-poor area in what is now Panama, to be the new home for millions of African Americans. Lincoln just had to convince them to leave. In August 1862, he lectured five black leaders whom he had summoned to the White House that it was their duty, given what their people had done to the United States, to accept the exodus to South America, telling them, "But for your race among us there could not be war."[10] As to just how and why "your race" came to be "among us," Lincoln conveniently ignored. His framing of the issue not only absolved plantation owners and their political allies of responsibility for launching this war, but it also signaled the power of racism over patriotism. Lincoln's anger in 1862 was directed at blacks who fully supported the Union and did not want to leave the United States of America. Many, indeed, would exclaim that, despite slavery and enforced poverty, "We will work, pray, live, and, if need be, die for the Union."[11] Nevertheless, he cast *them* as the enemy for wickedly dividing "us" instead of defining as traitors those who had fired on Fort Sumter and worked feverishly to get the British and French to join in the attack to destroy the United States.[12]

From this perspective flowed Lincoln's lack of clarity about the purpose and cause of the war. While the president, and then his successor, Andrew Johnson, insisted that the past four years had been all about preserving the Union, the Confederacy operated under no such illusions. Confederate States of America (CSA) vice president Alexander H. Stephens remarked, "What did we go to war for, but to protect our property?"[13] This was a war about slavery. About a region's determination to keep millions of black people in bondage from generation to generation. Mississippi's Articles of Secession stated unequivocally, "Our position is thoroughly identified with the institution of slavery . . . Its labor supplies the product which constitutes by far the largest and most important portions of commerce of the earth."[14] In fact, two thirds of the wealthiest Americans at the time "lived in the slaveholding South."[15] Eighty-one percent of South Carolina's wealth was directly tied to owning human beings.[16] It is no wonder, then, that South Carolina was willing to do whatever it took, including firing the first shot in the bloodiest war in U.S. history, to be free from Washington, which had stopped the spread of slavery to the West, refused to enforce the Fugitive Slave Act, and, with the admission of new free-soil states to the Union prior to 1861, set up the numerical domination of the South in Congress. When the Confederacy declared that the "first duty of the Southern states" was "self-preservation," what it meant was the preservation of slavery.[17]

To cast the war as something else, as Lincoln did, to shroud that hard, cold reality under the cloak of "preserving the Union" would not and could not address the root causes of the war and the toll that centuries of slavery had wrought. And that failure of clarity led to a failure of humanity. Frederick Douglass later charged that in "the hurry and confusion of the hour, and the eagerness to have the Union restored, there was more care for the sublime superstructure of the republic than for the solid foundation upon which it alone could be upheld"—the full rights of the formerly enslaved people.[18]

Millions of enslaved people and their ancestors had built the enormous wealth of the United States; indeed, in 1860, 80 percent of the nation's gross national product was tied to slavery.[19] Yet, in return for nearly 250 years of toil, African Americans had received nothing but rape, whippings, murder, the dismemberment of families, and forced subjugation, illiteracy, and abject poverty. The quest to break the chains was clear. As black residents in Tennessee explained in January 1865:

> *We claim freedom, as our natural right, and ask that in harmony and co-operation with the nation at large, you should cut up by the roots the system of slavery, which is not only a wrong to us, but the source of all the evil which at present afflicts the State. For slavery, corrupt itself, corrupted nearly all, also, around it, so that it has influenced nearly all the slave States to rebel against the Federal Government, in order to set up a government of pirates under which slavery might be perpetrated.*[20]

The drive to be free meant that 179,000 soldiers, 10 percent of the Union Army (and an additional 19,000 in the Navy), were African Americans. Humanity, therefore, cried out to honor the sacrifice and heroism of tens of thousands of black men who had gallantly fought the nation's enemy. That military service had to carry with it, they believed, citizenship rights and the dignity that comes from no longer being defined as property or legally inferior.[21]

To be truly reborn this way, the United States would have had to overcome not just a Southern but also a national disdain for African Americans. In New York City, for example, during the 1863 Draft Riots:

> *Black men and black women were attacked, but the rioters singled out the men for special violence. On the waterfront, they hanged William Jones and then burned his body. White dock workers also beat and nearly drowned Charles Jackson, and they beat Jeremiah Robinson to death and threw his body in the river. Rioters also made a sport of mutilating the black men's bodies, sometimes sexually. A group of white men and boys mortally attacked black sailor William Williams—jumping on his chest, plunging a knife into him, smashing his body with stones—while a crowd of men, women, and children watched. None intervened, and when the mob was done with Williams, they cheered, pledging "vengeance on every nigger in New York."*[22]

This violence was simply the most overt, virulent expression of a stream of anti-black sentiment that conscribed the lives of both the free and the enslaved. Every state admitted to the Union since 1819, starting with Maine, embedded in their constitutions discrimination against blacks, especially the denial of the right to vote. In addition, only Massachusetts did not exclude African Americans from juries; and many states, from California to Ohio, prohibited blacks from testifying in court against someone who was white.[23]

The glint of promise that had come as the war ended required an absolute resolve to do what it would take to recognize four million newly emancipated people as people, as citizens. A key element was ensuring that the rebels would not and could not assume power in the newly reconstructed United States of America. Yet, as the Confederacy's defeat loomed near, Lincoln had already signaled he would go easy on the rebel leaders. His plan for rebuilding the nation required only that the secessionist states adopt the Thirteenth Amendment and have 10 percent of eligible voters (white propertied males) swear loyalty to the United States. That was it. Under Lincoln's plan, 90 percent of the power in a state could still openly dream of full-blown insurrection and consider themselves anything but loyal to the United States of America.

As one South Carolinian explained in 1865, the Yankees had left him "one inestimable privilege . . . and that was to hate 'em." "I get up at half past four in the morning," he said, "and sit up till twelve midnight, to hate 'em."[24] *The Liberator* reported that in South Carolina, "there are very many who . . . do not disguise the . . . undiminished hatred of the Union."[25] The visceral contempt, however, extended far beyond the Yankees to encompass the formerly enslaved. One official stationed in the now-defeated South noted, "Wherever I go—the street, the shop, the house, or the steamboat—I hear the people talk in such a way as to indicate that they are yet unable to conceive of the Negro as possessing any rights at all." He further explained how murder, rape, and robbery, in this Kafkaesque world, were not seen as crimes at all so long as whites were the perpetrators and blacks the victims. Given this poisonous atmosphere, he warned, "The people boast that when they get freedmen affairs in their own hands, to use their own classic expression, 'the niggers will catch hell.'"[26]

To stop this descent into the cauldrons of racial hate, African Americans had to have access to the ballot box. The reasoning was simple. As long as blacks were disfranchised, white politicians could continue to ignore or, even worse, trample on African Americans and suffer absolutely no electoral consequences for doing so. The moment that blacks had the vote, however, elected officials risked being ousted for spewing anti-black rhetoric and promoting racially discriminatory policies.[27] But, in 1865, that was not to be. Suffrage was a glaring, fatal omission in the president's vision for Reconstruction—although one that was consistent with the position

Lincoln had taken early in his political career when he "insist[ed] that he did not favor Negroes voting, or," for that matter, "Negroes serving on juries, or holding public office, or intermarrying with whites."[28]

"I am not," Lincoln had said, "nor ever have been, in favor of bringing about in any way the social and political equality of the white and black races."[29]

The situation only worsened with the presidency of the man who stepped in after Lincoln's assassination.[30] To be sure, during the war, Andrew Johnson, a Tennessee Democrat, had blasted the Confederate leadership and plantation owners as "traitors" who "must be punished and impoverished."[31] But his resentment was rooted in the class envy of an embittered man who had grown up achingly poor, hardscrabble, and illiterate, utterly unlike the Southern gentry who had challenged the Union. Johnson's antipathy, however, did not translate into support for black equality or the abolitionists, whom he disdained.[32] Indeed, the contempt this sometime slave owner felt for black people was palpable. Addressing a regiment of African American soldiers who had just returned from a tour of duty in October 1865, the president lectured them. "Freedom is not simply the principle to live in idleness," he chided the men. "Liberty does not mean merely to resort to the low saloons and other places of disreputable character."[33] Never mind that these were men in uniform, men who had honorably served the United States. In this president's estimation, blacks—despite years of service to the nation and a willingness to put their lives on the line (forty thousand had died during the war)—were just immoral, drunken sluggards. How, then, could the epic violence that had consumed the United States have been about the nation recognizing the very humanity and citizenship of these beings? The new president, just like Lincoln, had convinced himself instead that the Civil War was only about preserving the Union. No more. No less. And therefore, he set about stitching the rebel South back into the fabric of the nation.

First, within weeks after taking office, Johnson pardoned scores of former Confederates, ignoring Congress's 1862 Ironclad Test Oath that expressly forbade him to do so, and handed out full amnesty to thousands whom, just the year before, he had called "guerrillas and cut-throats" and "traitors . . . [who] ought to be hung." Beneficiaries of his largesse included the head of the Confederate Army, Robert E. Lee, and even CSA vice president Alexander Stephens.[34] Even more shocking, given Johnson's decades-long resentment against and vilification of the "damnable aristocracy," his generosity and forgiveness extended to the plantation owners themselves.[35]

Still, there was hope of progress. In March 1865, Congress created an organization, the Bureau of Refugees, Freedmen, and Abandoned Lands, commonly known as the Freedmen's Bureau, which had a range of responsibilities including the reallocation of abandoned Southern land to the newly emancipated. The bureau's charge was to lease forty-acre parcels that would provide economic self-sufficiency to a people who had endured hundreds of years of unpaid toil. Already, in January 1865, Union general William Tecumseh Sherman had issued Special Field Order No. 15, which, to take some of the pressure off his army as thousands of slaves eagerly fled their plantations and trailed behind his troops, "reserved coastal land in Georgia and South Carolina for black settlement." Less than a year after he issued the order, forty thousand former slaves had begun to work four hundred thousand acres of this land.[36] Then, in July of the same year, the head of the Freedmen's Bureau, General Oliver O. Howard, issued Circular 13, fully authorizing the lease of forty-acre plots from abandoned plantations to the newly freed families. "Howard was neither a great administrator nor a great man," noted W. E. B. Du Bois, "but he was a good man. He was sympathetic and humane, and tried with endless application and desperate sacrifice to do a hard, thankless duty."[37] Howard made clear that whatever amnesty President Johnson may have bestowed on Southern rebels did not "extend to . . . abandoned or confiscated property."[38]

Johnson, however, immediately rescinded Howard's order, commanding the army to throw tens of thousands of freedpeople off the land and reinstall the plantation owners.[39] While this could have come from a simple ideological aversion to land redistribution, that was not the case and, for Johnson, not the issue; *who* received it was. Beginning in 1843, when he was first elected to the U.S. Congress, and over the next nineteen years, Johnson had championed the Homestead Act, which would *give*, not lease, 160 acres in the West to citizens who were "without money"—meaning poor whites. The intended beneficiaries were clear because from 1843 through 1862, when the law was finally passed, most African Americans were not citizens and therefore, regardless of how impoverished, were ineligible.[40] Doggedly pushing back on those who argued that a land giveaway program was unfair to those who had actually saved their hard-earned dollars and purchased their plots, he made no apologies for "standing by the poor man in getting him a home that he could call his."[41] Nor was it just acreage out West that Johnson eyed. In 1864, two years after the Homestead Act passed, he advocated taking the plantation owners' land as well and distributing it to "free, industrious, and honest farmers," which again was Johnson's way of helping poor whites, whose opportunities, he felt, had been denied and whose chances had been thwarted by the enslaved and masters alike.[42] In fact, he reveled in the charge that he was "too much of the poor man's friend."[43] But even his core constituency, first impoverished under the old plantocracy and then treated as cannon fodder, became readily expendable when it seemed that the only way to keep blacks as labor without rights was to reinstate the leadership of the old Confederacy.

Johnson's rash of pardons had the desired effect. The new congressional delegations looked hauntingly like those from the Old South: CSA vice president Stephens and cabinet officers, as well as ten Confederate generals, a number of colonels, and nearly sixty Confederate Congress representatives, were ready to be ensconced, once again, in the nation's capital.[44] The reigning leaders of the Confederacy, who had rightfully expected to be tried and hung as traitors, now were not only poised to sail back into power in the federal government but also, given Johnson's amnesty, allowed to regain control of their states and, as a consequence, of the millions of newly emancipated and landless black people there. As he welcomed one "niggers will catch hell" state after the next back into the Union with no mention whatsoever of black voting rights and, thus, no political protection, he effectively laid the groundwork for mass murder.[45]

One of the president's emissaries, Carl Schurz, recoiled as he traveled throughout the South and gathered reports of African American women who had been "scalped," had their "ears cut off," or had been thrown into a river and drowned amid chants for them to swim to the "damned Yankees." Young black boys and men were routinely stabbed, clubbed, and shot. Some were even "chained to a tree and burned to death." In what can only be described as a travelogue of death, as he went from county to county, state to state, he conveyed the sickening unbearable stench of decomposing black bodies hanging from limbs, rotting in ditches, and clogging the roadways.[46] White Southerners, it was obvious, had unleashed a reign of terror and anti-black violence that had reached "staggering proportions." Many urged the president to strengthen the federal presence in the South.[47] Johnson refused, choosing instead, to "preside over . . . this slow-motioned genocide."[48] The lack of a vigorous—or, for that matter, *any*—response only further encouraged white Southerners, who recognized that they now had a friend in the White House.[49] One former cabinet member in the Confederacy "later admitted that . . . the white South was so devastated and demoralized it would have accepted almost any of the North's terms. But . . . once Johnson 'held up before us the hope of a white man's government,' it led '[us] to set aside negro suffrage' and to resist Northern plans to improve the condition of the freedmen."[50] Thus emboldened, Virginia's rebellion-tainted leaders planned to "accomplish . . . with votes what they have failed to accomplish with bayonets."[51]

Like a hydra, white supremacist regimes sprang out of Mississippi, Alabama, Georgia, and the other states of a newly resurgent South. As they drafted their new constitutions, the delegates were defiant, dismissive of any supposed federal authority, and ready to reassert and reimpose white supremacy as if the abolition of slavery and the Civil War had never happened.[52] They praised their newfound ally on Pennsylvania Avenue, who saw things, it seemed, much as they did. The delegates at Louisiana's Constitutional Conference in October 1865 were so confident in the president's support and their reclaimed power that they resolved, "We hold this to be a Government of white people, made and to be perpetuated for the exclusive benefit of the white race; and in accordance with the constant adjudication of the United States Supreme Court"—specifically, the infamous *Dred Scott* decision of 1856, wherein Chief Justice Roger B. Taney had stated explicitly that black people have "no rights which the white man is bound to respect." The Louisiana delegates concluded "that people of African descent cannot be considered as citizens of the United States."[53]

In this reconstruction of the Reconstruction, with the reassertion of *Dred Scott*, the exclusion of blacks from the ballot box, and the rescission of forty acres and a mule, African Americans now had neither citizenship, the vote, nor land. Johnson, who saw black empowerment as a nightmare, insisted, "This is . . . a country for white men, and by God, as long as I'm President, it shall be a government for white men."[54] Therefore, Louisiana's declaration that "people of African descent cannot be considered citizens of the United States" aligned perfectly with Johnson's. One Georgia plantation owner agreed as he asserted that white Southerners now had "the right and power to govern our population in our own way." And, as Louisiana emphasized, that meant "getting things back as near to slavery as possible."[55]

Mississippi showed the way. In the fall of 1865, the state passed a series of laws targeted and applicable only to African Americans (free and newly emancipated) that undercut any chance or hope for civil rights, economic independence, or even the reestablishment of families that had been ripped apart by slavery. As noted by Du Bois, the notorious Black Codes "were an astonishing affront to emancipation" and made "plain and indisputable" the "attempt on the part of the Southern states to make Negroes slaves in everything but name."[56] The codes required that blacks sign annual labor contracts with plantation, mill, or mine owners. If African Americans refused or could show no proof of gainful employment, they would be charged with vagrancy and put on the auction block, with their labor sold to the highest bidder. The supposed contract was beyond binding; it was more like a shackle, for African Americans were forbidden to seek better wages and working conditions with another employer. No matter how intolerable the working conditions, if they left the plantation, lumber camp, or mine, they would be jailed and auctioned off. They were trapped. Self-sufficiency itself was illegal, as blacks couldn't hold any other employment besides laborer or domestic (unless they had the written consent of the mayor or judge) and were also banned from hunting and fishing, and thus denied the means even to stave off hunger. More galling yet was a provision whereby black children who had been sold before the war and hadn't yet reunited with their parents were to be apprenticed off, with the former masters having the first right to their labor. Finally, the penalty for defiance, insulting gestures, and inappropriate behavior, the Black Codes made clear, was a no-holds-barred whipping.[57]

Mississippi's success in reinscribing slavery by another name was undeniable. Nine of the other former Confederate States quickly copied the Black Codes, sometimes verbatim. These laws, despite their draconian nature, were not the work of extreme secessionists. Some of the South's most respected judges, attorneys, and planters crafted the Black Codes. From the cool marble halls of the statehouses, white opposition had done its job with the mere stroke of a pen. "If you call this Freedom," wrote one black veteran, "what do you call Slavery?"[58]

Not even Union general (and future president) Ulysses S. Grant saw anything wrong. Under Florida's Black Codes, disobedience or impudence was a "form of vagrancy and a vagrant could be whipped." In Louisiana black adults had to sign labor contracts within "the first ten days of each year that committed them and their children to work on a plantation." In North Carolina "orphans were sent to work for the former masters of their families rather than allowing them to live with grandparents or other relatives." But Grant, despite all brutal evidence to the contrary, was convinced that white Southerners had adjusted well to losing the Civil War. If African Americans resisted and complained bitterly about the Black Codes, this meant only that the Freedmen's Bureau was "encouraging unrealistic expectations among the former slaves." Grant did not attribute the turmoil in the South to the incredible levels of violence unleashed on the newly freed or to the barbaric Black Codes to which they were now subject; General Howard's staff, he felt, must be the source of the problem. Bureau and federal oversight were, in Grant's mind, "unnecessary, even harmful."[59]

One Philadelphia newspaper, a hair more realistic, acknowledged the odiousness of the Black Codes. Still, the article continued, the codes were necessary. Perhaps the form they took was a touch too severe, but the Black Codes, it argued, were not about trying to reestablish slavery. The Southern states "just wanted to stop vagrancy and put an end to the undeniable evils of idleness and pauperism arising from the sudden emancipation of so many slaves." By compelling them to work, the argument went, this measure prevented the newly freed from becoming a "burden upon society." What the paper failed to recognize was that black people's willingness to work had never been the problem. Having to work for free, under back-breaking conditions and the threat of the lash, was the real issue.

Nor did Johnson's policies or the Black Codes ensure that African Americans would not be a "burden upon society." If anything, they guaranteed the opposite. Blacks were denied access to land, banned from hunting and fishing, and forbidden to work independently using skills honed and developed while enslaved, such as blacksmithing. Under such conditions, self-sufficiency could never have been achieved.

The bottom line was that black economic independence was anathema to a power structure that depended on cheap, exploitable, rightless labor and required black subordination. But instead of honing in on this fundamental reality, the Philadelphia newspaper simply bemoaned the unforeseen and unfortunate consequences of the Black Codes for whites, complaining that, since "planters refuse to pay wages at all" to blacks, due to the landowners' claims that "negroes are so lazy as not to be worth paying," there was a downward pressure on overall wages that left poor whites unable to find work that provided enough "to keep soul and body together." And yet, even when the constituency for whom Andrew Johnson swore he served got caught in the blowback of these ruthless laws, he did not lift a finger to stop it.[60]

As another article in the paper asserted, the South was in much better shape than could have been expected, and this was because of the president's policies, which were "worthy of our admiration." Johnson understood, the paper contended, that the "war was for the Union, and the Union has been restored beyond our most sanguine expectations." The president, then, was to be commended for a "job well done."[61]

Andrew Johnson could not have agreed more. His message to Congress in December 1865 had that same upbeat, triumphal cadence: The war was over. The South was repentant. New governments had been formed. The federal government, he concluded, had done what it had set out to do and done it beautifully. He had heard some rumblings about voting and civil rights for the freedpeople, but any lingering questions about rights, despite the enforcement clause in the Thirteenth Amendment, Johnson felt, were matters for the states.[62]

This congratulatory, rose-colored vision of the State of the Union ignored the brutal conditions that greeted four million people by the war's end. Johnson dismissed the numerous reports of mutilated black bodies piled up like logs, did not hear the incessant crack of the whips tearing into black flesh, and found in the draconian Black Codes that reinstalled slavery by another name nothing but progress. How stunning, too, that such a prideful, stubborn man could swallow his dignity over and over again when the states he had just welcomed back into the fold defied even the very low standards he had set to rejoin the United States of America. South Carolina ratified the Thirteenth Amendment only after the state had attached a declaration with its own series of "if, then, but" clauses nullifying any federal right to enforce the anti-slavery provision. To make its point perfectly clear, the state also refused to renounce its Articles of Secession. Louisiana and Alabama attached their own addenda negating congressional authority over the status of slavery within their borders.[63] Florida held out against ratification until nearly the bitter end, December 28, 1865, and had to do it again in 1868; Texas held out even longer (1870). Mississippi, whose governor, a Confederate general pardoned three days *after* winning the gubernatorial election, just flat out refused to ratify the amendment.[64] Indeed, such was Mississippi's obstinacy that it delayed ratification of the Thirteenth Amendment until 2013.[65] But despite at least half the old Confederacy mocking and treating contemptuously his olive branch, Johnson was pleased with what he had done. Not only had the Union been preserved, but also the ratification of the

Thirteenth Amendment, no matter how halfhearted or tarnished, meant that the existence of chattel slavery would never threaten the sanctity of the nation again. As the president surveyed all that he had accomplished, he was satisfied. He simply could not fathom that Northern Republicans, concerned about the complete deprivation of rights for freedpeople, would criticize or try to undo what he had so painstakingly stitched together.[66]

For many Northern congressmen, the Black Codes sparked a general sense of outrage. Even some Southern whites thought the codes were just a bit too audacious and precipitous. "'*We showed our hand too soon*,' a Mississippi planter conceded. 'We ought to have waited till the troops were withdrawn, and our representatives admitted to Congress; then we could have had everything our way.'"[67] He was right. Voluminous testimony about whippings, killings, and virtual slavery were all too much for Congress to stomach. The sight of unrepentant leaders of the Confederacy, such as Gettysburg General Benjamin Humphreys, now Mississippi governor, fully ensconced in state governments, as if the war had never happened, was infuriating. The smugness of Andrew Johnson—who was president, as some said, only because of John Wilkes Booth—rebuilding the nation without even the advice and counsel of the legislative branch was unacceptable. For Congress, the core issue was the newly emancipated; without any rights, without any citizenship, they would be left without any hope. They would be at the mercy of the same slavocracy that had left more than six hundred thousand dead.

If the Radical Republicans, led by Representative Thaddeus Stevens (R-PA) and Senator Charles Sumner (R-MA), sought for African Americans a sweeping agenda—land, citizenship, and the vote (and that is what made them "radical")—the majority of Congress was unwilling to go that far.[68] Moderate Republicans did believe, however, that Johnson had not gone far enough. At a bare minimum, citizenship needed to be fully acknowledged and the Freedmen's Bureau, which by law was set to shut its doors in April 1866, had to continue setting up schools for the newly freed, because at the time of emancipation, just a little more than 3 percent of four million formerly enslaved were literate. Congress, therefore, passed both the Freedmen's Bureau Bill and the Civil Rights Act of 1866, which defined as citizens all persons born in the United States, except for Native Americans. The moderates believed they had stripped out the most objectionable clauses from the legislation—the right to vote and widespread land distribution—so that President Johnson could now easily sign both bills into law.[69]

They were wrong. So venomous was Johnson's veto of the Freedmen's Bureau Bill that it left even his supporters in Congress stunned. He railed against the unconstitutionality of the legislation, given that eleven rebel states, despite their newly formed governments, were not represented in Congress. He denounced the creation of a judicial system under the Freedmen's Bureau when there were perfectly good courts already in existence in the South. He raged against the beginnings of a bloated federal bureaucracy designed to tend to the needs of "one class of people" while ignoring "our own race." He demanded to know why the government would build schools for blacks when it did not even do that for whites. Johnson further lectured that the modest land provision still in existence from Sherman's Special Field Order No. 15 was just plain wrong and set a horrible precedent. The government "never deemed itself authorized to expend the public money for the rent or purchase of homes for the thousands, not to say millions, of the white race who are honestly toiling from day to day for their subsistence," so why would it do so for the freedmen?[70]

This bill, he was convinced, was designed to set up black dependency on the federal government. And he was having none of it. Negroes, he insisted, should have the wherewithal to fend for themselves. The president, despite evidence to the contrary, concurred with his advisers that "the current condition of a freedman was 'not so bad.'"

> *His condition is not so exposed as may at first be imagined. He is in a portion of the country where his labor cannot well be spared. Competition for his services from planters, from those who are constructing or repairing railroads, or from capitalists in his vicinage, or from other States, will enable him to command almost his own terms. He also possesses a perfect right to change his place of abode, and if, therefore, he does not find in one community or State a mode of life suited to his desires, or proper remuneration for his labor, he can move to another where labor is more esteemed and better rewarded.*

Johnson insisted that the "laws that regulate supply and demand will maintain their force, and the wages of the laborer will be regulated thereby." Moreover, given these very highly favorable conditions, the president asserted, blacks could build their own schools and buy their own land instead of waiting for a handout from the government. "It is earnestly hoped that instead of wasting away, they will, by their own efforts, establish for themselves a condition of respectability and prosperity."[71]

Even as he complained bitterly that Congress would not recognize the duly elected representatives from the eleven rebel states he had welcomed back into the Union, Johnson ignored the fact that seven of those states had either refused to ratify the Thirteenth Amendment or stated that they would do so only with clauses that negated any federal authority, and ten of them had instituted the Black Codes, which strongly suggested that slavery was alive and well in the Confederate South. Like Louisiana, those states proudly trumpeted the systematic exclusion of millions of African-descended people from the government.

Similarly, while the president supposedly fretted about government intrusion into the economy, he voiced no concern whatsoever when the leaders of the Confederacy, whom he had just pardoned, used the power of the state, via the Black Codes, to derail the very market forces he touted as the cure for the post-slavery blues. Government intervention ensured that African Americans could not take their labor to the best employer; could not move "to another abode" for fear of being arrested on vagrancy charges and auctioned off; could not use their skills for anything but cleaning the plantation owners' houses, picking cotton, chopping sugarcane, or planting tobacco and rice. The laws of supply and demand, Johnson's alleged panacea, could not operate. His determination to ensure that this was "a white man's government" had undercut not only democracy but the basic tenets of capitalism as well.

That same hypocrisy was evident in Johnson's vision of landownership. While claiming that the government had never provided access to land for "hard toiling whites," Johnson simply erased the nineteen years that he had worked for the passage of the Homestead Act to ensure that his constituency was given 160 acres wrested or browbeaten from Native Americans. Meanwhile, he cringed that the formerly enslaved would lease forty acres abandoned by those whom he had once called "traitors." Perhaps this disparity in treatment reflected Johnson's wish to reward those who embodied the "good old American work ethic." The truth was much more complicated.

Mississippi's Article of Secession, for example, while extolling the enormous wealth generated from planting and picking cotton, contended that the environmental conditions were too harsh in the Magnolia State for whites to actually do that work.[72] When, as a teenager, future president of the Confederacy Jefferson Davis had refused to go to school, his father sent him into the cotton fields. But he did not last long. "After the boy spent two days stooping under the Mississippi sun, the classroom became more appealing."[73] Shortly after the war, a Philadelphia newspaper reported that "all northern men visiting" the South had one "universal complaint": "White men are as averse to labor as ever. Rich or poor, they all ignore work."[74] Similarly, Carl Schurz reported that in his conversation with a plantation owner, who was beside himself that emancipation had left him without any slaves to do the heavy lifting, the man dismissed the idea of working the land himself. "The idea that he would work with his hands as a farmer seemed to strike him as ludicrously absurd. He told me with a smile that he had never done a day's work of that kind in his life."[75] U.S. Supreme Court justice Samuel Miller was equally astounded by the "pretence . . . that the negro won't work without being compelled to do so," especially when the charge was being "made in a country and by the white people, where the negro has done all the work for four generations, and where the white man makes a boast of the fact that *he* will *not* labour."[76] Nonetheless, Johnson had absolutely no qualms about using the power of government to ensure that plantation owners and poor whites gained or regained title to millions of acres of land, whereas those who had actually labored hard in the vast fields were treated as criminals and vagrants who needed the threat of the whip in order to work.[77]

The president's concerns about a proposed judicial system where freedpeople might be able to find some justice for the violence raining down on them proved a similar Janus-faced sophistry. Johnson insisted that the existing court structure was fair, equitable, and fully functioning. Southern courts, in fact, were "racist, biased, obstructionist, and oblivious to northern opinion. Southern judges and law enforcement officials . . . looked the other way when ex-rebels committed violent crimes against blacks and white Unionists. State courts forbade testimony by blacks, making crimes against African Americans nearly impossible to prove. Black veterans of the Union army were particular targets of unpunished violence," and the pile of corpses and dismembered bodies, whose perpetrators were walking around scot-free, showed that Johnson had misrepresented what Southern courts were in fact designed to do: provide legal cover for terror.[78] A second function came into sharper focus with the ramping up of an expanded and aggressive penal system reconfigured to capitalize on the economic potential of the recently emancipated and newly imprisoned.[79] In effect, Southern courts transferred full control of black people from the plantation owner to a carceral state.[80] The instrument of re-enslavement was a brutal deployment of sheriffs, judges, and hard-labor punishment for black-only offenses such as carrying a firearm, making an insulting gesture, or stealing a pig. African Americans were then swept into the prison system to have their labor fill the coffers of the state and line the pockets of the plantation, mine, and lumber mill owners.[81]

In fact, the authors of the Black Codes crafted the South's criminal justice system to enforce these brutal new laws to extract labor under the harshest conditions and provide wholly inadequate sustenance to the convicted. Those who died working the fields or in the mines could be easily replaced by more black bodies charged with vagrancy and handed a death sentence. As the flow of convict labor poured through the system, states either built or expanded the jurisdiction of their courts to handle the surge of cases.[82] Justice, however, contrary to anything the president said, was never on the docket.

Education, as well, received the Johnson treatment, with the president voicing utter disbelief at the suggestion of the government building schools for blacks. To be sure, the South did not have a tradition of public schooling for anyone, least of all poor whites or blacks. The "planters believed that state government had no right to intervene in the education of children and, by extension, the larger social arrangement." As in most oppressive societies, those in power knew that an educated population would only upset the political and economic order. Indeed, in the antebellum South, the enslaved were actively forbidden from learning to read and write. Many paid dearly for their literacy. One man "endured three brutal whippings to conceal his pursuit" of education. "In another instance a slave by the name of Scipio was put to death for teaching a slave child how to read and spell and the child was severely beaten to make him 'forget what he had learned.'"[83]

The South's defeat had little to no effect on that power dynamic. General Howard's appointee in Louisiana warned him that whites had made clear that all that stood between them and stripping blacks of any hope of land and education was a thin line of Union troops. Then he ominously added that if the soldiers were removed, black schools would be the first thing to vanish.[84] Indeed, one Louisiana legislator, when first seeing a school opened by the Freedmen's Bureau, exclaimed, "What? For niggers?"[85] Johnson was right in line with these attitudes. If blacks wanted schools, the president was clear, they would have to build their own.

In fact, African Americans did not wait for Johnson's blessing, let alone for government support or a white benefactor. One Freedmen's Bureau official recorded, "Throughout the entire South . . . an effort is being made by the colored people to educate themselves." He identified "at least 500 schools" built, staffed, and run by black people. In Georgia, for example, by the fall of 1866, African Americans "financed entirely or in part 96 of the 123 day and evening schools." Harriet Beecher Stowe remarked, "They rushed not to the grog-shop but to the schoolroom—they cried for the spelling-book as bread, and pleaded for teachers as a necessity of life."[86]

Although many poor whites languished, refusing to attend schools built under the supposed "nigger programs" of the Freedmen's Bureau, the formerly enslaved emerged "with a fundamentally different consciousness of literacy . . . that viewed reading and writing as a contradiction of oppression."[87]

Instead of offering any support to those who embodied the self-reliance he said he valued, Johnson was blind to the herculean and impressive effort that blacks had mounted in the South, and he demanded that they do even more without any help.[88]

The Civil Rights Bill of 1866 also came under attack by the president. In vetoing the proposed legislation, Johnson raised several telling objections. He argued that blacks had to earn their citizenship, reminding Congress that African Americans had just emerged from slavery and, therefore, "should pass through a certain probation . . . before attaining the coveted prize." There was to be no born-on-American-soil-lottery, he intoned; instead, they had to "give evidence of their fitness to receive and to exercise the rights of citizens."[89] For Johnson, nearly 250 years of unpaid toil to build one of the wealthiest nations on earth did not earn citizenship. And so, by his veto, he rendered the Civil Rights Bill null and void, fearing it would "establish for the security of the colored race safeguards which go infinitely beyond any that the General Government has ever provided for the white race. In fact," he continued, "the bill [is] made to operate in favor of the colored and against the white race."[90] This, a simple injunction against discriminating against blacks, was labeled as favoritism, and that is what made the proposed legislation so patently unacceptable. The Civil Rights Bill, Johnson complained, was just the opening salvo in the Radical Republicans' efforts "to protect niggers."[91]

Congress overrode both his vetoes and hoped that there might be some way to work with the president. But in the spring and summer of 1866, the South's descent into an orgy of anti-black violence signaled the final break between Johnson and the Republicans. In New Orleans, nearly fifty African Americans were slaughtered and more than a hundred injured for meeting to discuss voting. When one of the killers, who had just bludgeoned a black man to death, was warned that "he might be punished," he scoffed. "Oh, hell! Haven't you seen the papers?" he said. "Johnson is with us!"[92] In Memphis, there was another gory bloodbath, and another round of silence from the White House.[93] In Texas, from 1865 to 1868, nearly one thousand African Americans were lynched.[94]

A woman pleaded with President Johnson "to do something about the plight of the 'poor negro . . . their masters are so angry to loose [*sic*] them that they are trying to persecute them back into slavery.'" Justice Miller was livid with Southern leaders, who sat in silence while the violence raged around them. "Show me," he demanded, "the first public address or meeting of Southern men in which the massacres of New Orleans or Memphis have been condemned." The "single truth is undenied that not a rebel or secessionist was hurt in either case, while from thirty to fifty negroes and Union white men were shot down," which removed "all doubt as to who did it and why it was done." As the black body count mounted, with justice nowhere to be found, least of all from the president of the United States, the Reconstruction era descended into nothing less than an age of violence and terror.[95]

Congress, therefore, moved to provide some level of protection, passing the Reconstruction Acts of 1867, which divided the South into five military districts and tried to put U.S. troops between a still-smoldering, vengeful rebel population and the freedpeople. Then, in response to the rise of the Ku Klux Klan and organized, terrorist violence, Congress issued the Enforcement Acts. It also passed and the states subsequently ratified the Fourteenth and Fifteenth Amendments, weaving citizenship for all those born in the United States, except Native Americans, as well as the right to vote, into the Constitution.

Johnson did everything in his power to stop constitutional recognition of black people's citizenship and voting rights, including convincing most of the Southern states not to ratify the Fourteenth Amendment and launching a breathtaking and ultimately disastrous political campaign to unseat Radical Republicans in Congress.[96] Nevertheless, despite Johnson's wild fulminations about the "Africanization" of the South and the tyranny of "negro domination," the Fourteenth Amendment was ratified on July 9, 1868, followed by the Fifteenth on February 3, 1870.[97] Congress had just created a legal structure to begin to atone for America's "original sin."

The U.S. Supreme Court, however, stepped in and succeeded where Johnson had failed. Frederick Douglass lamented that by the time the justices had finished, "in most of the Southern States, the fourteenth and fifteenth amendments are virtually nullified. The rights which they were intended to guarantee are denied and held in contempt. The citizenship granted in the fourteenth amendment is practically a mockery, and the right to vote . . . is literally stamped out in face of government."[98]

The Supreme Court justices gave the aura of being "strict constitutionalists" whose job was not to interpret or create but merely to distinguish between the rights the federal government enforced and those controlled by the states.[99] But the supposedly legally neutral interpretations had profound effects. And the court, just like Johnson, demonstrated an uncanny ability to ignore inconsistencies and to twist rules, beliefs, and values to undermine the solid progress in black people's rights that the Radical Republicans had finally managed to put in place. The court declared that the Reconstruction amendments had illegally placed the full scope of civil rights, which had once been the domain of states, under federal authority. That usurpation of power was unconstitutional because it put state governments under Washington's control, disrupted the distribution of power in the federal system, and radically altered the framework of American government.[100] The justices consistently held to this supposedly strict reading of the Constitution when it came to African Americans' rights.

Yet, this same court threw tradition and strict reading out the window in the *Santa Clara* decision. California had changed its taxation laws to no longer allow corporations to deduct debt from the amount owed to the state or municipalities. The change applied only to businesses; people, under the new law, were not affected. The Southern Pacific Railroad refused to pay its new tax bill, arguing that its rights under the equal protection clause of the Fourteenth Amendment had been violated. In hearing the case, the court became innovative and creative as it transformed corporations into "people" who could not have their Fourteenth Amendment rights trampled on by local communities.[101] So, while businesses were shielded, black Americans were most emphatically not.

The ruling that began this long, disastrous legal retreat from a rights-based society was the 1873 *Slaughterhouse Cases*. New Orleans had passed a law not only to confine butcher shops, with their blood, entrails, and inevitable disease, to a discrete section of town but also to allow only city-authorized stores to operate. The butchers went to court, pleading that their right to due process under the Fourteenth Amendment had been violated. The justices ruled that that was impossible because the amendment covered only federal citizenship rights, such as habeas corpus and the right to peaceful assembly. Everything else came under the domain of the states.[102] As a result, "citizens still had to seek protection for most of their civil rights from state governments and state courts."[103]

Even the right to vote, despite the Fifteenth Amendment, was not federally protected. In *Minor v. Happersett* (1874), Chief Justice Morrison R. Waite wrote, "The Constitution of the United States does not confer the right of suffrage upon anyone," because the vote "was not coexistent with citizenship."[104] This was reaffirmed in *United States v. Reese* (1875). In Lexington, Kentucky, a black man, William Garner, had tried to vote. The registrars, Hiram Reese and Matthew Foushee, refused to hand Garner a ballot because he had not paid a poll tax. Yet, the black man had an affidavit that the tax collector had refused to accept his payment. The registrars scoffed. With one wing of local government demanding proof of payment and the other flat out refusing to accept the funds, Garner knew his right to vote had been violated. The U.S. Supreme Court, in an 8–1 decision, disagreed. In another opinion, Waite wrote that the Fifteenth Amendment did not guarantee the right to vote but "had merely prevented the states from giving preference to one citizen over another on account of race, color, etc." To emphasize the point, Waite reiterated, the "right to vote . . . comes from the states."[105]

In quick succession, the court had undermined citizenship, due process, and the right to vote. Next was the basic right to life. In 1873, Southern Democrats, angered that African Americans had voted in a Republican government in Colfax, Louisiana, threatened to overturn the results of the recent election and install a white supremacist regime. Blacks were determined to defend their citizenship rights and occupied the symbol of democracy in Colfax, the courthouse, to ensure that the duly elected representatives, most of whom were white, could take office. That act of democratic courage resulted in an unprecedented bloodbath, even for Reconstruction.[106] Depending on the casualty estimate, between 105 and 280 African Americans were slaughtered. Their killers were then charged with violating the Enforcement Act of 1870, which Congress had passed to stop the Klan's terrorism. Chief Justice Waite, in *United States v. Cruikshank* (1876), ruled that the Enforcement Act violated states' rights. Moreover, the only recourse the federal government could take was the Fourteenth Amendment, but, he continued, that did not cover vigilantes or private acts of terror, but rather covered only those acts of violence carried out by the states. The ruling not only let mass murderers go free; it effectively removed the ability of the federal government to rein in anti-black domestic terrorism moving forward.[107]

But the rollback of rights was not over yet; next on the list were dignity and equality. In the *Civil Rights Cases* (1883), the justices ruled that the 1875 Force Act that banned discrimination in public accommodations was also unconstitutional because the Fourteenth Amendment could be enforced only by the states, not the federal government. Moreover, in a wicked one-two punch, the justices added that the Thirteenth Amendment's ban on "badges of servitude" did not extend to discrimination in public accommodations, such as in hotels, restaurants, and railcars.[108] U.S. Supreme Court justice Joseph Bradley was exasperated with African Americans consistently seeking legal redress and laws to fend off the violence, state-sponsored discrimination, legalized terror, and the reimposition of "crypto-slavery" and a "netherworld of rightlessness" that had come to define their lives after the Civil War. He barked that "there must be some stage in the progress of his elevation when he takes the rank of a mere citizen, and ceases to be the special favorite of the laws."[109] Like Andrew Johnson, Bradley saw equal treatment for black people as favoritism.

Unequal treatment, however, became the law of the land. In *Hall v. DeCuir* (1877), the justices ruled that a state could not prohibit racial segregation.[110] Then, in a series of decisions, *Strauder v. West Virginia* (1880), *Ex parte Virginia* (1880), and *Virginia v. Rives* (1880), the U.S. Supreme Court provided clear guidelines to the states on how to systematically and constitutionally exclude African Americans from juries in favor of white jurors.[111] The crowning glory was *Plessy v. Ferguson* (1896). Homer Plessy, a black man who looked white, thought his challenge to a Louisiana law that forced him to ride in the Jim Crow railcar instead of the one designated for whites would put an end to this legal descent into black subjugation. He was wrong. The justices, in an 8–1 decision, dismissed the claims that Plessy's Fourteenth Amendment rights to equal protection under the law were violated. Justice Henry Brown unequivocally stated, "If one race be inferior to the other socially, the constitution of the United States cannot put them on the same plane." And when Plessy argued that segregation violated the Thirteenth Amendment's ban against "badges of servitude," the Supreme Court shot down that argument as well, noting: "We consider the underlying fallacy of [Plessy's] argument . . . to consist in the assumption that the enforced separation of the two races stamps the colored race with a badge of inferiority. If this be so, it is not by reason of anything found in the act, but solely because the colored race chooses to put that construction upon it."[112] Despite more than a generation of irrefutable evidence of widespread racial discrimination in the aftermath of the Civil War, the court created the mythic "separate but equal" doctrine to confirm racial segregation as the law of the land. The court then followed up with a ruling in *Cumming v. Richmond County Board of Education* (1899) that even ignored *Plessy*'s separate but equal doctrine by declaring that financial exigency made it perfectly acceptable to shut down black schools while continuing to operate educational facilities for white children.[113]

Just prior to that, the court had sanctioned closing off the ballot box. In a unanimous 9–0 decision in *Williams v. Mississippi* (1898), the justices approved the use of the poll tax, which requires citizens to pay a fee—under a set of very arcane, complicated rules—to vote.[114] Although the discriminatory intent of the requirement was well known prior to the justices' ruling, the highest court in the land sanctioned this formidable barrier to the ballot box. In fact, Justice Joseph McKenna quoted extensively from the Mississippi Supreme Court's candid admission that the state convention, "restrained by the federal Constitution from discriminating against the negro race," opted instead to find a method that "discriminates against its [African Americans'] characteristics"—namely, poverty, illiteracy, and more poverty.[115]

The repercussions were harrowing for American democracy; the poll tax not only ensnared black voters but also trapped poor whites. As late as 1942, for instance, only 3 percent of the voting-age population cast a ballot in seven poll tax states.[116] Just 3 percent of an electorate in these states decided who would sit in the U.S. Senate and House of Representatives to shape federal policy. This, in turn, strengthened the years of seniority and thus the stranglehold on federal law of these officials, who accordingly rose in the ranks to assume or hold on to key leadership positions, such as chairing the Foreign Relations Committee, judiciary committees, and others.

Senator Walter George (D-GA) was proud of how states like his beloved Georgia were able to legally disfranchise millions of voters. "Why apologize or evade?" he asked. "We have been very careful to obey the letter of the Federal Constitution—but we have been very diligent in violating the spirit of such amendments and such statutes as would have a Negro to believe himself the equal of a white man."[117]

From 1873, with the *Slaughterhouse Cases*, *Cruikshank*, *Plessy*, *Williams*, and others, the U.S. Supreme Court had systematically dismantled the Thirteenth, Fourteenth, and Fifteenth Amendments and rendered the Enforcement and Force Acts dead on arrival. For strict constructionists, the court willfully ignored congressional intent and the history behind the laws and amendments. At the onset of the twentieth century, in *Giles v. Harris* (1903), Justice Oliver Wendell Holmes wrote that "the federal courts had no power, either constitutional or practical, to remedy a statewide wrong, even if perpetrated by the state or its agents."[118]

The Supreme Court thus identified states as the ultimate defenders of rights, although Southern states had repeatedly proven themselves the ultimate violators of those rights. Through antiseptic, clinical, measured language, the learned jurists had entrusted the protection of life, liberty, and the pursuit of happiness for African Americans to the very same states that bragged "this is a white man's government"; that yearned for the moment to regain control of the freedmen and then "the niggers will catch hell"; whose citizens fretted, "*We showed our hand too soon*" with the Black Codes, which allowed Mississippi and its brethren to criminalize, auction off, and whip black people; and that were determined to "get things back as close to slavery as possible." The result was not lost on African Americans. One black man from Louisiana summed it up this way: "The whole South—every state in the South—had got into the hands of the very men that had held us as slaves."[119]

So while the United States may have won the Civil War, and blacks may have tasted freedom, the white opposition that ruled from the White House and the Supreme Court all the way down through every statehouse in the South meant that real change was infinitesimal at best. To quote one historian's paraphrase of Frederick Maitland: "The slave law of the South may have been dead, but it ruled us from the grave."[120]

Two

Derailing the Great Migration

It was 1918. The United States was in the midst of a global war "to make the world safe for democracy."[1] But in Georgia, it was anything but safe for black people. In the southern part of the state near Valdosta, a white plantation owner, Hampton Smith, had become notorious for his brutal treatment of black laborers on his farm. Because his standard employee management practices included beatings, theft of wages, and whippings, he had considerable difficulty hiring anyone to willingly work his land. With fields to plow and a crop to harvest, he turned to an old trusty labor supply. Drawing on the peonage system set up after the Civil War, the planter routinely went to the local jail, paid the fine of a black person, and then had the African American work on the plantation until the debt was paid. At least that was the way it was supposed to be. But Smith, although only thirty-one years old, was already a mean, hard man. He ruthlessly worked African Americans far past the point of any debt payoff and then refused to provide any compensation for the additional work. If challenged, he would pull out his whip.[2] In May 1918, he did that to the wrong black man.

After a dispute over work, Hampton Smith gave Sidney Johnson, an African American laborer whose thirty-dollar fine the plantation owner had paid, an unforgettable and unforgivable thrashing. Within a week after the beating, Johnson took out a rifle and put two bullets into the planter's chest. Smith died instantly. White retribution was swift, indiscriminate, and merciless. In a "five days lynching orgy," at least eleven African Americans, ten of whom had absolutely nothing to do with Smith's death, were hunted down and slaughtered.[3] Perhaps none more gruesomely than Mary Turner.

A lynch mob had already snatched her husband, Hayes, strung him from a tree, and let his body rot, dangling from that limb all weekend. Eight months pregnant with two small children, whom she had to send into hiding, she was enraged that he had been killed for no good reason. Feisty, strong-willed, and stubborn, Mary Turner threatened that "if she knew the parties who were in the mob she would have warrants sworn out against them."[4] She would never get the chance. On Sunday, the lynchers came for her.

They dragged Mary to a tree, stripped her, tied her ankles together, and strung her upside down. The men ran to their cars, brought back gasoline, and began "to roast her alive." Then they saw her naked, eight-month-pregnant stomach convulsing. That only sent the mob, made up of several of Hampton Smith's brothers, as well as a clerk in the post office, an auditor for Standard Oil, a furniture salesman, and several farmers, into a deeper frenzy, as one man took out his knife and sliced away at her charred flesh until the baby, now ripped out of the womb, fell to the ground and gave two cries. Someone in the lynch party then stepped forward and smashed the child's head into the red Georgia dirt with the heel of his boot.[5]

In one form or another, this scene was repeated over and over again throughout the South, including the lack of consequences: no arrests, trials, convictions, or prison sentences for murdering black people, even in broad daylight.[6] The economic, political, and legal vulnerability meant that no one, not even an eight-month-old fetus, was safe. Blacks in southern Georgia knew it. Within two months of Mary Turner's lynching, more than five hundred had already moved away.[7] They joined more than one million African Americans who were determined to leave the stultifying air of Jim Crow and, as one group fleeing Louisiana and heading North confided to W. E. B. Du Bois, "run any risk to get where they could breathe freer."[8]

The risks they took were, indeed, great. It required an unfathomable amount of courage. It required as well a level of cunning and guile that many, consistently underestimating African Americans, didn't believe they had. The states and their supporters had erected a series of traps, sinkholes, and barriers both legal and extralegal, to contain this clearly oppressed population. Yet, like those in Mary Turner's Georgia, they plotted their exodus. Southerner and novelist Richard Wright evoked perhaps most succinctly the desperation and the determination fueling it all: "I've got to get away; I can't stay here."[9]

They would soon find out that the stories of the North as the promised land, where drive, hard work, and ambition would be rewarded regardless of color, had little to no relationship whatsoever to the actual conditions above the Mason-Dixon Line.[10] Robert S. Abbott, owner of the *Chicago Defender*, the premier black newspaper, had experienced "firsthand just how cruel the North could be" as his education and ambition translated into nothing more than years of closed doors and poverty.[11] Still, the mirage of the promised land coupled with the reality of conditions in the South fueled the drive to leave.

Migration is the story of America. It is foundational. From Pilgrims fleeing oppression in Europe, to the millions who took advantage of the Homestead Act to "go West," to the erection of the Statue of Liberty in New York's harbor, all the way up to the U.S. Congress tying Most Favored Nation status to the human right of Soviet Jews to emigrate, the movement of people fleeing tyranny, violence, and withered opportunities is sacrosanct to Americans. In fact, "freedom of movement" is a treasured right in the nation's political lexicon.

Yet, when more than 1.5 million African Americans left the land below the Mason-Dixon Line, white Southern elites raged with cool, calculated efficiency. This was no lynch mob seeking vengeance; rather, these were mayors, governors, legislators, business leaders, and police chiefs who bristled at "the first step . . . the nation's servant class ever took without asking."[12] In the wood-paneled rooms of city halls, in the chambers of city councils, in the marbled state legislatures, and in sheriffs' offices, white government officials, working hand in hand with plantation, lumber mill, and mine owners, devised an array of obstacles and laws to stop African Americans, as U.S. citizens, from exercising the right to find better jobs, to search for good schools, indeed simply to escape the ever-present terror of lynch mobs. In short, the powerful, respectable elements of the white South rose up, in the words of then-secretary of labor William B. Wilson, to stop the Great Migration and interfere with "the natural right of workers to move from place to place at their own discretion."[13]

The Great Migration had been spurred initially by Northern industries' desperate need for labor. World War I, which began in August 1914, had exponentially increased orders for manufactured goods—guns, battleships, steel, etc.—while simultaneously reducing the traditional workforce of European immigrants responsible for producing those goods. The flow of immigrants dropped from more than 1.2 million in 1914 to just over 300,000 in 1915.[14] Business leaders, looking for an untapped source of labor, soon realized that there was a vast pool of African Americans who previously had been shut out of the industrial workforce. Corporations like the Pennsylvania Railroad Company hired labor agents to go below the Mason-Dixon Line and convince black people to abandon Dixie and come north.[15] For African Americans, this was a chance to escape, as Du Bois said, the "Hell" of the South.[16]

The inferno was nearly unbearable. In the wake of the Civil War, government and judicial officials had decimated the right to vote, the economic provisions of forty acres and a mule, the chance for good public schools, and equality before the law. Despite the

Thirteenth Amendment, African Americans had virtually no protection from a system that came painfully close to re-creating the exploitation and brutality of chattel slavery.[17] In the late-nineteenth and early-twentieth centuries, white Southerners had saturated the old Confederacy in black blood. By 1920, in fact, there had been more than a thousand lynchings per decade; and in the rebel South, almost 90 percent of those killed were African American. Five states—Mississippi, Georgia, Texas, Alabama, and Louisiana—accounted for more than half of all lynchings in the nation. One of the most macabre formats for the murders was a spectacle lynching, which advertised the killing of a black person and provided special promotional trains to bring the audience, including women and children, to the slaughter. These gruesome events were standard family entertainment; severed body parts became souvenirs and decorations hung proudly in homes. And while African American women were not spared, they were particularly vulnerable to systematic sexual violence as rape became part of a white man's "rite of passage." All the while, the newly freed found themselves subject to barren education deserts, and barely (if at all) remunerated labor.[18] Ambition was forbidden.

African Americans knew all too well the "'Dixie limit' beyond which no black could advance." "Whenever the colored man prospered too fast in this country," complained Ned Cobb, a black farmer and former sharecropper, "they worked every figure to cut you down, cut your britches off you." He understood that his success, indeed, the fact that he had acquired some land and managed to not be in debt to local whites, made him a threat. "They looked hard, didn't stop lookin . . . they didn't like to see a nigger with too much; they didn't like it one bit and it caused 'em to throw a slang word about a 'nigger' havin all this, that, and the other." Whites, Cobb explained, just "hated to see niggers livin like people." Similarly, an Alpharetta, Georgia, farmer, who just wanted to "be free . . . and vote free," explained that the South was no place for an honest, hardworking, ambitious man. "Better not accumulate much," he warned, because "no matter how hard and honest you work for it, as they—well, you can't enjoy it." In that stammer lay the bone-chilling truth that signs of prosperity could attract night-riders and the bloodletting, torture, and land seizure that inevitably followed.[19] Equally vicious was the practice of "whitecapping," which, since the horrors of Bosnia and Srebrenica, we now recognize as ethnic cleansing: In several Georgia and Mississippi counties, where plantations did not dominate the economy, local whites maimed, murdered, and terrorized African Americans and, as the persecuted fled, seized all the land until one could "ride for miles and not see a black face."[20]

In other areas dependent on the sharecropping system, a different type of persecution prevailed: peonage.[21] Fewer than 20 percent of all sharecroppers ever made a profit at the end of the year, with the rest consigned to an ever-widening cavern of debt slavery. The sharecropping system required those who worked a farm to purchase all their supplies and foodstuffs from the landowner, regardless of price or the staggering interest rates charged. At the end of the year, the accrued "debts" would be deducted from whatever amount the harvest had brought and the difference paid to the sharecropper. It was a system designed for abuse. The landowner having, as often as not, rigged the accounting, charged inflated prices for goods that were commonly never received, and engaged in systematized fraud. Most sharecroppers, therefore, never saw a penny and instead owed the employer. Thus, they would start the next year in the hole paying off debts they had never actually incurred. Those who did make a profit earned only between nine and forty-eight cents a day for a year's hard labor in the fields.[22] To challenge the system, however, could easily result in another lynching, spectacle or otherwise. The point was to send a powerful signal to the larger African American community that speaking up for one's rights and demanding appropriate compensation was a death sentence.[23]

These were the conditions that finally led the *Chicago Defender* to exclaim that African Americans "are going north to get some real freedom." Under no illusions about the conditions in Chicago and elsewhere above the Mason-Dixon Line, but with the labor shortage crisis growing because of the war in Europe, editor Robert Abbott deduced, "Now is our opportunity." Therefore, the *Chicago Defender* exhorted that the region where 90 percent of blacks currently lived should be considered uninhabitable. African Americans, the newspaper insisted, "are tired of lynchings and burnings in the south" and, equally important, "the lack of education."[24]

The latter grievance cut particularly keenly. Southern whites' belief that education spoiled the slave remained virtually unchanged well into the twentieth century.[25] In one county in Mississippi, 350 black children had only three teachers among them. The low priority the government placed on schools for African American children was reflected not only in the paucity of resources but in the truncated school year as well. The academic term for black children in Dawson County, Georgia, was six weeks. In Mississippi, because children were essential for picking cotton and would not be released until the last harvest was in, African Americans' schools routinely opened as late as mid-November.[26] Beyond sick and tired of the anemic and inadequate public education designed for blacks, African Americans were willing to go north to find good schools for their children.[27]

And so they collected what pennies they had to buy train tickets out of the South. They accepted free passes from labor agents for train rides. They waited anxiously for fare sent from relatives who had already made it north. They hid their Sunday best beneath their work clothes so as not to tip off their employers that they were leaving that night. They abandoned their tools in the fields and even their final paychecks to avoid alerting the bosses to their escape plans. They hitched rides on freight trains. They scoured the

Chicago Defender for information on housing and jobs. All told, the Great Migration moved nearly 10 percent of the black population out of the South.[28]

When five hundred thousand moved above the Mason-Dixon Line between 1917 and 1918, the South became alarmed.[29] As more and more fled, the Georgia Bankers Association, citing a figure of more than twenty-seven million dollars in losses, described "the exodus as comparable only to Sherman's march to the sea in its damage to agriculture in the state."[30] It is easy to see why. Black labor was the foundation of the region's economy, and African Americans were also the sine qua non of the South's social and political structure.[31] Chattel slavery had marked blacks at the bottom—economically, politically, socially, culturally, physically, and intellectually. The base. If blacks extricated themselves from the region, as they were clearly doing—and without the approval of whites—then the entire socioeconomic structure of the South dependent on the support of that base was in danger of collapsing.

Thus, while African Americans understood the exodus as grabbing at a chance for freedom and equality, white Southerners saw black advancement and independence as a threat to their culture and, indeed, their economy. For years, political and economic elites had deluded themselves into believing that African Americans were somehow satisfied with the brutal inequality of the status quo; comfortable with having their wages stolen year after year; pleased to be trapped in debt slavery; OK with black women having absolutely no right to their bodies; and happy to have their children illiterate, uneducated, and futureless. They, therefore, had no framework by which to understand the Great Migration, no grasp of what could lead a black man like Shreveport, Louisiana's Isaac West to assert that he would "just as soon be in hell" as remain in that state.[32]

Given African Americans' supposed contentment with Jim Crow, officials throughout Dixie were initially certain that this flight north could happen only at the instigation of outside agitators. Clearly, "somebody . . . had to be stirring up local blacks and causing them to leave the South."[33] One of the most influential newspapers in the region, the *New Orleans Times-Picayune*, singled out "unscrupulous . . . labor agents from the North" as the culprit. Sounding the alarm because "the movement has reached immense proportions," the newspaper declared that "the drain has, of late, become so great . . . as to call for action."[34]

White reaction, with its veneer of legality and respectability, answered, rising up to stop African Americans from controlling their own destiny. Soon the South was blanketed with anti-enticement statutes reminiscent of the Black Codes that again leveled exorbitant licensing fees and chain-gang prison sentences for those "luring" blacks away from their employers. In Macon, Georgia, policymakers "exacted $25,000 for a labor recruiting license," while also requiring "recommendation by ten ministers, ten manufacturers, and twenty-five other businessmen."[35] Not only was it highly unlikely that forty-five pillars of the community would vouch for a labor agent, but also the mandatory licensing fee—the equivalent in 2014 of $2.76 million—was pure extortion.[36] Jacksonville, Florida's city council required a thousand-dollar license. Failure to pay while recruiting the town's black workers to leave could result in a six-hundred-dollar fine and sixty days in jail.[37] The Georgia legislature considered it a felony punishable by three to seven years in prison for any labor agent who sought to entice blacks out of the state to work elsewhere.[38] In September 1916, the Montgomery City Commission enacted a law "that any person who would *entice*, persuade or influence any laborer or other person to leave the city of Montgomery for the purpose of being employed at any other place as a laborer" would be fined one hundred dollars and face six months' hard labor, or both.[39]

These were not idle threats. Suspected labor agents were arrested routinely whenever a trainload of African Americans left or when the fields were empty and there was no one to work the land.[40] The Reverend D. W. Johnson, a black labor agent in Mississippi, barely escaped detection, the sting of the whip, or worse for handing out free railroad passes north to African Americans. "About twelve o' clock," he recounted:

> *that door swung open and there was two great big, three great big red-faced guys . . . Now they had a bullwhip on they shoulder and a rope and a gun in each of their hands. And those pistols, them barrels looked like shotguns, you know? They gonna kill every so-and-so Negro that they found had a pass. Well, so they searched us one by one and they searched me . . . Had they pulled off my shoe, that'd been it for me. Because they swo' they was gonna kill the one who had it. Yeah, it was in the toe of my shoe.*[41]

City councils, state legislatures, and police forces were determined to punish those, who, in a capitalist economy, offered African Americans a better employment opportunity. The legalistic language about fines and prison sentences masked a barely contained fury at the dawning realization that blacks believed they could leave the South or the rural areas for decent wages, functioning schools, and more freedom. African Americans simply did not have that right: That was the message as white authorities went after labor agents.

When it became clear, however, that the exodus showed no signs of slowing down, the white elites searched for yet another outside agitator and found the most unapologetic, viscerally anti-South black newspaper published, the *Chicago Defender*.[42] Central to the Great Migration, the *Chicago Defender* served as one of the primary conduits of information about opportunities up north. Using a far-flung distribution system of African American railroad porters, the paper extended its influence well beyond Chicago and deep into the Mississippi Delta. The *Defender*'s stridency, its unrelenting embrace of blackness, and its open contempt for white racist regimes turned a simple newspaper into a symbol of African American pride and defiance. Though its circulation figures may have been in the hundreds of thousands, its impact was even greater as the illiterate and barely literate listened intently in churches, diners, shacks, and barbershops as the paper was read aloud.[43]

The message was revolutionary. Whereas Booker T. Washington, once the most powerful African American in the nation, and then his successor at Tuskegee Institute, Robert Moton, had openly accommodated Jim Crow, declaring that blacks would have to prove themselves worthy of rights, the *Defender* demolished that narrative.[44] Over and over again, the newspaper pounded on the idea that Dixie was going to have to prove that *it* deserved the presence of African Americans, not the other way around.[45] And, the *Defender* argued, what the region's governments and employers had delivered so far left but one option: "Get out of the South."[46]

Abbott's newspaper warned its readers not to be duped by entreaties from so-called black leaders like Moton that Dixie was African Americans' natural home. The *Defender* would have none of it: "You see they are not lifting their laws to help you, are they? Have they stopped their Jim Crow cars? . . . Will they give you a square deal in court yet? When a girl is sent to prison, she becomes the mistress of the guards and others in authority . . . something they don't do to a white woman. And your leaders will tell you the South is the best place for you. Turn a deaf ear to the scoundrel, and let him stay."[47]

The *Chicago Defender*'s threat to the old regime was clear. Nor did it flinch in the face of the outrage that greeted its message. The *Defender* discussed not only the Klan but also the governors, legislators, government officials, and business leaders who benefited from a system of oppression that robbed African Americans blind. At least as notably, the *Defender*'s pages published one ad after the next about job opportunities in the North with wages that were unheard of to Southerners. The newspaper prominently displayed information as well about the Chicago Urban League, which made itself available to help smooth the transition from the rural South to the urban North. And in its pages were ever-present pictures of schools, homes, and lush public spaces that held out the promise of all that was possible.

Freedom of the press and First Amendment rights are hallowed constitutional ground in the United States, and the *Defender* had not violated any libel law: The lynchings happened; the theft of wages was real; the rape of black women was no secret. The *Defender* had done nothing but report the truth.[48] But for that crime, Southern elites felt it had to be silenced.

The police chief in Meridian, Mississippi, "ordered the newspaper confiscated from dealers."[49] Other locales soon followed suit. Montgomery passed an ordinance that "any person, firm or corporation who published, printed or wrote or delivered or distributed or posted . . . any advertisement, letter, newspaper, pamphlet, handbill or other writing for the purpose of enticing, persuading or influencing any laborer . . . to leave the city of Montgomery for the purpose of being employed as a laborer" would be sentenced to up to six months' hard labor and fined one hundred dollars.[50] A judge in Pine Bluff, Arkansas, issued an injunction banning the distribution of the *Chicago Defender* anywhere in the county.[51]

However, these maneuvers succeeded only in forcing the paper underground. Like a resistance movement in a totalitarian society, a network of black railroad porters, ministers, and teachers, even under the stress of surveillance, worked to circumvent the ban using the postal system and smuggling the paper in bulk goods.[52] Indeed, the attempt to keep the *Defender* out of the hands of African Americans only increased the paper's credibility and importance.[53]

While the ban on the *Chicago Defender* cut right to the core of American democracy, Southern states' assault on the First Amendment extended far beyond that newspaper. As the law in Montgomery made clear, the very idea of freedom of movement, and the concept that labor could go wherever it could get the best package, had to be stopped. Thus, in Georgia two men who carried a poem railing against the sharecropping system, lynching, and unequal pay were arrested, convicted, and sentenced to thirty days in jail for carrying incendiary literature.[54] While in Franklin, Mississippi, an African American preacher who sold the National Association for the Advancement of Colored People (NAACP) magazine *Crisis* was hit with a four-hundred-dollar fine and sentenced to five months on the county farm.[55]

Regardless of Southern officials' efforts, wave after wave of black people continued to leave. Nothing seemed to stop the flow. The officials, therefore, decided to go after the railroad system. The logic was simple: If the ideas that led to the exodus couldn't be stopped, then certainly the physical means by which hundreds of thousands had already left the region could be. A variety of tactics was employed. One was to physically prevent the trains from moving. A waylaid train could wreak havoc with schedules even under optimal conditions, but conditions weren't optimal. With World War I raging, the shipment of personnel and matériel was crucial to supporting the Allies. Nevertheless, white Southern leaders prioritized their need to stop the advancement of African Americans above all other considerations, including victory over the nation that had sunk the *Lusitania* and killed nearly twelve hundred passengers and crew members. It was most egregious in Mississippi, where, in Greenville, Greenwood, and Brookhaven, trains were stopped and sometimes sidetracked for days.[56] The federal government finally stepped in when the police chief in Meridian, Mississippi, held up a train on a technicality. The U.S. marshal arrested the city's highest-ranking lawman on the spot.[57] Recognizing that there was more than one way to disrupt the flow, Jackson, Mississippi's officials threatened to rig pending court decisions if the railroads did not stop handing out passes for African Americans to go north.[58]

In addition to strangling interstate commerce and being willing to hijack the legal system to blackmail the railroads into submission, authorities went after African Americans directly. In Albany, Georgia, the police ripped up the tickets of black passengers who were on the platform waiting to board.[59] Jacksonville mayor J. E. T. Bowden was upset that there were so many black men near the labor recruiting station and trying to board trains that he had the police chief arrest them for vagrancy and told the nearly five hundred men that they would not be allowed to leave the city for better jobs.[60] Memphis police inspector Earl Barnard seized twenty-six northbound African Americans, charged them with vagrancy, and then routed them to a plantation in Arkansas in what can only be called "peonage."[61] In Hattiesburg, Mississippi, the ticket agent, under the advice and counsel of the town's citizens, simply refused to sell any tickets to African Americans.[62] When blacks tried to circumvent the dragnet by walking many miles to use another station, they were manhandled by police at the railroad stations and then charged with vagrancy.[63] In Americus, Georgia, blacks trying to go north faced a dense network of local police and county sheriffs who were armed with state-issued arrest warrants. Herded into the jails, even though none of the officials knew for sure whether it was legal to detain someone simply because they wanted to go north, African Americans weren't released until the trains had left the city.[64]

The Macon *Telegraph* grimaced at such far-flung efforts at coercion: "We are not slaveholders . . . We do not own the Negroes; we cannot compel them to stay here."[65] Indeed, all the heavy-handed tactics boomeranged. Blacks weren't intimidated; instead, they were more determined than ever to leave.[66] In desperation, the mayor of New Orleans wired the president of the Illinois Central Railroad, asking his company to "stop carrying negroes to the North." In a reply that was a primer on basic federal law and economics, the railroad executive explained that neither his company nor any other one, given the interstate commerce clause, could refuse to sell tickets or provide transport to paying customers. Moreover, he pointed out, given the relatively high wages that blacks were now getting in the North, the South needed to brace itself; the exodus would surely continue.[67]

Rather than brace themselves, the same Southern leaders who had always been such staunch and proud adherents of states' rights now lobbied the federal government for help. They recognized that the nation's mobilization for World War I could provide the perfect patriotic cover—despite their own string of transgressions—to stanch the flood of blacks out of the South. In 1918, the Selective Service Division of the federal government issued a "work or fight" order that required every able-bodied person to be either inducted into the armed services or employed in the key industries the nation needed to wage total war.[68] Instead, the white South took full advantage of the fog of war to keep African Americans from migrating north. Conjuring up a new version of the infamous vagrancy laws that had fueled the convict-lease labor system after the Civil War, Southern officials used so-called Councils of Defense to corral black bodies for planters, mill operators, and other employers.[69]

The justification of this new form of bondage—as a defense of God and country—was a fig leaf to cover the Southern states' true, self-serving motives. Assistant Secretary of Labor Louis F. Post admitted that he had "found that the work-or-fight order was being used for peonage purposes and that employers were conscripting labor for private use rather than for the service to the war effort." Equally revealing was his concession that the majority of workers were black. The NAACP added that it was no accident that the widespread abuse of the work-or-fight order lined up "exactly . . . with that portion of the territory of the U.S. in which the institution of chattel slavery formerly existed."[70] The chief of the United States Employment Services, a man from Meridian, Mississippi, in fact, vowed "that the first thing he was going to do was to see that Niggers were stopped from going North."[71]

The reason Southern officials rose up to try to stop the Great Migration of a people for whom they clearly had such contempt goes far beyond the easy default response of "labor." Black flight threatened much more than the economic foundation of a feudal society; African Americans' determination to achieve their full potential endangered the legalistic, biological, and philosophical tenets of a racially oppressive system. Black prosperity and success—indeed, black intelligence—were unimaginable and, thus, justified the disparate funding in education that had led to abysmal schools and made the brutality of the criminal justice system necessary. It propped up skewed, racially based pay scales. The whole culture of the white South was erected on the presumption of black inability. And the Great Migration directly challenged that foundation. Black success was the white South's bogeyman.[72] And the fear that this engendered erupted in ticketed passengers being dragged off trains, interstate commerce getting blocked, the wartime needs of the nation going ignored, and labor becoming criminalized for taking its skills to an employer willing to pay.

Still, African Americans continued to leave. As the *Chicago Defender* crowed in 1922, MORE THOUSANDS KISS THE SOUTH A LAST GOOD-BY: MISSISSIPPI DELTA IS BEING STRIPPED OF LABORERS, EVERY TRAIN BRINGS GUESTS NORTH.[73] Yet, the land above the Mason-Dixon Line was, as Du Bois remarked, no paradise, and certainly no haven from oppression.[74] African Americans who went to the North simply stepped into a new articulation of the seething, corrosive hatred underlying so much of the nation's social compact. Beginning in 1917 and going into the 1920s, so-called race riots, which were essentially lynchings on a grander scale, erupted in East St. Louis, Chicago, Washington, D.C., and numerous other cities.[75] Though labeled "riots," these outbursts were more like rampages, where whites went hunting for African Americans to pummel, burn, and torture. Killing was just an added bonus. In some instances, as in Chicago, blacks fought back. But in all instances, they were outnumbered. In Chicago alone, twenty-three African Americans were killed, and one thousand black families were left homeless.[76] During the Red Summer of 1919 there were, in fact, seventy-eight lynchings, including a man burned at the stake in Omaha, Nebraska.[77]

More than just white fears of black competition for jobs ignited rampant violence against African Americans. Anxieties about housing played a big role. Chicago, for example, had hemmed the black population into tight, confined areas with finite housing possibilities. In 1917, the Chicago Urban League found that real estate agents had so constricted the supply of homes for African Americans that on one day alone, only fifty houses were available for 664 black applicants. Given the basic economics of supply (limited) and demand (great), rents skyrocketed up to 50 percent higher for this decaying housing stock.[78] For decades afterward, when it appeared that African Americans were moving into white neighborhoods, race riots became an all-too-familiar drumbeat to drive blacks back to overcrowded, dilapidated slums.[79] In one case, a young Jewish couple, Aaron and Louise Bindman, was suspected of hosting an African American boarder. "Some of the mob was actually up on our porch, pushing on the door," the wife recalled. "We were terrified. We put empty bottles on the floor to slow them down if they actually got inside. We had already barricaded the doors, and I remember breaking the table legs off our kitchen table to defend ourselves. We started boiling water to throw on anybody coming in. We were pretty defenseless." Her husband then explained, "We didn't expect help from the police, who were obviously assisting the hoodlums." With five thousand to ten thousand whites coming to run them and the phantom African American boarder out of the Chicago neighborhood of Englewood, the couple *was* defenseless.[80]

While spared a full-blown riot during the first wave of the Great Migration (1915–40), Detroit simmered in unmasked hatred against the tens of thousands of blacks who now called that city home.

Previously, there had been an uneasy truce between the white community and the relatively small number of African Americans in Detroit. But during the exodus, in just eighteen months, the African American population in the Motor City quadrupled, as the automobile industry provided job opportunities and possibilities for advancement almost unimaginable to those who had dealt with Mississippi, Alabama, and Georgia.[81] Employees at Ford, with an industry-setting pay scale of five dollars a day, could make in a single week what it took a prosperous sharecropper some two months or more to earn.[82] And so they kept coming. By the mid-1920s, there were ten times as many blacks in Detroit as there had been in 1915.[83] And then the tenuous truce shattered.

While the Great Migration had led to nearly exponential growth in the number of African Americans who called Detroit home, the area where they were supposed to live, Black Bottom, had never expanded. Realtors, insurance agents, banks, and landlords had devised a witches' brew of schemes and machinations, such as redlining and restrictive covenants, to cordon off wide swaths of Detroit's housing stock from African Americans and carve a color line through the city.[84] And so, the small stretch of land called Black Bottom became engorged with ten times the number of people it once held.[85] Less than half the homes in this ghetto-in-the-making had indoor plumbing, although in the urban north a bathroom was the norm. More than 15 percent of families were forced to live in one-room apartments. Nearly one third of all black families were crammed into four-room homes.[86] But despite the clearly debilitating and disastrous effects of this brutal reality, Michigan's Supreme Court, relying on the precedents of *Cruikshank*, the *Civil Rights Cases*, and *Plessy*, upheld racially restrictive housing policies as constitutional in *Parmalee v. Morris* (1922).[87]

Tired of the cramped living conditions and exasperated with paying exorbitant rents for ramshackle housing that the landlords refused to repair, black professionals sought to move away from

Black Bottom. That aspiration, however, was fraught with danger. While a few managed to find homes in white neighborhoods, others faced the wrath of mobs and homeowners' associations. In the summer of 1925, for example, Dr. Alexander Turner, Dunbar Hospital's co-founder and head of surgery, tried to move into the home he had purchased in an all-white part of town, Tireman. Within five hours of his unpacking his first box, bricks and rocks rained down as a mob a thousand strong moved in to drive him out. With Detroit police officers watching, "he was compelled to sign a deed and relinquish ownership of the property" at gunpoint. The police then escorted Turner and his family back to the black side of town.[88]

Dr. Ossian Sweet, who was also on staff at Dunbar Hospital, like Turner, dared breach the color line in Detroit. It was unclear to him why Black Bottom had to be his only option. He had a medical degree from Howard University; he was married to a beautiful, sophisticated woman; and he was a loving father to a baby girl. Sweet, with his carefully trimmed hair, tailored suits, and tortoise-shell glasses, wanted a home befitting a man who had emerged from the abject poverty of the Deep South to become a physician with a thriving practice in Detroit. He was the embodiment of the American dream.[89]

On September 8, 1925, Sweet began to move into his new home on the corner of Garland Avenue and Charlevoix. It was a nice bungalow—perhaps the finest house in the neighborhood, though it was no upscale community but rather a marginal white neighborhood in Detroit.[90] Residents were not college-educated; there wasn't a doctor, a lawyer, or an accountant among them. They were pipe fitters, factory foremen, blue-collar workers.[91]

The next day a mob, spurred by a number of meetings of the homeowners' association, began to form outside his house. Sweet, well aware of what had already happened to his colleague Dr. Turner, was prepared and had asked his brother and some friends to help him protect his property. He had firsthand knowledge of what a mob could do. When Sweet was a young boy in Florida, an African American teenager who lived around the corner from him was accused of rape, tied to a tree, and burned alive.[92] Sweet had also been in Washington, D.C., during the Red Summer 1919, when police allowed whites to rampage for days slaughtering black people. The tide turned only after returning African American veterans had seen enough, polished their rifles, and began shooting.[93] The next year, Sweet's relatives in Ocoee, Florida, lived in the part of town that whites incinerated "in the single bloodiest day in American political history." Whites went hunting for a black man who had dared approach the ballot box in the 1920 presidential election, and, in the process, killed scores of African Americans and ethnically cleansed the town until it became all-white for nearly sixty years.[94] As a result of his experience, Ossian Sweet had packed, among all the moving boxes and satchels, a small arsenal of guns and four hundred pounds of ammunition.[95]

Sweet made sure to alert the police that trouble was brewing. Several officers arrived on the scene, but they hung back from the house, even as the crowd continued to grow. Then, as the sun set and two of Sweet's friends arrived in a taxi, rocks suddenly began to pummel the home on Garland Avenue. Sweet heard angry shouts of "Here's niggers! Get them! Get them!" As his friends rushed into the house, the mob was like a tsunami. Sweet saw "a human sea. Stones kept coming faster." Windows in the home shattered.[96]

Some of the men in the home, including Sweet's brother, Henry, grabbed guns, and as rocks continued to rain down, they fired a full volley, twenty rounds. Two white men went down. One, Leon Breiner, a factory foreman who lived just across the street, was fatally wounded. The police, finally shaken out of their lethargy, sprang into action. They stormed the house, arrested Sweet, his wife, and the ten men who had come to his aid, and hauled them out of there.[97]

The Sweets were clearly in trouble, but it was the neighborhood association that had made abundantly clear its main goal to get rid of them by any means necessary, including violence. Almost the moment they purchased the home, notices for a never-heard-of-before homeowners' association sprang up in the neighborhood, inviting all concerned residents to a meeting to determine how to act "in self-defense" and stop the invasion. The main speaker at the gathering was the president of the Tireman Homeowners' Association, which had made front-page news in Detroit as it forcibly expelled or repelled the Turners and two other black families that had tried to move into his all-white neighborhood. We have the model for how to do this, he told the throng of seven hundred. "Use legal means if possible, force if necessary. But put the niggers out. Put them out."[98] Then a mob, which the media and the police initially estimated to be anywhere between three hundred and five thousand people, encircled Sweet's home. Rocks crashed through the bedroom windows and sat on the floor surrounded by shards of glass. Other stones littered the lawn, porch, and roof. Racial epithets singed the air as the mob surged toward the house.

The clearly violent intent of the mob should have saved the Sweets from the legal trouble that loomed on the horizon. But his aspirations, his ambition, nullified if not justified that intent and triggered a concerted response from the police, the prosecutor's office, the liberal, "anti-Klan" mayor, and the media itself, as they set to turn self-defense into premeditated murder and throw eleven black people, including a physician, a law student, and a federal narcotics officer, in prison forever.

The police officer in charge at the Sweets' home that evening, Inspector Norton Schuknecht, who had had a ringside seat to the shooting, stated that there had been no crowd around Sweet's house on Garland Avenue. There had been people milling about, he claimed, chatting with each other, but nothing that suggested a "mob," and certainly nothing that indicated the Sweets were in danger. When he charged into the home after the bullets went flying, as he recalled, he yelled at Sweet, "For Christ's sake, what the hell are you fellows shooting about?" When the doctor pointed to the rocks shattering his windows and pounding against the roof, Schuknecht scoffed, "What have they done? . . . I haven't seen a man throwing stones, and I haven't heard any commotion or anything else."[99] In the police officer's estimation, Sweet's posse, for its own nefarious reasons, simply pointed its arsenal, took aim, and fired at neighborly whites out for an evening stroll.

Taking into account the rocks that officers had found in the upstairs bedroom amid so much broken glass, Schuknecht insisted that the stones came *after* the shooting. His sequence of events—shots, *then* rocks—made clear that this had not been self-defense. Rather, Leon Breiner had been executed. This was the story the officer repeated to the press, to the prosecutor, and then to the jury, never conveying the impressions of his brother-in-law, who, there with him that evening, "caught snatches of bitterness seething through the growing crowd," including someone saying, "'Damn funny thing . . . that the police wouldn't go in there and drag those niggers out.'"[100]

A reporter from the *Detroit Free Press* who trudged through the rocks and debris at the Sweets' home listened to Schuknecht repeat the tale of neighbors walking the streets on a warm summer evening and then add a tantalizing new piece of information. When the officer and his men searched the home on Garland, they found nothing less than a full-blown arsenal: rifles, handguns, and hundreds of rounds of ammunition when the place was barely furnished. The implication was clear: This was not a home where people intended on living. It was, instead, a sniper's nest from which bullets were sprayed into a peaceful, calm neighborhood, killing a husband and father, while sending another man to the hospital. Schuknecht's story was explosive, and the *Detroit Free Press* ran with it, and was quickly followed by its rival paper, the *Detroit Times*.[101]

A reporter for a third newspaper in town, the *Detroit News*, had also been there that night. "A nigger family has moved into the neighborhood and they're going to put them out," Philip Adler heard a woman say. As he worked his way through the throng, Adler saw the rocks rain down on the Sweets' home, and then he heard the shots. Contrary to Schuknecht's account, Adler saw the Sweets had been under unrelenting attack while the police stood by and did nothing meaningful to stop it.[102]

However, Adler's editor refused to run his story and instead reiterated Schuknecht's version. By evening, Detroit's three newspapers had five hundred thousand copies blanketing the city, each of them condemning the Sweets as killers.[103]

It was like throwing gasoline on a fire. Since the war, Detroit had become Klan country, thirty-five thousand members strong. Thus far, a coalition of white ethnics and blacks—arrayed around the slogan "Keep Detroit an American City!"—had managed to beat back the Klan's challenge for the mayor's office.[104] Now, Mayor Johnny Smith, who had helped weld that coalition and whom blacks had come to view as an ally, sucker punched his African American constituency in an open letter to the police commissioner. He saw the KKK's hand behind "the outrage" on Garland Avenue, which, given the violence that rained down on the Sweets, initially made sense. But as Smith unveiled his logic, it was not the mob that had incurred his wrath, but the Sweets, who had the temerity to move into a white neighborhood. The Klan, he railed, had worked overtime to "induce Negroes to go into districts populated entirely by persons who would . . . resent such an invasion." The point of such an incursion, he asserted, was to spark a race war that would blow Detroit apart and deliver the city to the KKK. Unfortunately, the mayor continued, the Ossian Sweets of this world had been willing pawns in this power play. If the Negro would just stay in his place, he wrote, and quit demanding to exercise every last little right "which the law gives him," then there would be peace in Detroit.

"I shall go further," Smith then added. "I believe that any colored person who endangers life and property, simply to gratify his personal pride, is an enemy of his race as well as an incitant of riot and murder."[105] Even for Detroit's liberal mayor, peace was based on black people quietly and gracefully accepting the fact that they had no right to their rights.

As he read the police reports, the interrogation transcripts, and the newspaper accounts of what happened that evening on Garland Avenue, Wayne County prosecutor Robert Toms, who would go on to be tapped as a judge to oversee the Nazi war crimes trials at Nuremberg, spotted an obvious weakness in his case: All those arrested, despite the fact that their stories rippled with inconsistencies, agreed that the house was under attack, that rocks were "pouring in like rain," and that a bloodthirsty mob had descended on the Sweets. By any measure, that established self-defense. But Toms remained determined "to bring those eleven Negroes to trial."[106]

Toms sent his assistant prosecutor, Ted Kennedy, out to conduct additional interviews with the police and neighbors to shore up the case against Sweet and his friends. Two key points needed to be nailed down: the size of the crowd and the time when the rocks were first thrown. Michigan law defined a mob as more than twelve armed people, or thirty unarmed "assembled to intimidate or inflict harm," which meant causing "twenty-five dollars in damage to a piece of property." It wasn't just the Sweets who had insisted that there was a mob; the very newspapers that had branded them as killers described hundreds of people swarming Garland Avenue.

Schucknecht's version, though, had to be supported, and Kennedy's job was to nail down the police inspector's story and then get independent corroborating testimony. After just a few questions, it was clear to him that the case rested on quicksand. The assistant prosecutor strongly suspected that Schuknecht's answers were rehearsed, informed not by the truth but by a quick glance at Michigan law books. But Kennedy had a job to do, and as he turned to the next-door neighbors, the tone of his questions, along with his body language, helped steer them to the right answers.[107]

These corroborating statements buttressing an "avalanche of police evidence" convinced Toms to proceed. He would, as well, ensure that "the Sweets would face an all-white jury . . . and if he couldn't convince twelve Caucasians to convict eleven Negroes who invaded a white neighborhood armed to the teeth," well, then he "didn't deserve his salary."[108] He had already seen to it that the Sweets were denied bail and would have to languish in jail until the jury decided their fate months later.[109]

As the trial began, Toms described the "empty rooms contrasted with the full supply of weapons," driving home the point that "the defendants agreed to a preconceived conspiracy to murder," which, plotting by the people holed up in the house on Garland, he explained to the jury, was evident from the results of the interrogations.[110] At the police station, Kennedy had kept after Dr. Sweet about the guns: When had they arrived, why were weapons in the house, and who had brought them? Sweet dodged and dodged, but the assistant prosecutor was relentless.

"When you moved in, you had the arsenal up there with you . . . knowing you were going to have trouble, didn't you?"

"Yes," the doctor finally said.

If Sweet knew there was going to be trouble, Kennedy probed, "why did [he] move in there, then?"

Sweet's response, "Because I bought the house . . . and it was my house, and I felt I had a right to live in it," carried no weight.[111] Blacks had no property rights in white neighborhoods.[112] Henry Sweet eventually admitted that he had fired a rifle, but only after the rocks "began coming in on me." Kennedy was unimpressed. "Did any of them hit you? . . . If you stayed out of the front room . . . you wouldn't have been hit, would you?"[113]

Toms summed up his case at the end of the trial: The invasion of a white neighborhood, the arsenal in a sparsely furnished house, the admission that shots had rung out from the upstairs window—it all meant only one thing: Leon Breiner was "shot through the back from ambush." And, as the prosecutor told the jury, "you can't make anything out of those facts . . . but cold-blooded murder."[114]

Watching the Sweet case unfold, Walter White, assistant secretary of the NAACP, immediately recognized that "if the ancient Anglo-Saxon principle that 'a man's home is his castle' were not made applicable to Negroes . . . we knew that other and even more determined attacks would be made upon the homes of Negroes throughout the country."[115] The Association declared that if black people in Detroit couldn't protect their home from a white mob, then no black person anywhere in America was safe.[116] The NAACP had, therefore, rushed to pull together a legal team to help the Sweets, including famed attorney Clarence Darrow, for whom this case was about "a sacred ancient right, that of protection of home and life."[117] And, as David Lilienthal wrote in the *Nation*, the question was "Did Negroes have the same right of self-defense as white people?"[118]

Patiently and meticulously, Darrow and his co-counsel, Arthur Garfield Hays, picked apart the lies, the coached testimony, and the half-truths of the neighbors, homeowners' association leaders, and police. The size of the crowd inched well above Schuknecht's twelve. The rocks were acknowledged as a hailstorm, and eventually a homeowners' association discussion concerning property values was revealed to have been about the level of violence necessary to oust the Sweets.[119]

During closing arguments, Darrow explained for the jurors' benefit that the prosecution's case was based on racism and lies. "Every one of them [the prosecution's witnesses] . . . perjured themselves over and over and over and over again to send [eleven] black people to prison for life." What was more, he added, they had "perjured themselves on behalf of what they think is their noble, Nordic race." "Acquit my clients," he insisted, "and repair the damage caused by America's shameful original sin."[120]

Several days of deliberations later, Darrow did not get what he wanted, but neither did Toms. Five jurors voted for acquittal. Seven, however, repeatedly voted to convict Ossian and Henry Sweet for murder.[121] It was, then, a hung jury. Yet, despite the fact that Darrow had exposed the perjured testimony and legal weaknesses in the case, Toms refused to drop the charges. And so there was a second trial at which Henry Sweet, an admitted shooter, was the first to be tried.

Darrow was more than ready.[122] This time he suspected that the lying would be all the more obvious, with "many of the prosecution witnesses [having] forgotten the testimony they gave at the first trial." Even the press, taking notice of these irregularities, had begun to tone down its polemics.[123] Having already managed to establish that so many cars had been in the area that night that the police had had to barricade the street, Darrow explained to the jurors, "There is nothing but prejudice in this case. If it was reversed, and eleven white men had shot and killed a black while protecting their home and their lives against a mob of blacks, nobody would have dreamed of having them indicted . . . They would have been given medals instead."[124]

With each crack in witnesses' testimony, Toms's case fell apart. By the time of his closing statement, therefore, he was reduced to arguing that "even if there were five hundred people out that night," Michigan law might call that a mob, but the doctor and his friends had no right to do so.[125] Toms went on to argue that "prejudice" and "intolerance" had nothing to do with this case.[126] Nevertheless, he said, it "wasn't unreasonable for the community association to want to maintain the racial purity of their neighborhood."[127]

Toms continued to minimize what a rock-throwing mob converging on the house at Garland Avenue actually meant to those trapped in the home. Even though the prosecution's own witnesses, under intense cross-examination, admitted to stones having positively pounded the bungalow, Toms remarked that it couldn't have been that intense because only two panes of glass had broken. The only thing that mattered was that Leon Breiner, a white man, was now dead. And Toms, as he continued his closing arguments, wanted the all-white jury to understand why: The killing of that family man happened because "the Sweets and their friends were uppity." They murdered Breiner "just to impress on the right people that they didn't propose to be driven out."[128] Sweet thought that he had "the right to live wherever he wanted to live by any means he chose to adopt."[129] "It was not fear that led Henry Sweet to pull the trigger," Toms stated by way of conclusion. "It was hate. It was arrogance."[130] Breiner was "sacrificed on the altar of Henry Sweet's rights and privileges."[131]

This time, though, the jury didn't buy Toms' argument and the foreman pronounced Henry Sweet "not guilty."

The costs of this legal victory, however, were painfully, staggeringly high. Gladys Sweet, the doctor's wife, who had been cooking dinner when the rocks and bullets started flying, contracted tuberculosis while being held for nearly a month in the dank, crowded, and unsanitary jail. Their baby daughter also became infected, as did Henry. All of them died. Ossian Sweet, who had fought so hard, tried to soldier on, but eventually he faced foreclosure, had to sell the home on Garland Avenue, and was forced to move to a small apartment in Black Bottom. He put a gun to his head one night and pulled the trigger.[132]

Three

Burning *Brown* to the Ground

Jim Crow dominated the lives of black people in America from 1890 well into the twentieth century. From conception to coffin, there was no nook or cranny of a black person's life that it did not touch. In the early 1930s, under the direction of brilliant legal tactician Charles Hamilton Houston, the NAACP launched a campaign in the courts to destroy Jim Crow and overturn the *Plessy v. Ferguson* decision that had made "separate but equal" the legal cornerstone of racial segregation in America. When the U.S. Supreme Court first announced that 1896 decision, the states had seized on the "separate" aspect of the edict almost immediately, instituting racially distinct facilities from telephone booths to cemeteries. For nearly six decades, the same states had consistently failed to provide anything approximating "equal" for America's black citizens.[1] This was the Achilles' heel that the NAACP's legal team attacked.

The Association's initial thrust was to force the states to equalize educational opportunities, as *Plessy* required, insisting they finance, create, and maintain black law schools and doctoral programs of the same caliber as the ones labeled "whites only." White Southern leaders tried to parry the NAACP's challenge and still meet *Plessy*'s threshold. Texas attempted to re-create the University of Texas at Austin's law school for black students in a run-down off-site basement and, as far as the justices could tell, failed miserably.[2] Missouri opted to define "equal" as paying for African Americans to get their legal education in Nebraska or Iowa; the U.S. Supreme Court would have none of it and ordered the University of Missouri to open its doors to African Americans.[3] Oklahoma hoped to keep *Plessy* intact by admitting blacks to its flagship university but then creating apartheid-like separate spaces on campus for them. But that hardly constituted "equal," as the justices noted, and they ruled that those internal racial barriers were unconstitutional.[4] Those results were not surprising. The states couldn't possibly build two comparable systems. But if they really wanted Jim Crow, the NAACP began to make painfully clear, they would have to pay for it.[5]

Already Jim Crow had cost America's black children dearly. Delaware, a border state, had abdicated all responsibility for the education of its African American citizens: "Blacks were pretty much left to their own devices as far as education was concerned." By 1910, they had built eighty-one schools throughout Delaware, but, given their lack of resources, these were no more than shacks without decent lighting, plumbing, or enough desks. Even when philanthropist Pierre S. Du Pont launched a program to bring these schools up to code, white residents made it clear that they not only opposed public funding for black schools but were equally resistant to private, philanthropic resources intervening as well.[6] The results were devastating. There was only one black public high school in the entire state. As a consequence, by 1950, African American adults in Delaware had finished, on average, only 7.2 years of school; whites had finished more than 10 years. Only 505 blacks in the entire state had earned at least a bachelor's degree. Not surprisingly, African Americans' income was "barely one-third of white families' earnings."[7]

Virginia, despite being the wealthiest Southern state and the fifth richest in the entire nation, with a constitution and statutes requiring the provision of public schools and compulsory attendance, was equally determined not to educate its black population.[8] In Prince Edward County, for example, no high school existed for blacks until 1939, and by 1947 Robert Moton High "was jammed with more than twice the number of students it was designed to hold." White residents, however, refused to use their tax dollars to relieve the overcrowding, ignoring the fact that 45 percent of the county's population was composed of African Americans, who had clearly contributed to the public till as well. Instead, to handle the overflow at Moton High, the all-white school board erected three tar paper shacks, with neither insulation nor electricity, to house the students. One teenager remembered visitors taking pictures of the shacks "to show the people back home how backward we were." An elementary school for African American children—"a one-room wooden schoolhouse that housed seven grades"—was no better.[9]

The other black schools in Prince Edward County, too, were poorly constructed with no indoor plumbing and thus serviced only by outhouses. The fifteen facilities for 2,000 African American students were valued at $330,000, whereas the seven brick schoolhouses for 1,400 white students, replete with indoor toilet facilities and modern furnaces, had been appraised at $1.2 million.[10]

In the Deep South, the educational opportunities were at least as bleak.[11] The disparity in student-to-teacher ratios in mid-1930s Atlanta, for example, was staggering. For blacks, there were 82 students for every teacher, while the ratio for whites was 35 to 1. The overcrowding led to significantly shortened school days, as African American students rotated through on staggered, truncated shifts. Even when public funding was finally increased, the disparities not only remained but also actually grew. In 1942, the Atlanta school board allocated $75 more in support per capita for white students than for black students. By 1946, that figure had climbed to a difference of almost $80. African Americans had to contend with "overcrowded classrooms, decrepit school buildings, inadequate numbers of textbooks, schools lacking libraries, cafeterias, gymnasiums," and double and triple sessions where "85 percent of all black elementary school students attended class for only half the day during the 1947–48 school year."[12]

In Louisiana during the 1943–44 academic year, similar funding disparities echoed throughout the school system. At the elementary level alone, for example, the East Baton Rouge parish spent $67.79 per capita on white children while doling out a mere third of that for each African American student. Orleans parish spent $103.65 on each white elementary school student and $66.76 on each black student. East Feliciana Parish, thirty miles north of Baton Rouge, had a per capita allocation of $121.64 for whites in kindergarten through sixth grades and a paltry $18.92 for each black child in those grades. Overall, Louisiana spent $76.34 per white elementary school child and only $23.99 for each African American one.[13]

South Carolina was just as discriminatory. In the early 1950s, the state spent nearly five times more per capita on school buildings for whites than it did on those for blacks, had no high school whatsoever for African Americans in nineteen counties, and assigned only eight school buses throughout the state to transport black children.[14] In Clarendon County, there were "thirty school buses for the white children . . . none for the black children." And when in 1947 a soft-spoken black preacher asked the all-white school board for just one bus, the chairman, R. W. Elliott, fired back, "We ain't got no money to buy a bus for your nigger children." Yet, they had funds to educate white students. The property value of black schools in Clarendon County, attended by 6,531 students, was "officially listed as $194,575. The value of the white schools, attended by 2,375 youngsters, was put at $673,850." Thus, the county spent nearly ten times more per capita on the white students' facilities.[15]

The result of such widespread disparities in funding was that the U.S. educational system, despite the demands of parents and students craving high-quality schools, had deliberately produced a sprawling, uneducated population that would bedevil the nation well into the twenty-first century. In Alabama, Georgia, Louisiana,

South Carolina, and Mississippi, with a combined population of 4.7 million African Americans, more than half of all black adults by the mid-1940s had less than five years of formal education. In South Carolina and Louisiana, more than 60 percent of black adult citizens had no more than a fourth- or fifth-grade education.[16]

In one court case after the next, from 1935 to 1950, the NAACP had convincingly demonstrated that southern governments were simply incapable of meeting *Plessy*'s Jim Crow standard of "separate but equal."[17] And because the legal bedrock of the South was predicated on that dictum, the proven inability to have both equal and separate simultaneously left Dixie in judicial danger, which was just as Charles Hamilton Houston intended.[18] With the legal precedent duly laid, the time to take down *Plessy* as fundamentally unconstitutional was now. Houston's protégé, Thurgood Marshall, led the next phase of this legal battle. Starting in 1950, the NAACP's lawyers had amassed cases from Delaware, Virginia, South Carolina, Kansas, and Washington, D.C., that were bundled into one, *Brown v. Topeka Board of Education*. In December 1952, Marshall argued before the U.S. Supreme Court that racial segregation violated the equal protection clause of the Fourteenth as well as the due process clause of the Fifth Amendment. And with that, a series of legal, political, and cultural explosions went off below the Mason-Dixon Line; it was clear that "Jim Crow in the classroom was fast approaching a fatal constitutional rendezvous," something white Southern politicians were determined to avoid at all costs.[19]

This legal challenge was no surprise. Every legislator, senator, congressman, and governor knew that the schools designed for black children were woefully inadequate and had been so for generations. As Roy Wilkins, executive secretary of the NAACP, explained, "By any fair calculation, governors and school boards had had nearly twenty years to see the train coming down the track. It didn't just roll up to them overnight." The Association's first lawsuit had been in 1935 against the University of Maryland, followed by cases against

Missouri, Oklahoma, and Texas; therefore, Wilkins wrote, "it should have been obvious that change in the high school and grade schools was coming next."[20]

As they had previously attempted with higher education, the states then dangled a series of school-equalization packages before the NAACP and the black community as a bribe to drop the lawsuits and accept separate schools as reality in America. President Dwight Eisenhower sympathized with the white South. At the behest of his "great friend," South Carolina governor James Byrnes, Eisenhower hosted a small dinner party at the White House to explain to Chief Justice Earl Warren that Southerners "are not bad people. All they are concerned about is to see that their sweet little girls are not required to sit in school alongside big overgrown Negroes."[21] At the same time, he warned Governor Byrnes, "the last-minute southern attempt to put some money into Negro schools" would be prohibitively expensive.[22] During World War II, the federal government estimated that it would have taken, in 2014 dollars, $1.2 trillion to equalize the schools in America.[23] Byrnes and others, however, believed the expense was worth it to keep Jim Crow the uncontested law of the land. And so, as a gesture of good faith, new black high schools suddenly popped up across the South, while property tax bonds earmarked for black schools sailed through, or were at least earnestly discussed in all-white legislatures.[24]

That was the carrot. The NAACP, however, refused to bite. Those new schools—"guilded [*sic*] citadels of segregation," the Association called them—were but a sorcerer's trick in the struggle for real equality. Politicians who had ignored or deliberately strangled black children's opportunities for decades had not miraculously experienced a change of heart. Only the NAACP's steady stream of victories in court had caused this sudden loosening of the wallet, and this all-too-recent concern about the overcrowded shacks called schools. African Americans had no doubt that the moment the Association backed off, underlying assumptions of black inferiority and inability would reemerge and continue to translate into public policy—and not just in the schools but also in housing, employment, health care, and the vote. So neither the NAACP nor the black community backed down or backed off.[25]

Roy Wilkins scoffed at white Southern leaders' "scramble . . . to upgrade black school shanties in the vain hope of heading off pressure to do away with them entirely."[26] The future was at stake here, and African Americans were determined to use every resource at their disposal to ensure that not one more generation fell into the abyss of illiteracy, poverty, and economic vulnerability. "I offered my life for a decadent democracy," pronounced the Reverend L. Francis Griffin, a black man who had served in the Jim Crow military during World War II and had been one of the firebrands in Prince Edward County behind *Brown*, "and I'm willing to die rather than let these children down."[27] For those whites who had hoped that equalization would defuse the "Armageddon" of *Brown*, that kind of trenchant response was as terrifying as it was surprising.[28]

When it was clear that the carrot wouldn't work, and when even once-reliable Negroes, whom the power structure had always been able to count on to preach patience, actually refused to lend their support to equalization schemes to convince the NAACP to withdraw *Brown* from the Supreme Court's docket, then the response was emphatic.[29] Senator James O. Eastland (D-MS) vowed, "We will protect and maintain white supremacy throughout eternity."[30] Mississippi governor Fielding Wright concurred, adding, "regardless of the consequences."[31]

In Georgia, beating back a 1949 challenge from black parents to equalize the schools, Governor Herman Talmadge had already proposed a constitutional amendment that would authorize the state legislature to scrap the public school system altogether and "channel state funds into tuition grants for [white] students attending private schools." In other words, while threatening to scuttle public education and provide state-funded tuition for whites to attend segregated private academies, Talmadge, who had vowed, "as long as I am Governor, . . . Negroes will not be admitted to white schools," never contemplated any educational alternatives for the 321,255 African American children in the state in 1950.[32]

Similarly, Mississippi's legislature crafted a constitutional amendment to abolish public schools and, in case that didn't pass, a pupil-placement law using race-neutral language—"ability," "whether a good fit or not"—to give school boards inordinate power to prevent more than 325,000 black children from gaining access to better-resourced white schools. In South Carolina, Byrnes, who had been a congressman, a U.S. senator, a U.S. Supreme Court justice, and then secretary of state before becoming governor, "added dignity and a sense of solemn purpose to the segregationist cause." The aura of respectability he lent to a slew of legislative proposals—selling public school property to private individuals, pupil-placement laws, and "a constitutional amendment relieving South Carolina of its obligation to provide a free public school system"—made them seem the work of reasonable, learned statesmen. "Of only one thing can we be certain," he swore. "South Carolina will not now, nor for some years to come, mix white and colored children in our schools" even if, he continued, that meant shutting down the entire education system.[33] Similar reaction spread throughout the South, and threatened to erupt more seriously in the event that the Supreme Court ruled *Plessy*, and therefore Jim Crow, unconstitutional.[34]

That day of reckoning came. After nearly sixty years of racial purgatory, the U.S. Supreme Court ruled in *Brown* that Jim Crow schools violated the equal protection clause of the Fourteenth Amendment and, in the D.C. case, the due process requirement of the Fifth Amendment. Even the taciturn Roy Wilkins could barely contain himself. "May 17, 1954, was one of life's sweetest days," he later recalled.[35] Nor was the significance of this judgment confined to the education of black children. "If segregation is unconstitutional in educational institutions," observed Charles Johnson, president of Fisk University, "it is no less so unconstitutional in other aspects of our national life."[36] At that moment, it appeared that citizenship—true citizenship—might finally be at hand for African Americans. It was "the greatest victory for the Negro people since the Emancipation Proclamation," wrote the *New York Amsterdam News*. Robert Jackson, a black professor in Virginia, exclaimed that "a heavy burden has been lifted from [black students'] shoulders. They see a new world opening up for them and those that follow."[37]

To Southern leaders who had already been readying their political arsenal, the decision in *Brown* was but a declaration of war. Wilkins later admitted, "My sense of euphoria was a bit naïve. Swept away, elevated, exalted, I failed to anticipate the ferocity of the resistance that quickly grew up in the Deep South." There was a "cold, clinical cruelty of the response."[38]

Traditionally, white Southern resistance to *Brown* has been captured by the visual images of violence that followed the Supreme Court decision: the horribly mutilated body of Emmett Till; the angry mob of housewives surrounding traumatized Elizabeth Eckford on the first day of school at Central High in Little Rock, Arkansas; and the disturbing Norman Rockwell painting of little, pigtailed six-year-old Ruby Bridges surrounded by towering National Guardsmen and racial epithets scrawled on the wall as she walked up the steps to desegregate her elementary school in New Orleans. None of that violence would have happened, however, and certainly would not have been given the broader societal stamp of approval, if the respected elements in white society—governors, legislators, U.S. senators, congressmen, and even, more tepidly, the president of the United States—had not condoned complete defiance of and contempt for the Supreme Court and the constitutional provision that its decisions are the law of the land.

In the North, where racial segregation was intense, the defiance was subtle but effective. In 1957, for example, Milwaukee's school board instituted "intact busing" that carried black children to white schools, kept them isolated in a separate classroom, and then ferried them back home again.[39] The overt, even violent response to *Brown* did not occur until much later, in the 1970s, most spectacularly in Boston.[40]

On the other hand, the Southern states made clear that they were ready for war. The first step was to ensure that only those who felt threatened by *Brown* could vote.[41] Ever since the rise of Jim Crow in the 1890s, Southern officials had been vigilant in eviscerating black access to the ballot box. By 1944, in the states of the old Confederacy, only 5 percent of age-eligible African Americans were registered to vote, which left millions of blacks politically voiceless.[42] In the late 1940s, the NAACP launched a series of voter registration drives to provide local Southern communities with resources to deal with the tangle of requirements—the poll tax, literacy tests, understanding clauses—blocking African American access to the ballot box. But the going was hard and, in places like Mississippi, lethal, with well-coordinated campaigns of racial terrorism leading to the murders of residents aiding the NAACP's efforts.[43]

As difficult as voter registration had been before *Brown*, it became much more so after the ruling. Mississippi reinforced an amendment requiring superior literacy and an ability to "understand" and interpret the state's constitution.[44] Given that nearly 53 percent of Mississippi's adult African American population had fewer than five years of education, compared with only 10 percent of whites of voting age, the emphasis on literacy and interpretation of a complicated legal document, while appearing race-neutral, was, in fact, targeted directly at black Mississippians.[45] Even more, state authorities required already registered African Americans to go through the gauntlet of literacy tests, understanding clauses, and the whims of registrar scrutiny once again to re-register. That move alone caused the number of black registered voters in Mississippi to plummet by two thirds.[46] Moreover, the ever-present threat of violence was pervasive, with the full support, and sometimes participation, of law enforcement. As J. W. Milam, the Mississippian who tortured and murdered fourteen-year-old Emmett Till only to be found "not guilty" in 1955 by a jury of his peers, remarked, "Niggers ain't gonna vote where I live. If they did, they'd control the government. They ain't gonna go to school with my kids."[47] The same sentiment animated officials 110 miles away in the capital of Jackson, who worked tirelessly to reduce the power of the black vote until in many counties not a single African American was on the voter rolls.[48] Even as late as 1960, more than 98 percent of Mississippi's black adults were not registered to vote.[49]

Similarly, in 1953, in Alabama's so-called Black Belt, "where the black population equaled or exceeded that of whites," only 1.3 percent of eligible African Americans were registered. Two counties had no black voters whatsoever.[50] In 1954, the year of *Brown*, the Alabama legislature modified the state's constitution to raise significantly the threshold on access to the polls by adding comprehensive-understanding and good-character clauses.[51] Just as in Mississippi, in Alabama the disparity between white and black adults with five years or less of education was so wide (16.3 percent versus 54.1 percent, respectively) that a requirement to read and interpret the state's constitution could yield only one result.[52]

Within five years, black defiance, courage, and sheer will in the face of such impediments pushed that 1.3 percent registration percentage to a little over 5 percent. Yet, by 1960, Wilcox and Lowndes Counties, with more than 11,000 voting-age African Americans, still had no registered black voters, while in Bullock County a mere 5 blacks had registered out of a total of 4,450 (or

0.1 percent). In Dallas County, with Selma as the major city, just 0.9 percent of eligible African Americans were registered to cast a ballot. On the other hand, six Alabama counties in the Black Belt actually listed more than 100 percent of eligible whites registered to vote, with Lowndes County topping the list at 117.9 percent.[53]

States relied as well upon another mechanism of insidious discrimination to silence blacks and ensure that the rule of a few would shape the course of the South and the nation for years to come: Legislative apportionment gave overwhelming and disproportionate power to rural counties, especially those that held the most ardent white segregationists and the largest black populations outside the urban areas. For example, Alabama, up to the 1960s, used the census from 1900, when the state was overwhelmingly rural, to determine the number of representatives each county sent to the state legislature. The result was that growing urban centers like Birmingham were underrepresented while Black Belt counties generally had twice as many legislators as their populations warranted. That disproportionate power was further aggravated by the massive disfranchisement of the black population. With cities thus electorally emasculated, and blacks in the rural counties silenced, there would be no countervailing force in the legislature to moderate or curtail the stranglehold at the statehouse.[54]

On May 31, 1955, the Supreme Court handed down an implementation decision, *Brown II*, stating that desegregation in public schools must happen "with all deliberate speed."[55] Recognizing that disfranchisement and legislative apportionment would not be enough to stop the progress stemming from *Brown*, the Deep South and Virginia soon added to their arsenals the discredited legal hocus-pocus of interposition, which argued that the state could put itself between federal law and U.S. citizens to stop enforcement of any ruling with which the state disagreed. State representative Sam Engelhardt declared that interposition would "serve notice on the rest of the nation that Alabama and the South will not accept integration." At a January 1956 meeting in Richmond, Georgia governor Marvin Griffin announced that the Southern leadership, all by itself, had determined that the federal courts did not have "jurisdiction over any State of the Union except in the case of suits between States respecting boundary disputes." Mississippi declared *Brown* "unconstitutional and of no lawful effect within the territorial limits of the state of Mississippi," while South Carolina's new governor, George Bell Timmerman, endorsed the unanimous legislative resolution that "condemns . . . the illegal encroachment by the central government" on the state's sovereignty.[56]

Just as at Fort Sumter at the start of the Civil War, the first shots were aimed at the federal government, which, in the Southern states' view, had no authority that they were bound to respect. Georgia's legislature even went so far as to pass a resolution to "repeal the 13th, 14th, and 15th amendments to the Constitution of the United States of America and to impeach the members of the Supreme Court."[57] On July 1, 1956, the state adopted a new flag, designed by segregationist John Sammons Bell, which "featured a prominent confederate battle flag. It was Georgia's way of letting the NAACP and the rest of the nation know that white Georgians, once willing to die to protect slavery, were also willing to die to protect segregation."[58] Meanwhile White Citizens' Councils, made up of the "sort found at Rotary meetings or dancing at the country club," sprang up throughout the South with but one objective: destroy *Brown*.[59] The Texas White Citizens' Council issued the disclaimer, "We do not advocate violence or any form of illegal activity." But the organization vowed to "prevent the integration of Negroes into white schools" and "do so by any means at [its] command which falls within the law." The Texas Council therefore proposed an amendment to the U.S. Constitution that would require the Supreme Court to answer to Congress.[60] First, this would, by design, destroy the central concept of checks and balances in the Constitution. Second, the proposed amendment would also ensure that the Supreme

Court, given the stranglehold that Southern Democrats had on both the U.S. Senate and the House of Representatives, would be at Dixie's beck and call. And in Louisiana, the governor empowered state police to arrest any federal judge or U.S. marshal who tried to implement *Brown*.[61]

The so-called Southern Manifesto, however, was the shot heard around America. On March 12, 1956, Representative Howard Smith (D-VA) and Senator Walter George (D-GA) introduced "the Declaration of Constitutional Principles" before their respective chambers in Congress, asserting that the Supreme Court had violated states' rights, abused judicial authority, and undercut the separation of powers. Signed by 101 members of Congress, all from states of the old Confederacy—Senator Lyndon Johnson (D-TX) was one of only a handful of holdouts—the Southern Manifesto signaled to their constituencies that Massive Resistance to *Brown* was not some base, primeval white supremacy but rather a principled, patriotic stand to defend the Constitution. The Southern Manifesto gave sanction from the highest levels to use the levers of government to defy the U.S. Supreme Court until, with the federal judiciary and African Americans tiring of the fight, *Brown* simply collapsed.[62]

The game plan of stall and defy was now in place. Southern states used and abused the legal process to pass one unconstitutional law after the next, knowing that the process to overturn the statutes would be costly. "We might as well be candid," Georgia attorney general Eugene Cook admitted. "Most of the laws will be stricken down by the Courts in due course."[63] But in the meantime, all the motions, hearings, affidavits, rulings, and appeals kept *Brown* at bay. Those extended legal battles allowed year after year to drizzle by while the continued existence of separate and decidedly unequal schools consigned black children to some of the worst education that America had to offer. Proud of the consequences, one man bragged, "As long as we can legislate, we can segregate."[64] Indeed, by 1963, not one black child attended a public school with a white child in South Carolina, Alabama, or Mississippi. In Virginia, the birthplace of Massive Resistance, a full decade after *Brown*, only 1.63 percent of blacks were attending desegregated schools.[65] In North Carolina, generally billed as having a "more genteel" Jim Crow, fewer than 1 percent of black pupils in the state attended schools with whites.[66] African American students who once saw in *Brown* their "opportunity to step forward and prove to the world that the Negro is as capable as any human being," now saw the lives and futures of nearly 2.7 million black children hanging precariously in legal purgatory in the old Confederacy.[67] African Americans faced a Hobson's choice: back down and accept the inferior, unequal, and unconstitutional education that states insisted black children deserved, or call the South's bluff and risk no public schools at all.[68]

Black parents chose to fight and hauled the states back to court. Arkansas became the site of a landmark lawsuit and U.S. Supreme Court decision. African Americans were furious at how Little Rock, with a district judge's approval, shut down the city's schools after "violence and disorder" caused by "the actions of the Governor and Legislature" rained down on nine black teenagers.[69] The subsequent U.S. Supreme Court decision in *Cooper v. Aaron* was unequivocal: *Brown* "was the supreme law of the land and had to be obeyed."[70] The "state could not deprive black children of their constitutional rights in the face of the violence and disorder that the state had brought upon itself." But that ruling, like *Brown*, only baited white officials in the South. In an amazingly wrongheaded interpretation of the U.S. Constitution, Arkansas argued that it was the state's governor, not the U.S. Supreme Court, who had the right and power to determine the law of the land. With Governor Orval Faubus "doing just about everything he could to secede from the Union," Roy Wilkins defined it as an "insurrection."[71]

Faubus's Fort Sumter moment happened the minute the governor closed the public schools in Little Rock and all the legislative machinery of privatization that had been previously holstered came out blazing.[72] Between donations totaling more than $300,000, state funding of $176 per year per student, and taxpayer-subsidized busing to private academies, Little Rock had the means for most white children to remain in school while the state simultaneously defied the Supreme Court by keeping blacks locked out.[73] As one white student recalled, "When they said there was going to be a private school" and that "it would not cost you anything, my parents said 'you're going.'"[74] As a disconsolate Wilkins understood, though, while "white parents sent their children to private academies" funded by the state, "we had no such recourse"; "black children in Little Rock were without school altogether."[75]

Delaware had witnessed the first act of Massive Resistance to *Brown* in the town of Milford, where approximately 1,500 people descended on the high school shouting "Keep our schools white!" and "Dynamite the schools!" A subsequent district court ruling snubbed both the landmark 1954 decision and *Cooper v. Aaron* by authorizing a twelve-year delay in implementing *Brown*—or, essentially, another complete era of black children in the swamp of Jim Crow education, despite the well-stated law of the land. "At least implicitly," the federal judges "conceded . . . that white people's prejudices and lack of self-restraint were justification for continuing to deny blacks their constitutional protections."[76]

In Virginia, when local school boards in Charlottesville, Norfolk, and Front Royal were under federal court orders to admit black students, Governor James Lindsay Almond closed, in his words, every "school threatened with desegregation." Ironically, because the white, well-funded schools in those cities matched that description (no one was clamoring to integrate overcrowded Moton High in Prince Edward County), he had shut out nearly thirteen thousand white children from getting an education.[77] But despite their own actions in bringing Virginia to this point, Governor Almond and his supporters "placed full blame for education disruption at the feet of the 'NAACP agitators.'"[78]

School closures spread now to besieged Prince Edward County. This time, black children were in the crosshairs, where they would remain for nearly a generation. With *Brown* looming over their heads, Virginia's political officials passed a series of laws to close the public schools, siphon tax dollars into private academies, and pay tuition for white students, while ensuring that there was nothing in place for African American children to continue their education. On November 11, 1955, the Gray Commission (named after State Senator Garland Gray) rolled out a phalanx of recommendations to keep Virginia's schools separate and unequal. Gray first cherry-picked the commission's members, providing disproportionate representation to those in Black Belt counties, and then narrowed discussion even further by tapping only the most ardent segregationists to sit on the all-important executive council.[79] Another, more "moderate" alternative, the Perrow Plan (named for State Senator Mosby Perrow), would have at least saved the public schools, but just barely. This plan developed a formula to divert the lion's share of tax dollars into a private school system while cutting public schools' funding and operational abilities to the bone. The governor shelved that one and eventually chose Gray's.[80] The state of Virginia was hurtling toward an educational apocalypse. Since 1954, nearly 20 percent of the state's public schools had closed in response to *Brown*. Moreover the Gray Plan required Virginia to spend one million dollars for every 1 percent of the student population that chose the private school system. Savoring this Pyrrhic victory, State Senator Gray proudly boasted, "I guess we won the Civil War."[81]

The Gray Commission's plan was put into action after a 1959 Fourth Circuit decision reversed a district court ruling that had given Prince Edward County a full seven years to comply with

Brown. With the Fourth Circuit now ordering the schools to integrate by the fall of 1959, county supervisors immediately abolished the property tax that funded public schools and diverted the money into a cache for tuition grants to support the all-white Prince Edward Academy.[82] The supervisors added their county funds to grants offered by the state to ensure that the costs for this private education were covered with public dollars. In addition, sixty-seven of the sixty-nine teachers at Prince Edward Academy were all from the now-closed public schools.[83]

While white children were educated, 2,700 black children were locked out. The defiance of Prince Edward County was singular—no other school system in the nation remained closed for five years (1959 to 1964) rather than comply with *Brown*.[84] The impoverished but determined African American community managed to send some children away to relatives, but only thirty-five black students were able to attend those out-of-state schools on a full-time basis.[85] During those five long years, critical in terms of child development, most African American students spent their formative education time in activity centers that the black community cobbled together.[86] The Baltimore *Afro-American* reported that these makeshift centers, some in basements, some in churches, others in abandoned shacks, staffed overwhelmingly by housewives and those with only a high school diploma, could not provide anything approximating an adequate education. The resources were simply not available to be open more than three days a week, for half a day and have a curriculum of "little more than a scant program of reading, singing and discussion."[87] These years had taken a great toll on the children.

Once again, black parents, with the determined Reverend L. Francis Griffin as the plaintiff, had to haul Virginia back to court. But as the *Washington Post* reported, when the lawsuits hit, Prince Edward County supervisors simply "denied that the Virginia constitution requires the operation of public schools in any county."[88]

Finally, cutting through that absurdity, the U.S. Supreme Court handed down two unequivocal decisions that forced the schools to reopen.[89] Even then local and state authorities "employed every weapon in their arsenal to ensure that the newly reopened system remained segregated, impoverished and academically substandard."[90] The most popular method of foot-dragging was the school board's freedom-of-choice plan, which ensured that white parents could move their children away from any school "threatened" with desegregation.[91] The result was that by 1969, Prince Edward County Schools were now 98 percent black, and, once again, starved of resources.[92] Stall and defy had transformed into stall and undermine, but the results were the same: devastating.[93]

During the series of court cases swirling around Prince Edward County, a judge had noted that "an interrupted education of one year or even six months at that age places a serious handicap upon a child, which the average one may not overcome."[94] The federal government agreed and in 1963 backed the privately funded Free School to serve as an educational bridge to get the black children of Prince Edward County academically ready for when the public schools finally reopened.[95] But it was too late. One black teen, Skip Griffin, spoke of how "embarrassing" it was to sit in a classroom and look at an assignment, unable to do anything more than write his name at the top of the page. He had two crippling words to describe himself: "very dumb." His mother had tried to help him, but the schools she herself had attended in Prince Edward County were nothing but shanties and hovels with the equipment to match.[96] The psychological devastation was equally debilitating. Henry Cabarrus recalled one of Prince Edward County's white officials declaring that he would "rather his children be baked in the oven" than go to an integrated school. Cabarrus was taken aback. "When you have such strong white resistance against you as a person such that they can take away the most fundamental thing—education—if someone can take that away from you, your esteem is so small that . . . you're always looking over your shoulder for who is going to attack or criticize."[97] The damage had been done. Eventually, Skip Griffin, along with legions of African American children, became discouraged and simply dropped out.[98]

Prince Edward County is emblematic of the way that systematized racism not only destroys black lives but also undermines the very strength of the United States. Even as thousands of African American children were left behind educationally, the economy was beginning a seismic transformation that would require even more of its citizens. Factory jobs, the ones that President Franklin Roosevelt had once called "the arsenal of democracy"—the living-wage-with-barely-a-high-school-diploma jobs—were rapidly disappearing.[99] It wasn't quite perceptible then that a sector that at one time had accounted for some 25 percent of all paid employment in the United States would be near collapse by the 1970s.[100] But the first cracks in the armor of industrial America were already there in the 1950s.[101] By the time Prince Edward County finally decided to implement at least parts of *Brown* in the 1970s, the heyday of industrial America, where gainful employment had not required a strong education—just a strong back—was already well over, with the knowledge-based economy taking hold.[102] That economy was primed for those who had had the benefit of years of good schools and, in particular, for whites who had a well-funded public school system that went all the way through the twelfth grade and graduated the lion's share of them as college-ready.

By contrast, an entire generation of black children who had fought long and hard to receive a quality education was now forced to face this cold, hard new economy with neither the necessary education nor work skills. It was not just black America, however, that suffered the cost of this waste of human lives and talent. The brutally relentless tactics of stall and defy, then stall and undermine—tactics that went on for at least four decades—left the United States with millions of citizens who lacked the education needed to be competitive in a global, technology-driven economy. This, in turn, left the United States lagging far behind other developed countries and placed the nation at enormous economic risk.[103]

White leaders in the South saw no such thing; they saw themselves as defenders of the Constitution and saviors of states' rights against a federal Leviathan. In their minds, they were patriots not racists. In this reworking of history, "black parents were to blame for the interruption of their children's education, since blacks had chosen integration over education" and had joined "the federal courts and the NAACP as the aggressors."[104]

Because the National Association for the Advancement of Colored People was supposedly at the epicenter of the tumult and rebellion in the South, the next round in the chamber of Massive Resistance had the NAACP's name all over it.[105] Wilkins would shudder as he recounted how "there was nothing abstract about the South's hatred of the N.A.A.C.P. at that time."[106] Starting in 1956, legislatures from Virginia to Texas passed a series of laws that banned the Association from operating within the Southern states' borders. An especially pernicious law, barratry, cast the NAACP's formidable legal team as nothing more than ambulance chasers, drumming up business by cajoling both the unwitting and the amoral into a series of dubious lawsuits alleging violations of constitutional rights. Not only did the cynical enforcement of barratry statutes stop the Association from providing legal counsel to those taking the brunt of Jim Crow, but it prevented the NAACP from giving financial support to those suing the state as well.[107]

Southern governments also went after the Association where it hurt, demanding that the organization either hand over or publicly post its membership lists. Louisiana, in a rather unsavory twist, resurrected an old anti-Klan law and used it against the NAACP, which was now required to file membership lists with the state. That would have meant putting a bull's-eye on every dues-paying member, inviting, at bare minimum, economic extortion as credit was cut off, mortgages called in, and jobs suddenly withdrawn. Indeed, in five states, NAACP members were banned from holding public employment. Moreover, identifying who paid dues to the Association meant that NAACP members would also be targeted for violence. Fully comprehending that black people's lives and livelihoods hung in the balance, the Association refused to comply. That noncompliance led to a series of injunctions and fines, some totaling one hundred thousand dollars, that effectively crippled the NAACP below the Mason-Dixon Line. For eight years, at the peak of the Civil Rights Movement, which had been spurred on by *Brown*, the Association was severely hampered in the South. Not until 1964 could the NAACP resume operations in Alabama.[108]

One year after *Brown II* and the same year that segregationists in Congress issued the Southern Manifesto, Attorney General Eugene Cook of Georgia capriciously decided that the NAACP was, despite its tax-exempt status, a for-profit organization that owed the state $17,000 in back taxes, or the equivalent in 2014 of $150,000. Cook then insisted, and a local judge concurred, that until the NAACP paid what it supposedly owed Georgia, the Association would not be able to operate in the state. Just to drive home the point, authorities arrested the head of the NAACP's branch in Atlanta. Similarly, in 1956, Texas attorney general John Ben Shepperd instructed armed Texas Rangers and state highway patrolmen to raid local NAACP offices searching for proof of failure "to pay taxes and engaging in unlawful political activity." Despite an utter lack of evidence, a local judge issued the requisite injunction to put the NAACP, which refused to turn over its membership lists, out of business in Texas.[109]

The recalcitrant South swaddled itself in the American flag, portraying its efforts as the last holdout of patriotism.[110] Georgia's Eugene Cook, Mississippi senator James O. Eastland, and Arkansas congressman Ezekiel Gathings combined two of their favorite villains—the NAACP and the Communist Party, USA—into one treasonous behemoth, which they unveiled during a series of congressional and state hearings.[111] Senator Eastland, for example, ignoring that in his own Mississippi, Amite County officials spent only $3.51 per black student while providing $30.24 for every white one, claimed that *Brown* "was the result of communist manipulation." Drawing on questionable records from the infamous House Un-American Activities Committee (HUAC), the Mississippi senator insisted that the scholars the Association had relied on in *Brown*, such as sociologist E. Franklin Frazier, had "no less than 18 citations" before HUAC. It "is evident," Eastland roared, "that the decision of the Supreme Court in the school segregation cases was based upon the writings and teachings of pro-communist agitators and other enemies of the American form of government." Gathings, to give an air of legitimacy to the charges, filled more than eighty pages in the *Congressional Record* with assertions that the NAACP's effort to destroy Jim Crow was actually an "Anti-White Plot Hatched in Moscow." Cook similarly sounded the alarm that the NAACP seized the racial issue "as a convenient front for their more nefarious activities" including "delivering this nation into the hands of international Communism."[112]

Sensitivity to such arguments, no matter how specious, only increased when a Cold War crisis hit in 1957. On Friday, October 4, of that year, America's sense of nuclear invincibility was shattered by the faint *beep*, *beep*, *beep* sound heard over a radio receiver. The Soviets had successfully launched a satellite, Sputnik, that circled Earth every ninety-six minutes. Until then, the threat of the Kremlin's nuclear arsenal had been mitigated by the USSR's seeming inability to send a payload of destruction across the Pacific or Atlantic Oceans. Suddenly, though, with that ominous beeping, traveling thousands of miles had been reduced to the equivalent of crossing the street.

The *New Republic* feared that Sputnik was "proof of the fact that the Soviet Union has gained a commanding lead in certain vital sectors of the race for world scientific and technological supremacy."[113] The *New York Times* glumly reported that the Department of Defense's missile experts were "shaken by Sputnik," because it was "evidence of Soviet superiority in rocketry."[114] The *Washington Post* intoned, "This is confirmation, if any really is needed, of Soviet progress with the intercontinental ballistic missile and intermediate range ballistic missile." The grave consequences were not just military, however; they also threatened the entire structure of U.S. Cold War foreign policy. "Let no one mistake the political significance of the Soviet accomplishment," continued the *Post*'s gloomy editorial, "It will have a strong psychological effect in intimidating wavering allies and uncommitted countries, for it will seem to say that the Soviet Union is irresistible."[115]

This was a national security crisis. President Eisenhower had earlier commissioned a blue-ribbon panel, led by the head of the Ford Foundation, H. Rowan Gaither, to prepare an analysis for the National Security Council on the state of America's military preparedness. Sputnik had launched right before the final report hit the president's desk. The reaction to the report was as thunderous as that to the Soviet satellite itself. The top-secret Gaither Report detailed America's shocking descent into "a second-class power . . . in the face of rocketing Soviet military might," and "portray[ed] a United States in the gravest danger in its history."[116] Even Eisenhower, who had received enormous criticism for his "apparent complacency," had to shake off the charge peppering newspaper op-eds that the White House was the "Tomb of the Well-Known Soldier" and admit that if things didn't change soon, the United States would not be able to recover.[117]

In some measure of silver lining, the Sputnik debacle, many agreed, could be traced right back to the schoolhouse door. There was a general consensus that this Cold War defeat was a direct result of something the nation's educational institutions did or did not do.[118] Some pointed to the trend toward progressive education and the lack of attention to the basics, especially math and science. Most had identified the source of the problem, however, as the unconscionable waste of intellectual talent as poor and unmotivated youth failed to go on to college. Changing his tune, Eisenhower now asserted that the United States had to do everything it could to prevent "the loss of a student with real ability."[119] He "stressed" that it was vital that this generation of American youth get the education necessary to be "equipped to live in the age of intercontinental ballistic missiles." Delay or failure to act, Eisenhower insisted, would leave the United States "irretrievably behind."[120]

In fact, the president, politicians, educators, and pundits all hammered on this imperative against waste, arguing that the hundreds of thousands of students who did not go on to college were being "lost" to the nation. Alabama congressman Carl Elliott, who would take the lead in this crusade to transform education in the United States by backing the National Defense Education Act, argued that "in the context of critical national needs . . . a valuable national resource must not be lost through lack of action." And, he warned: "Whatever happens in America's classrooms during the next fifty years will eventually happen to America."[121]

What was happening to millions of students in America's classrooms in 1957, as Elliott well knew, was the direct outcome of Jim Crow. The long shadow it cast on a nation struggling to produce enough scientists and engineers should have signaled a turning point in the war over *Brown*: an acknowledgment that schools with no libraries and no labs had no chance of training the next generation of inventors and theoreticians. Grappling with America's trenchant refusal to open up the doors to quality education, *Time* announced that the "gap between what the Negro now achieves and what he might achieve indicates that he is the nation's most wasted resource."[122]

For all his hand-wringing, Representative Elliott had no intention of doing anything to repair the structural threat to national security posed by a system that deliberately starved millions of its citizens of adequate education. While he was clear that, after Sputnik, the nation had to "mobilize [its] brainpower, including schoolchildren and undergraduate and graduate students, on an emergency basis," he was equally resolute in his conviction that maintaining racial segregation and the built-in inequality that came with it, was more critical to the nation.[123]

Thus, while bills for the National Defense Education Act bounced through Congress, seeking ways to provide unprecedented federal financial support to schools and universities, Elliott, along with his fellow Alabamian senator Lister Hill, both of whom had signed the Southern Manifesto, were insistent that any movement on education funding, even if for national security, could not, in any way, dismantle Jim Crow or penalize Southern schools and universities for refusing to integrate.

The Alabamians had a strong ally in Eisenhower. Even before *Brown* he had voiced great skepticism about the validity of integration that did not spring organically from, say, Mississippi or South Carolina. He was a states' rights man. Therefore, in his eyes, the Supreme Court was wrong to insert the federal government into local race relations. In 1953, he complained that "two or three court decisions of recent years . . . have tended to becloud the original decision of 'equal but separate' facilities." He was especially piqued at the *McLaurin* decision, which ruled that "a Negro in graduate school attending exactly the same classes as whites, but separated from them by some kind of railing was . . . the victim of discrimination."[124] That just seemed preposterous.

After the *Brown* decision and despite the rumblings in the South about a declaration of war, the president still wanted implementation "to accord a maximum of initiative to local courts."[125] The Southern Manifesto, the outlawing of the NAACP, and the murder of Emmett Till led Eisenhower in 1957 to write to his best friend, Edward "Swede" Hazlett, that "no other single event has so disturbed the domestic scene in many years as did the Supreme Court's decision of 1954 in the school segregation case." To find some manner of peace, the president laid out his priorities: empathy for how hard it would be for the South to jettison its way of life on the basis of a "mere decision of the Supreme Court," especially after building and maintaining a legally segregated society for more than "three score years"; and respect for the Supreme Court's authority. The president hoped to reconcile the two. "The plan of the Supreme Court to accomplish integration gradually and sensibly," he conveyed to Hazlett, "seems to me to provide the only possible answer if we are to consider on the one hand the customs and fears of a great section of our population, and on the other the binding effect that Supreme Court decisions must have on all of us if our form of government is to survive and prosper."[126] Noticeably absent from the president's list of priorities were the rights and educational needs of African Americans.

Thus, as the National Defense Education Act was being debated and crafted, Eisenhower had no intention of using tens of millions of federal dollars to finally gain compliance with *Brown* by "threatening to withhold funds from segregated educational institutions."[127] Wilkins, who later assessed Eisenhower's leadership in the face of Massive Resistance, could say only that at virtually every turn "the president had left us all out in the cold."[128]

The White House's icy stance was affirmed by the attorney for the Department of Health, Education, and Welfare (HEW), Richard Conley, who explained during the House-Senate conference proceedings on the proposed National Defense Education Act that although *Brown* was the law of the land, his agency had no intention of enforcing that ruling. "Integration," he assured Representative Elliott, "would not be a precondition for obtaining funds unless" the Southern-dominated "Congress decided it should be"—which was highly unlikely. In addition, when selecting universities to house the federally sponsored language-training centers, the lawyer continued, the overall quality of the school would determine choices, rather than the "segregation practices of the institution," which "would not be a controlling factor." Similarly, Conley explained to Congress, HEW would have no problem providing fellowships and student loan funds to institutions that "still practice[d] segregation," so long as those awards to students were made "without discrimination."[129] Thus, the University of Georgia, Ole Miss, and the University of Alabama, among other universities in the South, could continue to deny African Americans admission on the basis of race, as long as fellowships went to any of the enrolled white students on a nonracially discriminatory basis.

Assured that *Brown* would have no effect on the proposed National Defense Education Act, Elliott and Hill, desperate to pour federal dollars into the white schools in Alabama, marshaled all their legislative wizardry to guide the bill through both houses of Congress and dodge the amendment from Representative Adam Clayton Powell Jr. (D-NY) that restricted federal funding to only those institutions in full compliance with the Supreme Court decision. And so, when House Resolution 13247 successfully emerged, allocating $183 million in 1959 and another $222 million in 1960 to schools and universities for fellowships, facility upgrades, and state-of-the-art equipment, the desperate conditions that faced African American students remained in full force.[130]

Given Congressman Elliott's prediction that whatever happened in America's classrooms in the 1950s would determine what the United States would look like half a century later, the deliberate omission of African Americans from the National Defense Education Act bore its bitter fruit.[131] In 2004, fifty years after *Brown*, "not a single African American earned a Ph.D. in astronomy or astrophysics," according to the *Journal of Blacks in Higher Education*. In fact, of the 2,100 Ph.Ds. awarded in forty-three different fields in the natural sciences, not one of these doctoral degrees went to an African American.[132] The refusal to implement *Brown* throughout the South even in the face of Sputnik—not only as the law or as simple humanity might have dictated but also as demanded by national interest and patriotism—compromised and undermined American strength. Now, in the twenty-first century, the sector of the U.S. economy that accounts for more than 50 percent of our sustained economic expansion, science and engineering, is relying on an ever-dwindling skilled and educated workforce. Whereas at one point, "about 40% of the world's scientists and engineers resided in the U.S.," according to Rodney C. Adkins, senior vice president of IBM, "that number [had] shrunk to about 15%" by 2012.[133]

The 1950s, then, should be seen as a fateful moment in America when history failed to turn and alter the trajectory of the nation. *Brown* held out hope to millions desperately seeking a quality education. Children clamored to go to school, fought for it, even. A teenage Barbara Johns, for example, rallied her classmates in 1951 to take a stand against the horrible conditions at Moton High in Prince Edward County. Yet, for fighting to be educated, she had to be spirited out of the state by her parents to go live with her uncle, the Reverend Vernon Johns, in Alabama. Black adults, too, put their lives on the line for the children. Reverend Joseph DeLaine, who sued Clarendon County, South Carolina, for gross unequal education and became one of the cases bundled in *Brown*, faced the unbridled wrath of local whites: "They fired him . . . they fired his wife and two of his sisters and a niece . . . And they sued him on trumped-up charges and convicted him in a kangaroo court and left him with a judgment that denied him credit from any bank. And they burned his house to the ground while the fire department stood around watching the flames consume the night."[134]

Since the days of enslavement, African Americans have fought to gain access to quality education. Education can be transformative.

It reshapes the health outcomes of a people; it breaks the cycle of poverty; it improves housing conditions; it raises the standard of living. Perhaps, most meaningfully, educational attainment significantly increases voter participation.[135] In short, education strengthens a democracy.

As if sensing this threat, white opposition careened from the Massive Resistance of disfranchisement, interposition, school closures, and harassment of the NAACP to the passive resistance of pupil placement laws, residential segregation, token integration, and "neighborhood schools."[136] In Little Rock, when the schools were forced to reopen, the most liberal member of the school board, sounding eerily similar to Georgia attorney general Eugene Cook, proposed using the law to undercut *Brown* and limit how integrated Little Rock schools would be. He argued that pupil-assignment plans, using the same factors that Mississippi had considered—"ability," "whether a good fit or not"—could ensure that most African Americans stayed right where they were in their "well-segregated neighborhoods." Meanwhile, a handful of blacks could be enrolled in white schools; just enough, he explained, to "satisfy the federal courts," but at the same time, "small enough to satisfy the reluctant and vocal whites in the community."[137] This tactical shift from stall and defy to stall and undermine effectively "clogged" court dockets for more than forty years, as African Americans struggled to nail down a moving target whose goal had not changed: Stop black advancement.[138]

African Americans weren't the only ones who took a hit. The states of the Deep South, which fought *Brown* tooth and nail, today all fall in the bottom quartile of state rankings for educational attainment, per capita income, and quality of health.[139] Prince Edward County, in particular, bears the scars of a place that saw fit to fight the Civil War right into the middle of the twentieth century. Certainly it is no accident that, in 2013, despite a knowledge-based, technology-driven global economy, the number one occupation in the county seat of Farmville was "cook and food preparation worker." Nor is it any accident that in 2013, while 9.9 percent of white households in the county made less than ten thousand dollars in annual income, fully 32.9 percent of black households fell below that threshold.[140] The insistence on destroying *Brown*, and thus the viability of America's schools and the quality of education children receive regardless of where they live, has resulted in "the economic equivalent of a permanent national recession" for wide swaths of the American public.[141]

Four

Rolling Back Civil Rights

The Civil Rights Movement was so much more than Rosa Parks refusing to give up her bus seat in Montgomery, Alabama, or Martin Luther King Jr.'s iconic "I Have a Dream" speech on the National Mall before 250,000 people. The movement was a series of hard-fought, locally organized campaigns, supported at times by national organizations such as King's Southern Christian Leadership Conference (SCLC), shining the klieg lights of the press on gross inequities in employment, accommodations, and the right to vote. Adopting the strategy of nonviolence, African Americans skillfully used the media to expose the horrors of Jim Crow to the world—from snarling dogs lunging at unarmed demonstrators in Birmingham, to schoolteachers yanked onto the concrete for trying to register to vote in Selma, to four little girls in Birmingham dynamited in church right after a Sunday-school lesson on "A Love That Forgives."[1]

This was a battle, as the SCLC noted, "to redeem the soul of America."[2] It was obvious that a series of congressionally neutered Civil Rights Acts, one in 1957 and another in 1960, was so ineffectual that the conditions of mass disfranchisement and overt discrimination remained virtually untouched. African Americans and their white allies would, therefore, put their bodies on the line to shake the American public and the U.S. government out of a fog of moral and legal lethargy. Thus, a triple murder of civil rights workers in Mississippi led eventually to the Civil Rights Act in 1964, and the killings in Selma and the horrific spectacle of Bloody Sunday—where nonviolent protesters were tear-gassed, whipped, and trampled by horse-bound troopers—resulted in the Voting Rights Act (VRA) in 1965.

The impact of this civil rights struggle had been slow but significant. Inequality had begun to lessen. Incomes had started to rise. Job and educational opportunities had expanded.[3] And just as with Reconstruction, the Great Migration, and the *Brown* decision, this latest round of African American advances set the gears of white opposition in motion. Once again, the United States moved from the threshold of democracy to the betrayal of it, within two decades having locked up a greater percentage of its black males than did apartheid South Africa.[4] Given the power of this iconic movement, the descent into "the new Jim Crow" should have been virtually impossible. But by the 1968 presidential election, white opposition had once more coalesced into an effective force. And in the years that followed, its response was carefully implemented.

Both the Nixon and Reagan administrations, with the support of the Burger and Rehnquist Supreme Courts, executed two significant tasks to crush the promise embedded in the Civil Rights Act of 1964 and the Voting Rights Act of 1965. The first was to redefine what the movement was really "about," with centuries of oppression and brutality suddenly reduced to the harmless symbolism of a bus seat and a water fountain. Thus, when the COLORED ONLY signs went down, inequality had supposedly disappeared.[5] By 1965, Richard Nixon asserted, "almost every legislative roadblock to equality of opportunity for education, jobs, and voting had been removed."[6] Also magically removed, by this interpretation, were up to twenty-four trillion dollars in multigenerational devastation that African Americans had suffered in lost wages, stolen land, educational impoverishment, and housing inequalities. All of that vanished, as if it had never happened.[7] Or, as Patrick Buchanan, adviser to Richard Nixon and presidential candidate himself would explain decades later: "America has been the best country on earth for black folks. It was here that 600,000 black people, brought from Africa in slave ships, grew into a community of 40 million, were introduced to Christian salvation, and reached the greatest levels of freedom and prosperity blacks have ever known."[8] Similarly, chattel slavery, which built the United States' inordinate wealth, molted into an institution in which few if any whites had ever benefited because their "families never owned slaves."[9] Once the need for the Civil Rights Movement was minimized and history rewritten, initiatives like President Lyndon Johnson's Great Society and affirmative action, which were developed to ameliorate hundreds of years of violent and corrosive repression, were easily characterized as reverse discrimination against hardworking whites and a "government handout that lazy black people 'choose' to take rather than work."[10]

The second key maneuver, which flowed naturally from the first, was to redefine racism itself. Confronted with civil rights headlines depicting unflattering portrayals of KKK rallies and jackbooted sheriffs, white authority transformed those damning images of white supremacy into the sole definition of racism. This simple but wickedly brilliant conceptual and linguistic shift served multiple purposes. First and foremost, it was conscience soothing. The whittling down of racism to sheet-wearing goons allowed a cloud of racial innocence to cover many whites who, although "resentful of black progress" and determined to ensure that racial inequality remained untouched, could see and project themselves as the "kind of upstanding white citizen[s]" who were "positively outraged at the tactics of the Ku Klux Klan."[11] The focus on the Klan also helped to designate racism as an individual aberration rather than something systemic, institutional, and pervasive.[12] Moreover, isolating racism to only its most virulent and visible form allowed respectable politicians and judges to push for policies that ostensibly met the standard of America's new civil rights norms while at the same time crafting the implementation of policies to undermine and destabilize these norms, all too often leaving black communities ravaged.

The objective was to contain and neutralize the victories of the Civil Rights Movement by painting a picture of a "colorblind," equal opportunity society whose doors were now wide open, if only African Americans would take initiative and walk on through.[13] Ronald Reagan breezily shared anecdotes about how Lyndon Johnson's Great Society handed over hard-earned taxpayer dollars to a "slum dweller" to live in posh government-subsidized housing and provided food stamps for one "strapping young buck" to buy steak, while another used the change he received from purchasing an orange to pay for a bottle of vodka. He ridiculed Medicaid recipients as "a faceless mass, waiting for handouts." The imagery was, by design, galling, and although the stories were far from the truth, they succeeded in tapping into a river of widespread resentment.[14] Second- and third-generation Polish Americans, Italian Americans, and other white ethnics seethed that, whereas their own immigrant fathers and grandfathers had had to work their way out of the ghetto, blacks were getting a government-sponsored free ride to the good life on the backs of honest, hardworking white Americans.[15] Some Northern whites began to complain that civil rights apparently only applied to African Americans. One U.S. senator, who asked to remain anonymous, confided, "I'm getting mail from white people saying 'Wait a minute, we've got some rights too.'"[16]

During his 1968 presidential bid, Alabama governor George Wallace understood this resentment. He had experienced a startling epiphany just a few years earlier after trying to block the enrollment of an African American student in the state's flagship university at Tuscaloosa. For that act of defiance, the governor received more than one hundred thousand congratulatory telegrams, half of which came from north of the Mason-Dixon Line. Right then he had a revelation: "They all hate black people, all of them. They're all afraid, all of them. Great God! That's it! They're all Southern! The whole United States is Southern!"[17] But even then, he recognized, it couldn't be business as usual. The Civil Rights Movement meant that "the days of respectable racism were over."[18] And so in his bid for the presidency, Wallace mastered the use of race-neutral language to explain what was at stake for disgruntled working-class whites, particularly those whose neighborhoods butted right up against black enclaves. To the thousands, sometimes tens of thousands, who came to his campaign rallies in Detroit, Boston, San Francisco, New York, Chicago, and San Diego, he played on the ever-present fear that blacks were breaking out of crime-filled ghettos and moving "into *our* streets, *our* schools, *our* neighborhoods," signaling in unmistakable but still-unspoken code that "a nigger's trying to get your job, trying to move into your neighborhood."[19] For working-class whites whose hold on some semblance of the American dream was becoming increasingly tenuous as the economy buckled under pressure from financing both the Great Society and the Vietnam War (on a tax cut), this was naturally upsetting.[20] Black gains, it was assumed, could come only at the expense of whites.[21] Not surprisingly, polls showed that as African Americans achieved greater access to their citizenship rights, white discomfort and unease mounted. By 1966, 85 percent of whites were certain that "the pace of civil rights progress was too fast."[22]

Despite Wallace's premise that "Negroes never had it so good," by the mid-1960s African Americans' median family income was only 55 percent that of whites, while the black unemployment rate was nearly twice as high.[23] By 1965, just 27 percent of African American adults had completed four years of high school; whereas more than half of whites twenty-five years and over had achieved that basic threshold of education.[24]

African Americans simply refused to accept those disparities as natural. Refused to concede that a reality of just a quarter of black adults holding a high school diploma was as good as it was ever going to get. Refused to believe that double-digit unemployment rates were just fine for people who actually wanted to work. Refused to tolerate a practice where their labor was worth only 55 percent of that of whites doing the same job. Instead, blacks insisted that inequality was the result of a series of public policies that must be changed. Therefore, they continued to file a series of lawsuits to equalize education.[25] They used the courts to pry open closed labor unions.[26] They elected black political leadership in numbers that hadn't been seen since Reconstruction.[27]

Their resolve to dismantle racial inequality led one white woman in Dayton, Ohio, to assert, "Oh, they are so forward. If you give them your finger, they'll take your hand." The growing consensus was that blacks wanted too much too fast.[28] White angst rose further with the more overtly militant shift in the Civil Rights Movement. More than a decade of being beaten, jailed, and sometimes killed while using methods of nonviolent protest had begun to wear thin, especially on the youth involved in the demonstrations. Nor had the initial Southern focus of the movement addressed the discrimination that millions of African Americans faced in the urban North, Midwest, and West. Thus, nonviolence gave way to an ethos of self-defense, best articulated by the Black Panther Party, a group founded in 1966 which openly brandished guns and challenged the police. The goal of integration, so fundamental to the SCLC and the NAACP, was now forced to openly compete with the more sharply articulated demands of Black Nationalism and Black Power. Soon, in response to police brutality, rioting consumed wide swaths of Newark, Detroit, Los Angeles, and Cleveland, and this served only to intensify the white backlash that had begun with the second wave of the Great Migration during World War II, while also providing whites exasperated by what they perceived as threats to the status quo with the cover of "reasonableness" and "moderation."[29]

Like Wallace, Richard Nixon tapped into this general resentment. The "Southern Strategy," as his campaign handlers called it, was designed to pull into the GOP not only white Democratic voters from below the Mason-Dixon Line but also those aggrieved whites who lived in northern working-class neighborhoods. Using strategic dog-whistle appeals—crime, welfare, neighborhood schools—to trigger Pavlovian anti-black responses, Nixon succeeded in defining and maligning the Democrats as the party of African Americans, without once having to actually say the words. That would be the "elephant in the room."[30] In fact, as H. R. Haldeman, one of the Republican candidate's most trusted aides, later recalled, "He [Nixon] emphasized that you have to face the fact that the whole problem is really the blacks. The key is to devise a system that recognizes this while not appearing to."[31]

Nixon, therefore, framed America's issues as "excesses caused by . . . bleeding heart liberalism." The Civil Rights Act and the Voting Rights Act, he asserted, had removed the legal barriers to equality; they had also, he continued, raised unrealistic expectations in the black community. When equality didn't immediately emerge, he explained, lawlessness and rioting soon followed. On the presidential campaign trail, Nixon's basic mantra was that "it was both wrong and dangerous to make promises that cannot be fulfilled, or to raise hopes that come to nothing." The point, therefore, was to puncture blacks' expectations.[32]

That downward thrust would come through the iron fist of law and order.[33] Crime and blackness soon became synonymous in a carefully constructed way that played to the barely subliminal fears of darkened, frightening images flashing across the television screen.[34] One of Nixon's campaign ads, for example, carefully avoided using pictures of African Americans while at the same time showing cities burning, grainy images of protesters out in the streets, blood flowing, chaos shaking the very foundation of society, and then silence, as the screen faded to black, emblazoned with white lettering: THIS TIME VOTE LIKE YOUR WHOLE WORLD DEPENDED ON IT: NIXON.[35] The point, longtime aide John

Ehrlichman explained, was to present a position on crime, education, or public housing in such a way that a voter could "avoid admitting to himself that he was attracted by a racist appeal."[36] Nixon, after screening the ad, enthusiastically told his staff that the commercial "hits it right on the nose . . . It's all about law and order and the damn Negro–Puerto Rican groups out there."[37] Yet, in the ad he didn't have to say so explicitly. It was clear who was the threat, just as it was clear whose world depended on Nixon for salvation.[38]

In the 1968 election against Vice President Hubert Humphrey, Nixon, in addition to playing on the growing disenchantment with the Vietnam War, won by making the unworthiness of blacks the subtext for his campaign. Following his inauguration, the president targeted "two of the civil rights movement's greatest victories, *Brown* and the Voting Rights Act of 1965."[39] This was more than a cynical political ploy to curry favor with a particular constituency.[40] The Civil Rights Movement had raised the ante, because now, as in the years of Reconstruction, there appeared to be a strong Constitutional basis, in the newly invigorated Fourteenth and Fifteenth Amendments, for African Americans' claim to citizenship rights.

Given the landmines in the new post-civil-rights political terrain, outright opposition to the new statutes would have backfired. Thus, Nixon's strategy—one that would play out well into the twenty-first century—was to "weaken the enforcement of civil rights laws."[41] The Voting Rights Act in particular was the bête noire of the Republican Party's new Southern wing, empowering African Americans as it did through the ballot box. The VRA, which was able to muster only enough votes for initial passage by carrying the unprecedented provision requiring renewal within five years, was set for what its opponents hoped would be its death knell in 1970.

As the renewal hearings started, the Republican co-chair of the House Judiciary Committee, William McCulloch of Ohio, a fiscal conservative and civil rights advocate, explained that he had hoped the basic foundation of democracy, the vote, would now be accepted and honored. But "resistance to the program has been more subtle and more effective than I thought possible," he said. "A whole arsenal of racist weapons has been perfected." Instead of outright denial of access to the ballot, the South had begun to use dilution of black electoral strength through rigging precinct boundaries and requiring at-large elections. Mississippi, for example had passed a series of laws that turned the elected position of school superintendent into a political appointee and changed the selection of county supervisor from district-based to at-large elections. And Virginia, which prior to the VRA had assigned election officials to help the illiterate vote, in 1966 mandated that ballots had to be handwritten. The states argued that Section 5 of the VRA, which requires that the U.S. Department of Justice or the district court in Washington preapprove changes to election requirements, pertained only to mechanisms that directly affected access to the ballot box, such as the poll tax. In *Allen v. State Board of Elections* (1969), Chief Justice Earl Warren stopped Mississippi and Virginia in their tracks as he laid out that the VRA was "aimed at the subtle, as well as the obvious, state regulations which have the effect of denying citizens their right to vote because of their race." Representative McCulloch, therefore, noted in his support for renewal of the act that it was painfully obvious that "350 years of oppression cannot be eradicated in 5 years."[42]

While McCulloch saw the need to protect the ballot box, Attorney General John Mitchell announced that the Department of Justice, which he viewed as "an institution for law enforcement, not social improvement," opposed the renewal of the Voting Rights Act because it targeted, and therefore discriminated against, the South.[43] This upside-down framing of the VRA (and the sense that it was somehow not about the law but social engineering) purposely whitewashed the brutal electoral history of Jim Crow, somehow transforming ruthless perpetrators into innocent victims.

Alabama, Georgia, Louisiana, Mississippi, South Carolina, Virginia, and thirty-nine counties in North Carolina were singled out in the Voting Rights Act because they had mocked the Fifteenth Amendment and then contemptuously toyed with electoral discrimination lawsuits brought under the anemic Civil Rights Act of 1957. In addition, many of these states had also sanctioned or even fomented widespread terrorism against voting rights activists. The bullet-riddled corpses of James Chaney, Andrew Goodman, and Michael Schwerner, unearthed after months spent beneath tons of dirt in Neshoba County, Mississippi, served as a warning that those advocating the right to vote were, as one local woman scoffed, "just looking for trouble."[44] The televised fury unleashed on peaceful demonstrators in Selma, Alabama, as they tried to symbolically carry to the state capital of Montgomery the casket of slain voting rights activist Jimmie Lee Jackson, who had been killed by law enforcement, was only larger in scale than the day-to-day brutality that led to less than 1 percent of blacks in Selma being registered to vote. The horror on the Edmund Pettus Bridge was punctuated shortly thereafter by the bludgeoning death of Reverend James Reeb, who had come to Selma in support of voting rights.[45] The ambush and execution of Herbert Lee, who was helping to register blacks to vote, by a Mississippi legislator, followed soon after by a shotgun blast that blew off Louis Allen's face, sent a signal that the death sentence awaited those who believed that the Fifteenth Amendment applied to African Americans too.[46]

Despite Mitchell's insinuation, the Voting Rights Act was neither capricious nor punitive. It was, as the Department of Justice noted, "targeted at those areas of the country where Congress believed the potential for discrimination to be the greatest."[47] In 1966, in *South Carolina v. Katzenbach*, the Supreme Court, in an 8–1 decision, affirmed the need for federal oversight, ruling that:

> *Congress had found that case-by-case litigation [based on the 1957 Civil Rights Act] was inadequate to combat wide-spread and*

> *persistent discrimination in voting, because of the inordinate amount of time and energy required to overcome the obstructionist tactics invariably encountered in these lawsuits. After enduring nearly a century of systematic resistance to the Fifteenth Amendment, Congress might well decide to shift the advantage of time and inertia from the perpetrators of the evil to its victims.*[48]

Indeed, the impact of the Voting Rights Act was profound. Just prior to its passage, only 6.7 percent of black adults were registered to vote in Mississippi. Three years later, with federal oversight and Section 5 preclearance that required the Department of Justice or district court in Washington, D.C., to approve any changes to the state's election laws, the number of black registered voters had skyrocketed to 59.4 percent.[49]

Because the Voting Rights Act was clearly working, the first civil rights legislation Nixon sent to Congress proposed eliminating Section 5 and stretching the VRA's scope to the entire country.[50] Far from trying to disfranchise black voters, Nixon disingenuously explained, the amended legislation sought simply to address an imbalance that, when other areas of the nation also discriminated against segments of their citizenry, left the South unfairly singled out.[51] What eventually became clear during the congressional hearings, however, was that Nixon's new "civil rights legislation" would create a wholly uncivil America. "With the entire nation covered," the attorney general admitted, "it would be impossible for the Civil Rights Division of the Department of Justice to screen every voting change in every county in the nation." And thus, his staff would be unable to enforce the Voting Rights Act at all. Those who believed their rights had been violated at the ballot box, Mitchell continued, just needed to go through the courts. In essence, Nixon's plan was to hurl African Americans and the nation back to the slow, litigious route carved out in the long-since-discredited Civil Rights Act of 1957.[52]

During the VRA's extension hearings, South Carolina senator Strom Thurmond embraced the Nixon administration's idea as he floated a narrative of racial innocence that minimized the terror and walled off the brutal history of disfranchisement. Thurmond was emphatic that it was just wrong "to continually charge a state and a people with any alleged injustice that occurred many years ago." The NAACP's Clarence Mitchell looked Thurmond in the eye and countered that the injustices were hardly "alleged" but, in fact, well documented. "We could fill this room with the record of discrimination in the state of South Carolina," Mitchell informed the senator. Nor was Thurmond's "many years ago" accurate. At every turn in the civil rights struggle, the NAACP's representative asserted, "South Carolina has fought us all the way." Indeed, in 1966, one year after the VRA had passed, the state went before the U.S. Supreme Court, arguing that the Voting Rights Act infringed on states' rights, had illegally inserted federal registrars in counties that had literacy tests (which had been outlawed by the VRA), and presumed the state's guilt simply because far into the twentieth century, only 0.8 percent of South Carolina's voting-age black population was registered to vote. As Mitchell well knew, the court's *South Carolina v. Katzenbach* decision dismantled every one of the state's arguments and found the VRA constitutional. "Now that it appears we have won," Mitchell observed, "we don't want to have a situation develop where the White House gives back to South Carolina all the rights to discriminate that we have succeeded in wresting from them."[53]

The House and Senate agreed, refused to scuttle "the single most effective piece of civil rights legislation ever passed by Congress," and instead renewed the Voting Rights Act for another five years.[54] Still, the attorney general's initial thrust had made it all too clear how vulnerable the VRA was now, with its very strength—the increase in black voting—exposing its political jugular. Under the right circumstances and in the right venue, the vaunted Voting Rights Act could be taken down.

The Nixon administration turned its sights as well on *Brown*, which was already weakened by Massive Resistance and the subsequent tactic of stall and undermine. Almost fifteen years after the landmark Supreme Court decision, Mississippi, ever recalcitrant, had yet to desegregate its public school system. When, on July 3, 1969, the federal court ordered the state to implement *Brown* by that fall, Nixon's attorney general, as well as his secretary of Health, Education, and Welfare, convinced the judges to reverse the decision because "time was too short and the administrative problems too difficult to accomplish . . . before the beginning of the 1969–1970 school year."[55] In other words, by rejecting the *Cooper v. Aaron* decision about the unacceptability of kowtowing to state-sponsored obstruction, the Department of Justice, in league with HEW, ignored that Mississippi had already had more than a decade to develop a plan.

Nixon's four new appointments to the Supreme Court would follow through by eviscerating the constitutional right of black children to an education and then some. As vacancies opened on the bench, the president was drawn to the "law and order" writings of Warren Burger, who would replace Earl Warren as chief justice. Nixon also approved of the "strict constructionists" decisions and southern roots of Virginian Lewis Powell, and remained impressed by the "moderately conservative philosophy" and relative youth (at forty-seven years old) of William Rehnquist. The most contentious battles came over two of Nixon's Southern nominees, Clement Haynsworth, a "laundered segregationist," in the opinion of Joseph Rauh, counsel to the Leadership Conference on Civil Rights; and G. Harrold Carswell, who had ruled that "segregation of the races is proper and the only practical and correct way of life in our states." After a bruising series of confirmation hearings, the Senate rejected both. Nixon then turned to his default choice, a Northerner, Harry Blackmun. Admiring his handiwork years later, the president reflected, "I consider my four appointments to the Supreme Court to have been among the most constructive and far-reaching actions of my presidency . . . The men I appointed shared my conservative judicial philosophy and significantly affected the balances of power that had developed in the Warren Court."[56] This was an understatement, even for Richard Nixon. The court's subsequent decisions shut down access to quality education while allowing blatant racial discrimination to run rampant in criminal procedures.

Two important 5–4 Supreme Court decisions in which Nixon's appointees were in the slim but decisive majority undercut the possibility that *Brown* would ever fully be implemented. The first was the 1973 *San Antonio Independent School District v. Rodriguez* case. Parents from an impoverished, overwhelmingly minority neighborhood took Texas to court because the school funding mechanism, which relied on property taxes, created such disparate revenues as to make equal educational opportunity impossible. Of course, the value of property, on which school funding was heavily based, derived from government enforcement of residential segregation and discriminatory housing laws, as well as a series of public policy and zoning decisions such as where to put landfills, erect sewage treatment plants, allow liquor stores, and approve industrial plants.[57] Zoning had had a particularly deleterious effect on the Edgewood neighborhood of San Antonio, which was 96 percent Mexican American and black. That section had the lowest property value in the city, as well as the lowest median income.[58]

So committed were the parents to their children's education, however, that they voted for school levies that taxed their property at the highest rate in the area, which, even then, generated only $21 per student per academic year. Whereas the affluent, predominately white San Antonio neighborhood of Alamo Heights, whose property tax rate was significantly lower than Edgewood's, still produced enough revenue to expend $307 per pupil. Or, to put it another way, Alamo Heights secured nearly 1,500 percent more in funding with a significantly lower tax rate.[59]

Seeing the inequity, the parents in Edgewood screamed foul and sued. The U.S. district court, using *Brown* as the template, agreed. In a survey of 110 school districts throughout the state, the judges found that while the wealthiest districts in Texas taxed their property at 31 cents per $100, the poorest were "burdened" with a rate of 70 cents. Nevertheless, the district court continued, even with their low tax rate, the rich districts netted $525 more per pupil than the poor districts did. Clearly, the judges concluded, Texas's funding scheme "makes education a function of the local property tax base." The district court, therefore, ruled that "education is a fundamental right," that the state's use of "wealth" was a synonym for race and thus subject to judicial "strict scrutiny," and that Texas's funding scheme was irrational and violated the equal protection clause of the Fourteenth Amendment.[60] As the case moved up to the U.S. Supreme Court, Texas pleaded racial innocence and claimed not only that it was meeting the bare minimum requirements for access to education but also that it could not and should not be held responsible for the differences between what poor districts and wealthy ones amassed.

Nixon's four appointees to the court, as well as Potter Stewart, who had been tapped by Eisenhower, agreed. In a March 1973 ruling that pulled the rug out from under *Brown*, they found that "there is no fundamental right to education in the Constitution." The justices concluded, too, that the state's funding scheme "did not systematically discriminate against all poor people in Texas," and, because reliance on property taxes to fund schools was used across the country, the method was not "so irrational as to be invidiously discriminatory." For the court, then, the funding scheme, in which, for example, Chicago allocated $5,265 for African American pupils while the adjacent suburban school district of Niles appropriated $9,371 per student, was perfectly constitutional. Thus, despite the same kinds of rampant funding disparities that had led to *Brown*, Justice Lewis Powell declared that he saw no discriminatory public policy at all. With residential segregation no longer enforced by the government, whites and minorities alike, he felt, were free to move wherever they wanted in search of better schools. The fact that most minorities—after centuries of government-enforced racism in education and employment—simply did not have the economic wherewithal to move was overlooked.

And so, even in the waning days of the Civil Rights Movement, entrenched, constitutionally unequal education was once again an important part of the nation's way of life. "The Equal Protection Clause does not require absolute equality," Powell declared in a powerfully worded edict, "or precisely equal advantages."[61] What was at work here was class, not race; and class, unlike race, was not a "suspect category" that required "strict scrutiny." If Texas had a rational basis for its property tax system, the justices concluded, then the mechanism met judicial standards, despite producing a 975 percent disparity in school funding between white and minority children in Texas.

Fully recognizing the implications of *Rodriguez*, Justice Thurgood Marshall was apoplectic. More than 40 percent of black children fourteen and under lived with families below the poverty line, as compared with about 10 percent of white children.[62] Under those circumstances, Marshall feared, African American children wouldn't stand a chance. The decision, he wrote in his dissent, could "only be seen as a retreat" from a "commitment to equality of educational opportunity" as well as an "unsupportable" capitulation to "a system which deprives children . . . of the chance to reach their full potential as citizens." He was simply dumbfounded that the majority would acknowledge the existence of widely disparate funding for schools across Texas but then, instead of focusing on the cause of that disparity, clumsily pirouette to all of the state's supposed efforts to close the gaps. "The issue," Marshall explained, "is not whether Texas is doing its best to ameliorate the worst features of a discriminatory scheme but, rather, whether the scheme itself is in fact unconstitutionally discriminatory."[63]

Moreover, he found it the height of "absurdity" that Texas could actually argue there was no correlation between funding and school quality and then, from that faulty premise, deduce that there were "no discriminatory consequences for the children of the disadvantaged districts." Given the slew of amicus curiae briefs flooding the court supporting Texas's school funding scheme against the poor's challenge, Marshall wryly observed that if "financing variations are so insignificant to educational quality it is difficult to understand why a number of our country's wealthiest school districts . . . have nevertheless zealously pursued its cause before this Court." He was equally unimpressed with Texas's tendency to parade before the justices stories of children who had excelled despite living in under-resourced districts as some sort of proof that funding was irrelevant. That a child could excel even when "forced to attend an underfunded school with poorer physical facilities, less experienced teachers, larger classes," and a number of other deficits compared with "a school with substantially more funds," Marshall barked, "is to the credit of the child not the State."[64] *Rodriguez* placed the onus solely on the backs of the most vulnerable, while walling off access to the necessary resources for quality education, and played beautifully into the "colorblind," post-civil-rights language of substituting economics for race, yet achieving a similar result. The simple truth was that, by virtue of the sheer demographics of poverty, *Rodriguez* would have not only a disparate impact on African American children but also a disastrous one.

The next year, Nixon's Supreme Court appointees landed yet another powerful blow to *Brown*. This time the case emerged out of the North, in Detroit, which, by the early 1970s, was a predominately black city surrounded by overwhelmingly white suburbs. The K–12 system mirrored the racial geography, with virtually all the schools in the city more than 90 percent African American. Those schools were overcrowded, sometimes with classrooms holding as many as fifty students, and buildings so decayed and unsafe that classes were taught in trailers parked on the school grounds. Vera Bradley, a black mother of two sons, Richard and Ronald, wanted more for her children and turned to the NAACP for help. On August 18, 1970, Association general counsel Nathaniel Jones filed suit in the federal district court on Bradley's behalf against a number of officials including Governor William Milliken because, Jones noted, "these children were kept in schools that the Supreme Court said . . . were unconstitutional." City leaders, hoping to have the case withdrawn, devised a number of plans to integrate the K–12 system, but, as the district court noted, each scheme left the schools overwhelmingly identifiable racially and Detroit even blacker than before. The judge therefore ordered a metropolitan Detroit desegregation plan that spread beyond the city's borders. The suburbs immediately protested.[65]

The U.S. Supreme Court, however, calmed their fears. Just as *Rodriguez* ensured that funding in overwhelmingly white suburbs would never leak into the city schools, *Milliken v. Bradley* (1974) ensured that whites would not have to attend schools with African Americans. To accomplish this feat, the court had to ignore the role the law had played—in residential segregation; white flight; discriminatory public policy that financed, subsidized, and maintained white suburbs; and legislation that drew and redrew boundaries and curtailed transportation options—in keeping black children trapped in impoverished cities and subpar schools. Five justices held there was no evidence whatsoever that the outlying school districts had discriminated against blacks or been responsible for the racially distinct condition of inner-city Detroit. And if the suburbs were not part of the problem, the court reasoned, they could not be part of the solution. Then, as if to underscore the full retreat from *Brown*, the justices emphasized the importance of "local control" of schools and chastised the district court for overstepping its bounds. In a final coup de grâce, they added that *Brown* did not require "any particular racial balance in each school, grade, or classroom."[66]

Thurgood Marshall's dissent was a roaring eulogy to a once-promising landmark decision. He was astounded at the majority's "superficial" reasoning that had now resulted in the "emasculation of our constitutional guarantee of equal protection." Marshall balked at the notion of suburban innocence and scoffed at the contention that the Detroit public schools were locally controlled. The state of Michigan, he laid out, devised, tweaked, contorted, and, in fact, ran the K–12 system. Michigan, then, had the power to consolidate school districts and chose time and time again to keep white suburban ones separate and distinct from those in the city. Moreover, Marshall pointed out, when the city tried to exert some authority to implement *Brown*, the state legislature crushed Detroit's efforts. And while Michigan provided funding for buses in suburban schools, the same law actually banned the use of state transportation funds for students in the city of Detroit. This, Marshall noted, led to the "construction of small walk-in neighborhood schools, . . . which reflected, to the greatest extent feasible, extensive residential segregation." How the justices, given this firmly documented track record of discrimination, could absolve the state from responsibility for the racially divided metropolitan school system it created, Marshall had no idea: It "simply flies in the face of reality." For Marshall, the court's decision had less to do with "the neutral principle of law" than it did with public sentiment that "we have gone far enough in enforcing the Constitution's guarantee of equal justice." The consequences of this kind of cowardice for the United States, he warned, are "a course . . . our people will ultimately regret."[67]

As black access to quality public schools drifted further and further away, entrance into colleges and universities, increasingly essential in America's postindustrial economy, became even more difficult as well—thanks in no small part to the Supreme Court's 1978 *Bakke* decision. Allan Bakke, a white male, had applied to the University of California, Davis, medical school and was turned down twice. Bakke sued, arguing that the university's quota system allowed the admission of blacks and Latinos who had lower MCAT scores than his. There were, of course, whites who had also gained entry into the medical school program with scores lower than Bakke's, but their entrance was not the focus of his suit. Nor was the medical dean's tendency to guarantee admission to a number of his friends' and politicians' children (despite their lack of qualifications). Admissions based on alumni connections and high-level friendships, while generally dovetailing with whiteness, were not explicitly based on race and therefore not subject to "strict scrutiny." Instead, the university's policy to admit sixteen blacks and Latinos in a class of one hundred, Bakke charged, had denied him equal protection under the law.[68]

In the highly contentious and fractious 4–1–4 decision, a plurality of judges agreed, demanding concrete evidence that black students who had been admitted had personally been discriminated against by the university. The five justices further asserted that they would only countenance the use of race in admissions for well-defined diversity purposes, while preferring the broader, more multicultural scope of "disadvantaged," which would, for example, recognize what a "farm boy from Idaho" could bring to Harvard. Finally, they focused the court's concern on the "reverse discrimination" heaped on whites applying to colleges and universities who, like Bakke, "bore no responsibility for any wrongs suffered by minorities." As for admissions policies designed to atone for past discrimination against minorities, Justice Byron White was unequivocal: "I do not accept that position."[69]

Attempting to observe the law while also living up to an ethos they had now taken to heart, universities frantically turned to vaguer notions of "diversity," but the definition of that word soon became so expansive that by the twenty-first century white males would actually be the primary beneficiaries of affirmative action in college admissions.[70]

Even as the court rejected history, Thurgood Marshall's dissent in *Bakke* recounted 350 years of "the most pervasive and ingenious forms of racial discrimination" against African Americans. He then expressed disbelief that the court would deny California the right to apply a remedy in the face of that kind of sordid history.[71] Astounded as Marshall may have been, though, the decision, viewed through the opposite lens, made calculated sense. African Americans had rushed right through the barely opened door of opportunity pushed ajar by the Civil Rights Movement: From 1970 to 1978, the number of blacks enrolled in college had literally doubled. And in just a little more than a decade, the percentage of African Americans who had a college degree climbed to 6 percent from 4 percent.[72] A combination of their own determination and aspiration—coupled with the protections of affirmative action, which actively sought black students rather than shutting them out, and federal student financial aid, which helped defray tuition costs for a people overwhelmingly impoverished—had significantly changed the game.[73] Nixon's policies and the Supreme Court choices had set the stage to reverse those gains. Much of this reversal, though, would not be carried out until the Reagan administration.

Hailed as one of the most popular and even greatest presidents, Ronald Reagan oversaw the rollback of many of the gains African Americans had achieved through the Civil Rights Movement. Between 1981 and 1988, conditions regressed to levels reminiscent of the early 1960s.[74]

Journalist Hodding Carter described Reagan as "part Wallace and part Nixon and a more effective southern strategist than both put together."[75] Reagan's aura of sincerity and "aw shucks" geniality lent a welcoming, friendly facade to any harshness of the Southern Strategy—something that neither Nixon's brooding nor Wallace's angry countenance had ever been able to convey. Reagan, therefore, positively oozed racial innocence in his declaration of fealty to states' rights at the all-white 1980 Neshoba County Fair in Mississippi, site of the triple murder of civil rights workers.[76] In a 1981 interview, GOP consultant Lee Atwater explained the inner logic of, as one commentator noted, "racism with plausible deniability."[77] "You start out in 1954," Atwater laid out, "by saying, 'nigger, nigger, nigger.' By 1968, you can't say 'nigger'—that hurts you. Backfires. So you say stuff like forced busing, states' rights and all that stuff. You're getting so abstract now you're talking about cutting taxes, and all these things you're talking about are totally economic things and a byproduct of them is blacks get hurt worse than whites. And subconsciously maybe that is part of it. *I'm* not saying that," he then deflected.[78]

It was a role tailor-made for the former Hollywood actor. Reagan cast himself as a traditional conservative, but his disdain for supposed big government was geared not so much toward New Deal programs that had provided paid employment to millions of out-of-work Americans like his father; or social security, which had overwhelmingly benefited whites during the Great Depression. What President Reagan loathed was the Great Society that, despite its dispersal of benefits to middle-class whites and its measurable effectiveness in lifting the elderly out of poverty, he succeeded in coding as a giveaway program for blacks.[79] His budget priorities reflected that contempt, as he ordered a scorched-earth policy through the Great Society from education, to housing, to employment.

Despite his profession of, and supposed obsession with, a "color-blind" society where, as he said, "nothing is done to, or for, anyone because of race," Reagan's budget proposals targeted very specifically those programs in which blacks were overrepresented even as he protected the other portions of the "social safety net," such as social security, where African Americans were but a small fraction of the recipients.[80] For example, almost five times as many black college-bound high school seniors as white came from families with incomes below twelve thousand dollars. The administration reconfigured various grants and loan packages so that "the needier the student, the harder he or she would be hit by Reagan's student-aid cuts." Not surprisingly, nationwide black enrollment in college plummeted from 34 percent to 26 percent. Thus, just at the moment when the postindustrial economy made an undergraduate degree more important than ever, fifteen thousand fewer African Americans were in college during the early 1980s than had been enrolled in the mid-1970s (although the high school graduation numbers were by now significantly higher). Nor had the fallout happened only at the baccalaureate level; the plunge in undergraduate enrollment—which no other racial or ethnic group suffered during this time—cascaded into a substantial decline in the number of African Americans in graduate programs as well.[81]

While access to higher education was crumbling, the Reagan administration also established enormous roadblocks to quality K–12 public schools for African American children. The president cavalierly stated that he was "under the impression that the problem of segregated schools has been settled."[82] The assistant attorney general for civil rights, William Bradford Reynolds, agreed, and when he learned of an effort in South Carolina to dismantle what amounted to Jim Crow education, he was determined that black parents, whom he referred to as "those bastards," would have to "jump through every hoop" to file a lawsuit to desegregate the public schools in Charleston. "We are not going to compel children who don't choose to have an integrated education to have one," Reynolds insisted.[83] Under Reynolds and Attorney General Edwin Meese, the Department of Justice used virtually every legal strategy to dismantle, obstruct, and undermine the only remaining alternative to integrate schools—busing—including torpedoing a plan to finally desegregate a school district in Louisiana that had openly fought *Brown* since 1956.[84]

Already hampered by the Scylla and Charybdis of *Milliken* and *Rodriguez*, black children's passage through the education system became even more difficult during the Reagan years. The Detroit decision meant that children were, for the most part, locked inside their cities and their neighborhoods, while *Rodriguez* meant that those city and neighborhood schools would remain or become even more impoverished. And now the Department of Justice seemed determined to advocate segregated schools as a "remedy," putting its considerable weight on the side of the status quo of inequality.[85] Moreover, the Reagan administration exacerbated that inequality even further as it shredded the safety net.[86] Not even school lunch programs, geared toward those in greatest economic need, were sacred, the *Christian Science Monitor* reported, as they came under attack when "President Reagan trimmed $1.46 billion from $5.66 billion earmarked for child nutrition programs."[87] He also leveled a double-digit cut for a program designed to provide educational support for poor children in the classroom at the very moment when the share of black youth living below the poverty line had increased to almost 43 percent.[88]

The 1980s revealed just how fragile the economic recovery of African Americans was in the wake of 350 years of slavery and Jim Crow. From the 1960s to the 1970s, the black unemployment rate had declined, and the gap between black and white unemployment rates had actually narrowed. By the time Reagan's policies had taken effect, however, not only had the black unemployment rate increased, but also the unemployment gap between blacks and whites had widened to unprecedented levels.[89] During the early 1980s, the overall black unemployment rate stood at 15.5 percent—"an all time high" since the Great Depression—while unemployment among African American youth was a staggering 45.7 percent. At this point Reagan chose to slash the training, employment, and labor services budget by 70 percent—a cut of $3.805 billion.[90] The only "'urban' program that survived the cuts was federal aid for highways—which primarily benefited suburbs, not cities." In keeping with Lee Atwater's mantra that "blacks get hurt worse than whites," Reagan gutted aid to cities so extensively that federal dollars were reduced from 22 percent of a city's budget to 6 percent. Cities responded with sharp austerity measures that shut down libraries, closed municipal hospitals, and cut back on garbage pickup. Some cities even dismantled their police and fire departments.[91]

Reagan further destabilized the economic foundation for African Americans by ordering massive layoffs in federal jobs while deliberately weakening the enforcement of civil rights laws in the workplace. Blacks are disproportionately employed by the government, not least because the public sector suffers demonstrably less discrimination in hiring and compensation than private industry.[92] More than 50 percent of the growth in employment for black workers in the United States between 1960 to 1976, in fact, was in the public sector. But that avenue into economic stability, even for the college educated, was now threatened by two key developments: First, the federal government's layoffs were concentrated in the social service agencies, where many African Americans worked. Reagan had exempted the Department of Defense, for example, while making it clear that "other divisions of Government would be hit especially hard by the employment reductions." When one agency was abolished in 1981, jobs for nine hundred workers, 60 percent of them black, were wiped out. Then, the Department of Health and Human Services, a major agency for black employment, absorbed about half of the six thousand layoffs scheduled for 1982.[93]

The second development assaulting the job security of black civil servants was the administration's decision to put the Equal Employment Opportunity Commission (EEOC), which was the federal watchdog for employment discrimination, "on ice" by making the agency utterly ineffective.[94] Reagan appointed inadequate and often incompetent leadership. He was especially keen to select African Americans, such as future Supreme Court justice Clarence Thomas, who believed there was no group discrimination against minorities or women, certainly nothing that would warrant class-action lawsuits.[95] Under this new management, the agency slowed down to a crawl its investigation and processing of complaints. The result was a growing backlog whose legal shelf life expired before the EEOC even got around to investigating.[96] The watchdog had been effectively muzzled.

With the rollback now in full force, the "civil rights gains of the past," as National Urban League president Vernon Jordan remarked, were "now under attack and in danger."[97] The median family income for African Americans had been higher in the 1970s than it was under Reagan, even as the white median income, despite the economic downturn, continued to grow. As a result, the actual spending power of blacks decreased while that of whites rose, increasing the gap by 12 percent. "In virtually every area of life that counts," wrote David Swinton, future president of the United Negro College Fund, "black people made strong progress in the 1960s, peaked in the 70s, and have been sliding back ever since." The Reagan administration's "deplorable" policies and efforts "to turn back the clock" ensured it. Indeed, by 1990, blacks in the bottom 20 percent were poorer in relation to whites than at any time since the 1950s. Not surprisingly, the National Urban League labeled the president's policies "a failure" that has "usher[ed] in a new era of stagnation and decline" for the "vast majority of average black Americans."[98] Reagan's job cuts, retooling of student financial aid to eliminate those most in need, and decimation of antipoverty and social welfare programs "virtually ensured that the goal of the African American community for economic stability and progress would crumble and fade."[99]

In March 1981, Reagan assured reporters that "he would offer a national drug-abuse program that would put its main effort into warning young people about the dangers of drug use rather than into attacks on narcotics smuggling."[100] But by October 1982, the president had obviously changed his mind. In a gripping address, he explained that a scourge had invaded the nation's borders, taken hold of American families and children, and was laying siege to cities across the land. Hardest hit, the president conveyed, was the "garden spot" of South Florida, which had "turned into a battlefield for competing drug pushers who were terrorizing Florida's citizens." The president then laid out a potent multi-agency strategy using military intelligence and radar that could hone in on drug traffickers and execute brilliant interdiction strikes "to cut off drugs before they left other countries' borders."[101]

There was just one problem. There *was* no drug crisis in 1982. Marijuana use was down; heroin and hallucinogens use had leveled off, even first-time cocaine use was bottoming out.[102]

But, as Reagan well knew, such a crisis was certainly coming, for it had been manufactured and facilitated by his staff on the National Security Council (NSC) along with the Central Intelligence Agency (CIA). In these last throes of the Cold War, Nicaragua was the target. But the collateral damage would spray South Central Los Angeles and then radiate out to black communities all across the United States.

In 1979, after a coalition of moderate and Marxist Nicaraguans overthrew longtime U.S. ally and ruthless dictator Anastasio Somoza, communist Sandinistas came to power in Managua. Reagan did not see this as a homegrown revolution borne out of intolerable conditions of greed, torture, and human rights violations. Instead, he was sure that the Sandinistas were no more than Soviet stooges ensconced by Moscow to foment revolution in America's backyard.[103] The president was, therefore, obsessed with eliminating the Sandinistas.[104]

Shortly after taking office, Reagan ordered CIA director William Casey to do whatever was necessary to support a small band of anti-Sandinista guerrillas, known as the Contras, most of whom were strays from Somoza's feared and hated National Guard. Reagan followed up on November 23, 1981, with a directive to funnel $19.3 million through the CIA to the Contras. But that was not enough, argued Enrique Bermúdez, the founder of the guerrilla group. They needed much more.[105] Then, in December 1981, "Reagan signed a secret order authorizing Contra aid for the purpose of deposing the Sandinistas." The only question was where to get those funds; there was simply a limit to the depths that the CIA and National Security Council budgets could tap into to finance the Contras.[106] Congress, meanwhile, already stung by the debacle in Vietnam, was not about to loosen the purse strings.[107]

And so, at a December 1981 meeting, Contra leaders, whom Reagan referred to as the "moral equivalent of the Founding Fathers," floated the idea that trafficking cocaine into California would provide enough profits to arm and train the anti-Sandinista guerrillas.[108] With most of the network already established, the plan was rather straightforward: There were the Medellín and Cali cartels in Colombia; the airports and money laundering in Panama run by President Manuel Noriega; the well-known lack of radar detection that made landing strips in Costa Rica prime transport depots; and weapons and drug warehouses at Ilopango air base outside San Salvador. The problem had been U.S. law enforcement guarding key entry points into a lucrative market. But with the CIA and the National Security Council now ready to run interference and keep the FBI, the U.S. Customs Service, and the Drug Enforcement Administration (DEA) in check, the once formidable line of defense had dwindled to a porous nuisance. Reagan's "moral equivalent of the Founding Fathers" was now ready to saturate the United States with cocaine.

Initially, Nicaraguan exiles Oscar Danilo Blandón and Norwin Meneses, whose nickname was El Rey de las Drogas (the King of Drugs), set up their wholesale operations in San Francisco. But although they had the product, they didn't yet have the distribution network to move the initial shipment of cocaine into the retail markets. That came only when they managed to link up with Rick Ross, an illiterate yet entrepreneurial black man who became the conduit between the Contra drug runners and the Crips and Bloods gangs in L.A.[109]

The result was nothing less than explosive. From the Contra wholesalers, top-quality cocaine was then packaged and sold in little rocks of crack that reaped more than $230,000 per kilo in retail profit. Now, drug money, and all its attendant violence, pounded on a population with double-digit unemployment and declining real wages. The logistical strength of the Bloods and Crips, with an estimated fifty thousand gang members, spread the pain as they set up drug franchises throughout the United States to sell crack like it was on the dollar menu.[110] Soon crack was everywhere, kicking the legs out from under black neighborhoods.[111]

While the new self-created drug crisis threatened the security of millions of African Americans, the administration focused its efforts on facilitating greater access to weapons for the rebels purchased with off-the-books money. In 1982, Vice President George H. W. Bush (the former director of the CIA) and his national security adviser, Donald Gregg (a former CIA agent), worked with William Casey to run a program named Black Eagle, which was designed to circumvent Congress and funnel weapons to the Contras. As the logistical pipelines solidified, it became clear that Manuel Noriega would be essential to this operation. Through a series of top-secret negotiations, U.S. officials worked out landing rights at Panamanian airfields for the Black Eagle planes to transport weapons to the Contras and the use of Panamanian companies to launder money.[112]

Noriega, who was already in a four-hundred-million-dollar partnership with the Medellín cartel, seized on the profitability of this deal with the White House and began to divert Black Eagle planes and pilots for drug-running flights to the southern United States. The Reagan administration's response to what should have been seen as a diplomatic affront—especially since the president had tapped George H. W. Bush to lead the drug interdiction activities in South Florida—was telling and disturbing. The administration simply required the Panamanian president to use a percentage of his drug profits to buy additional weapons for the Contras.[113]

Thus, although Reagan bragged to the American public about using U.S. military resources "to cut off drugs before they left other countries' borders," his staff's shielding of Noriega and the Colombian traffickers in fact actively allowed cocaine imports to the United States to skyrocket by 50 percent within three years. The Medellín cartel's cut alone was ten billion dollars a year in sales.[114] The Reagan administration's protection of drug traffickers escalated further when the CIA received approval from the Department of Justice in 1982 to remain silent about any key agency "assets" that were involved in the manufacturing, transportation, or sale of narcotics.[115]

This network of White House protection for major drug traffickers swung into full gear once Congress, through a series of amendments in 1982 and 1984, shut off all funds to the Contras and banned U.S. material and financial support for the overthrow of the government in Nicaragua.[116] Undeterred by the law, the Reagan administration simply ramped up the alternate and illegal streams of revenue it had already devised: drug profits and arms sales to Iran.[117] At this point Lieutenant Colonel Oliver North, deputy director of the National Security Council, stepped in to create the larger, more dynamic operation that would soon replace Bush's Black Eagle.

North brought to the work both a military efficiency and a truly amoral focus. Years later, even when under congressional klieg lights, he seemed to imply that the breaking of laws was appropriate.[118] "I remain convinced that what we tried to accomplish was worth the risk," he said.[119] North understood that his role, working with his CIA counterpart Duane Clarridge, was to ensure that the Contras had weapons. Congress had cut off all funding, so profits from cocaine would have to become an alternate source. That warped framing of the Contras' needs led North to facilitate the trafficking of cocaine into the United States, which included working with the CIA to transport 1,500 kilos of Bolivian paste; diverting hundreds of thousands of dollars in "humanitarian aid" to indicted narcotics traffickers; and refusing to pass the names of known drug runners on to the appropriate authorities.[120] He also saw to it that the millions of dollars in profits from the sale of narcotics were then funneled safely out of the U.S. and that those funds went to arms dealers, especially in El Salvador and Honduras, who could equip the Contras with everything from boots to grenades.[121] The FBI learned that North's NSC, brandishing the pretext of "the interest of national security," routinely intimidated Customs and DEA officials to back off from making good narcotics cases. Moreover, Blandón and Meneses, who trafficked at least five tons of cocaine, or the equivalent of 16.2 million rocks of crack, into California, "led a charmed life" as the NSC and CIA blocked police, sheriffs, and the DEA from stopping the flow of drugs and money.[122] Similarly, in the summer of 1986 North was Manuel Noriega's champion in the halls of power. The *New York Times* had run a series of articles citing well-placed sources and a Defense Intelligence Agency report that the Panamanian president had "tight control of drug and money-laundering activities" in and out of the country and, therefore, although making only $1,200 a month, had a personal fortune of several hundred million dollars. It was too much even for Senator Jesse Helms (R-NC), an ultra-right-wing senior member of the Foreign Relations Committee, who then went on *Meet the Press* and branded Noriega "head of the biggest drug trafficking operation in the Western Hemisphere." The barrage hit too close to the truth and North's attempt at damage control swung into action. He confided to his boss, National Security Advisor John Poindexter, "You will recall that over the years Manuel Noriega in Panama and I have developed a fairly good relationship" and now, given the media onslaught, the dictator needed the Reagan administration's help in cleaning up his image. North was eager but, he continued, it was going to cost. The dictator's terms were simple. In exchange for one million dollars and a PR blitz from the White House, Noriega offered to destabilize the Sandinista government. At first, Poindexter wobbled. Was this a setup "so that he can blackmail us to lay off?" Reagan's National Security Advisor, however, quickly set aside those initial qualms and authorized North to open negotiations with Noriega noting "I have nothing against him other than his illegal activities." Secretary of State George P. Schultz was on board, as well. The CIA, this time, refused to play along. The agency "didn't want to do it . . . just didn't want to touch that one." But North was adamant. Noriega, who was instrumental in flooding the United States with cocaine, was a valued asset. North even swooped in to rescue a major Contra ally who was arrested by the FBI with 345 kilos of cocaine. The lieutenant colonel, using the full authority and aura of the NSC, weighed in on the court and had the drug kingpin's sentence reduced by 75 percent (down to five years) and the locale of incarceration changed from a maximum- to a minimum-security ("Club Fed") facility.[123]

While there was inordinate concern about avoiding prison sentences and the legal consequences for those who poured tons of cocaine into the United States, there was an equal determination to lock up and imprison the communities bearing the brunt of the White House's narco-funding scheme.[124] Unlike in 1981, when Reagan had indicated that treatment for addicts was the route he would take, his speeches and policies now became focused on enforcement, criminals, and harsh, no-mercy punishment.[125] With the onset of the epidemic of crack, a drug that had become thoroughly associated with African Americans, notions of treatment went out the window, despite numerous studies proving that treatment was not only more effective but also more fiscally sound and prudent. And, as one DEA agent remarked, "no one has yet demonstrated that enforcement will ever win the war on drugs."[126] Nonetheless, Reagan dragged America down the road of mass incarceration.

Each of the Reagan administration's decisions undercut the supposed stated goals of protecting American families, preventing the flow of drugs from washing onto the nation's shores, or bringing democracy to a war-torn society. The decision to fund the Contras with profits from the sale of cocaine, for example, came at a time when the economic downturn had created high unemployment, increasing homelessness, the depletion of savings, and other major stressors, which only heightened the possibility of creating a drug-addicted society at the very moment when narcotics use had actually stabilized or decreased.[127]

As the horrific toll crack cocaine caused in the inner city became more and more obvious, the administration's response was not to fund a series of treatment facilities but to demonize and criminalize blacks and provide the federal resources to make incarceration, rather than education, normative. "Drugs are menacing our society," the president told the nation in a September 1986 speech delivered from the White House. "They're threatening our values and undercutting our institutions. They're killing our children." The United States, he conveyed, was a nation under attack.[128]

"Despite our best efforts," Reagan added with a hint of shock and dismay, "illegal cocaine is coming into our country at alarming levels." At that point, in what looked like the nadir of surrender, Reagan identified public enemy number one: "crack." And then, just to reaffirm the heroes and villains in this set piece, the president sent out a clarion call, proclaiming, "Drug abuse is a repudiation of everything America is." He positively vibrated with a sense of righteous, patriotic indignation. No one, he intoned, has the right to destroy the dreams and shatter the lives of the "freest society mankind has ever known."[129] In this important speech, the president not only laid out an epic tale of good, freedom-loving Americans locked in a mortal battle for the nation's soul against crack addicts and drug dealers, but in doing so, he also defined the racial contours of this war.

Media fanned the flames, and then some. With little to no evidence, news outlets warned that crack, reputedly the most addictive drug known to mankind, was galloping out of the crime-filled inner cities and, as *Newsweek* claimed, "rapidly spreading into the suburbs." The *New York Times* echoed the refrain identifying "epidemic" crack use from Long Island to "the wealthiest suburbs of Westchester County."[130] The media's overwhelming tendency to blacken crack only added to this national panic. Between 1986 and 1987, 76 percent of the articles in the *New York Times*, the *Chicago Tribune*, the *Washington Post*, and the *Los Angeles Times* dealing with crack referenced African Americans either directly or through code words—*urban*, *inner city*, etc. Whites were mentioned only one third of the time.[131] The message was clear: the black "plague" was coming.[132]

The crack plague had already swept through African American neighborhoods around the country with absolutely no warning. There had been minor use of crack in the 1970s, but it began to visibly show up in 1984 and exploded in 1985 and 1986—just as Congress cut off funding to the Contras, leaving the administration desperate to finance the war against the Sandinistas.[133] As battles over lucrative drug turf escalated, black communities were besieged with rampant gang violence. Most had no idea how this crack scourge had arisen or how those who had once toted simple handguns now carried AK-47s and other automatic, military-grade weapons. It was clear immediately that something had gone horribly wrong.[134] A National Urban League report declared that the "gains made over the past 25 years, many the result of the Civil Rights Movement in the 1960s, will . . . unravel unless steps are taken to arrest the pervasive problem of crime in the black community."[135]

A research team from Harvard and the University of Chicago explained, "Between 1984 and 1994, the homicide rate for Black males aged 14–17 more than doubled and homicide rates for Black males aged 18–24 increased almost as much."[136] The magnitude of the firepower and the sheer number of killings were, in fact, critical factors that led African American life expectancy rates to actually decline—something that not even slavery or Jim Crow had been able to accomplish.[137] Moreover, many other sectors of the black community were also horribly affected by murders and crack—fetal death rates, low-birth-weight babies, and children now in foster care. The researchers concluded that the perilous decline of African Americans on so many quality-of-life indicators "represents a break from decades of convergence between Blacks and Whites on many of these measures."[138]

The divergence, however, was about to get exponentially worse. In 1986, Congress passed the Anti-Drug Abuse Act, which stipulated mandatory sentencing, emphasized punishment over treatment, and created the 100-to-1 disparity in sentencing between crack and cocaine based on the myth that the cheap narcotic rock was more addictive than its powder form. As the NAACP explained the law's 100-to-1 formulation, "a person must possess 500 grams of powder cocaine before they are subject to the same mandatory prison sentence (5 years) as an individual who is convicted of possessing just 5 grams of crack cocaine (despite the fact that pharmacologically, these two drugs are identical)."[139] The National Urban League was convinced that tougher sentencing policies were not the answer. The incarceration rate would be so high, it warned, that society would not be able to bear the costs.[140] Congress, nonetheless, followed up in 1988 with an even harsher version of the Anti-Drug Abuse Act that instituted mandatory sentencing for even a first-time offense, added the death penalty for certain crimes where drugs were an aggravating factor, and denied housing and other human rights to those whose greatest crime was having a friend or a family member in the drug trade even visit.[141]

The Supreme Court had played a critical role in tightening the noose. A series of cases, beginning in 1968 but escalating dramatically in the Burger and Rehnquist eras, legalized racial discrimination in the criminal justice system.[142] The Court

- affirmed that police, even though their overall racial bias is well documented, can stop anyone based on something far below the understood threshold of probable cause;[143]
- approved racial profiling;[144]
- upheld harsh mandatory sentencing for drug offenses;[145]
- tossed out irrefutable evidence of racial bias in sentencing because of its implications for the entire criminal justice system and required, instead, proof of overt, visible discrimination against the individual defendant to support a claim of violation of equal protection under the law;[146]
- approved, as the justices openly admitted, "ridiculous" peremptory strikes to eliminate blacks from a jury so long as the prosecutor's stated rationale was not based on race;[147]
- shielded district attorneys from disclosing the role the defendant's race played in prosecutorial discretion;[148]
- ruled that police could use their discretion instead of probable cause to search motorists for drugs;[149]
- determined that Title VI of the Civil Rights Act cannot be used by private individuals to sue entities, such as prosecutors or police, in the criminal justice system on grounds of racial bias; and[150]
- found that pretext traffic stops—for example, having a busted taillight or not using a turn signal—are a legal and permissible ruse for police to hunt for drugs.[151]

Taken together, those rulings allowed, indeed encouraged, the criminal justice system to run racially amok. And that's exactly what happened on July 23, 1999, in Tulia, Texas. In the dead of night, local police launched a massive raid and busted a major cocaine trafficking ring. At least that's how it was billed by the local media, which, after having been tipped off, lined up to get the best, most humiliating photographs of forty-six of the town's five thousand residents, handcuffed, in pajamas, underwear, and uncombed bed hair, being paraded into the jail for booking. The local newspaper, the *Tulia Sentinel*, ran the headline TULIA'S STREETS CLEARED OF GARBAGE. The editorial praised law enforcement for ridding Tulia of "drug-dealing scumbags."[152]

The raid was the result of an eighteen-month investigation by a man who would be named by Texas's attorney general as "Outstanding Lawman of the Year." Attached to the federally funded Panhandle Regional Narcotics Task Force, based in Amarillo, about fifty miles away from Tulia, Tom Coleman didn't lead a team of investigators; instead, he singlehandedly identified each member of this massive cocaine operation and made more than one hundred undercover drug purchases. He was hailed as a hero, and his testimony immediately led to thirty-eight of the forty-six being convicted, with the other cases just waiting to get into the clogged court system. Joe Moore, a pig farmer, was sentenced to 99 years for selling two hundred dollars' worth of cocaine to the undercover narcotics agent. Kizzie White received twenty-five years, while her husband, William "Cash" Love, landed 434 years for possessing an ounce of cocaine.[153]

The case began to unravel, however, when Kizzie's sister, Tonya, went to trial. Coleman swore that she had sold him drugs. Tonya, however, had video proof that she was at a bank in Oklahoma City, three hundred miles away, cashing a check at the very moment he claimed to have bought cocaine from her. Then another defendant, Billy Don Wafer, had timesheets and his boss's eyewitness testimony that Wafer was at work and not out selling drugs to Coleman. And when the Outstanding Lawman of the Year swore under oath that he had purchased cocaine from Yul Bryant, a tall bushy-haired man, only to have Bryant—bald and five feet six—appear in court, it finally became very clear that something was awry.[154]

Coleman, in fact, had no proof whatsoever that any of the alleged drug deals had taken place. There were no audiotapes. No photographs. No witnesses. No other police officers present. No fingerprints but his on the bags of drugs. No records. Over the span of an eighteen-month investigation, he never wore a wire. He claimed to have written each drug transaction on his leg but to have washed away the evidence accidentally when he showered. Additional investigation led to no corroborating proof of his allegations, and when the police arrested those forty-six people and vigorously searched their homes and possessions, no drugs were found, nor were weapons, money, paraphernalia, or any other indications at all that the housewife, pig farmer, or anyone else arrested were actually drug kingpins.[155]

What was discovered, however, was judicial misconduct running rampant in the war on drugs in Tulia, Texas, with a clear racial bias. Coleman perjured himself on the stand when he claimed to be an upstanding, law-abiding citizen. In fact, he was under indictment for theft in his previous position as a deputy sheriff in another county. The prosecutor, Terry McEachern, knew about this but failed to disclose it to the defense attorneys. The district attorney also ensured that there were no African Americans on the jury in each trial. Moreover, Judge Edward Self, who presided over the lion's share of the trials, publically expressed his support for the prosecutors and sealed Coleman's employment records, including the charge of embezzlement as a deputy sheriff.[156]

The judicial malfeasance immediately took on racial undertones. Coleman, a white man who routinely referred to African Americans as "niggers," had accused 10 percent of Tulia's black population of dealing in cocaine.[157] Based on his word alone, 50 percent of all the black men in the town were indicted, convicted, and sentenced to prison. Of the six whites and Latinos who were arrested in the raid, all had relations—familial or friendly—with Tulia's black community.[158] Although the white community consistently denied that race played any role in this, the speed and efficiency in which the criminal justice system worked to sentence black defendants and their white and Latino friends to decades in prison, based solely on the unsubstantiated testimony of a man under indictment, suggests otherwise.[159] Randy Credico of the William Moses Kunstler Fund for Racial Justice, called Tulia "a mass lynching . . . Taking down 50 percent of the male black adult population like that, it's outrageous. It's like being accused of raping someone in Indiana in the 1930s. You didn't do it, but it doesn't matter because a bunch of Klansmen on the jury are going to string you up anyway."[160]

But this wasn't 1930. It was the beginning of the twenty-first century, and a powerful Civil Rights Movement had bridged those two eras. Yet now, felony convictions, chiefly via the war on drugs, replaced the explicit use of race as the mechanism to deny black Americans their rights as citizens. Disfranchisement, permanent bans on jury service, and legal discrimination in employment, housing, and education—despite the civil rights legislation of the 1960s—are now all burdens carried by those who have been incarcerated. That burden has been disproportionately shouldered by the black community, which, although only 13 percent of the nation's population, makes up 45 percent of those incarcerated.[161]

Even more disconcertingly, these felony convictions have had little to do with ensuring the safety and security of the nation and in most cases target the wrong culprits.[162] Logically, given the poor state of the schools, crushing poverty, and the lack of viable living-wage options for large swaths of the black population, African Americans' drug use should mirror their staggering incarceration rates. According to Human Rights Watch, "the proportion of blacks in prison populations exceeds the proportion among state residents in every single state." In Missouri, for example, African Americans make up 11.2 percent of the state's residents but 41.2 percent of those incarcerated. In fact, "in twenty states, the percent[age] of blacks incarcerated is at least five times greater than their share of resident population."[163] But, there is no direct correlation between drug use and incarceration.

Despite all the economic and social pressures they confront, blacks have shown an amazing resilience in the face of drugs; indeed, they are among the least likely drug users of all racial and ethnic groups in the United States.[164] And despite all the stereotypes, they are among the least likely to sell drugs too. As a major study out of the University of Washington revealed, even when confronted with irrefutable evidence of whites' engagement with the illegal-drug trade, law enforcement has continued to focus its efforts on the black population.[165]

Thus, after the Civil Rights Movement, when African Americans were making incredible strides in education, voting, and employment, those gains were a threat to the status quo of inequality. Thus, the "United States did not face a crime problem that was racialized; it faced a race problem that was criminalized."[166]

Five

How to Unelect a Black President

On November 4, 2008, the United States seemed to be crossing the racial Rubicon. For a brief moment, the mirage of hope hung in the air, mesmerizing those not just in the United States but also around the world. Barack Obama's historic presidential victory led an observer in Tehran to note, "The country that they called 'the great Satan,' [declaring] it the symbol of all kinds of tyranny, has enough respect for democratic values that [it has] allowed a black candidate to come this far and even become a president." And from Moscow: "The U.S., that is a country that is really majestic . . . I feel it is a country where everything is possible."[1] Nobel Peace Prize winner Desmond Tutu agreed. Obama's victory, he said, told "people of color that for them, the sky is the limit."[2] CHANGE HAS COME TO AMERICA blazed the headline in the *Philadelphia Inquirer*.[3]

Not everyone was ecstatic. As the Republican postmortems on the election poured in, it immediately became apparent that the voting patterns spelled trouble for the GOP. Obama had captured a significantly higher share of the white vote than John Kerry had managed to secure in the 2004 election. Moreover, 66 percent of Hispanics voted overwhelmingly for Barack Obama, not to mention 62 percent of Asians, 56 percent of women, 66 percent of voters under thirty years of age, and 95 percent of African Americans.[4] The last of these, in some ways, was to be expected. What wasn't anticipated, however, was that for the first time in history, the black voter turnout rate nearly equaled that of whites.[5]

The only demographics John McCain could claim to have run away with were the elderly white and evangelical Christian vote.[6] And therein lay the problem; for those sectors of the American voting population are not growing. Republican South Carolina senator Lindsey Graham, taking stock of the nearly inevitable demographic apocalypse, put it best: "We're not generating enough angry white guys to stay in business for the long term."[7]

This dawning of demographic extinction was all the more troubling because the largest percentage of eligible voters in forty years had cast a ballot in the 2008 election.[8] It was not only a record turnout; it was one that delivered an 8.5 million vote differential in Obama's favor, with 15 million new voters overall. "It's a bad thing for Republicans when you drill down into all these states, and see lots of new voters, newcomers," groaned Rich Lowry, editor of the conservative *National Review*. "It's like, where did all the Republicans go? Did they move to Utah?"[9]

This was no idle question either, because the surge in voters came from all across the racial and ethnic ranks—blacks, Latinos, and Asians—of which only 8 percent identified as Republican.[10] While the number of whites who voted remained roughly the same as it had been in the 2004 election, two million more African Americans, two million additional Hispanics, and six hundred thousand more Asians cast their ballots in 2008.[11] Even more unsettling to the GOP was the youth and relative poverty of those who had now joined the ranks of voters. Those making less than fifteen thousand dollars a year nearly doubled their turnout to the polls, going from 18 percent in 2004 to 34 percent in 2008. And naturally these new voters had a policy agenda that favored a greater role for government in making education affordable and accessible, using the might of the federal government to institute a program to rebuild the nation's infrastructure, and raising the minimum wage to begin to put in place elements that could increase the quality of life for millions of Americans.[12]

The ardent supporters of McCain were simply not, as census projections soon enough confirmed, on the demographic ascendant. As a consequence, they were on the verge of losing both their electoral clout and the ability to control key public offices that could maintain the status quo.[13] Meanwhile, first-time voters cast almost 69 percent of their ballots for Obama. While that reality could have—or more to the point *should* have—signaled an opportunity for the GOP to reexamine its platform, the sclerotic hardening of the "conservative" notions that moved the Republican Party from centrist right to right-wing made it increasingly difficult if not impossible to adapt the GOP's policies to address the overriding concerns of this wave of newly engaged voters.[14] One party official, while offering assurances that racism wasn't the driving motivation, admitted, "It's simply that the Republican Party gave up a long time ago ever believing that anything they did would get minorities to vote for them."[15] Trapped between a demographically declining support base and an ideological straitjacket that made the party not only unresponsive but also unpalatable to millions of Americans, the GOP reached for a tried and true weapon: disfranchisement.

Once it became clear that the voter turnout rate of blacks had nearly equaled that of whites, as Penda Hair of the progressive Advancement Project has noted, "Conservatives were looking at it and saying 'We've got to clamp things down.' They'd always tried to suppress the black vote, but it was then that they came up with new schemes."[16] Those efforts hid the anger and determination behind a legitimate-sounding, noteworthy concern: protecting the integrity of the ballot box from voter fraud. Still, Paul Weyrich, a conservative activist and the founder of the American Legislative Exchange Council (ALEC), was explicit early on: "I don't want everybody to vote," he said, noting that the GOP's "leverage in the elections quite candidly goes up as the voting populace goes down."[17] But with fifteen million new voters already and with African Americans exercising their citizenship rights at rates virtually equal to whites, something had to be done. That is where ALEC stepped in to draft "model voter-ID legislation . . . that . . . popped up in very similar form in states like Pennsylvania and Texas and Wisconsin."[18] These laws require, among other things, particular types of identification that—properly and mercilessly applied—make it difficult for African Americans and others to vote.

Hans von Spakovsky, a former George W. Bush appointee to the Federal Election Commission and one of the primary catalysts behind the new intensified wave of voter suppression, actually took umbrage that anyone would call the nationwide efforts to crack down on supposed irregularities at the polls a "restoration of Jim Crow."[19] Just as African Americans' so-called genetically induced moral and intellectual failings provided the rationale for Jim Crow, the GOP created a similar series of hypotheses to rationalize voter suppression. The Southern Strategy's long-term efforts to link the Democratic Party with blacks and to make African American synonymous with crime, thus made tying Democrats to widespread fraud a simple, logical leap. "Corruption, election fraud, and Democrats," one man noted, "they went hand-in-hand-in-hand."[20]

Obama's victory, by this line of interpretation, was not the result of a brilliant strategy, that had already outmaneuvered the Clinton juggernaut by energizing the youth and the poor to believe that they had an actual stake in America, but rather the sordid outcome of a brazenly stolen election tied directly to all those new voters. Key to this charge was the Association of Community Organizations for Reform Now (ACORN), a community-based group that had launched extensive voter registration drives throughout the country. Even before the first vote was cast, McCain accused ACORN of "perpetrating one of the greatest frauds in voter history in this country, maybe destroying the fabric of democracy."[21] By the time the election was over, as *Newsweek*'s Katie Connolly reported, "a 52% majority of GOP voters nationally [thought] that ACORN stole the presidential election for Barack Obama last year, with only 27% granting that he won it legitimately."[22]

ACORN was many things, but a well-oiled machine able to pull off nationwide voter fraud was not one of them. In this case, it was terribly sloppy, lacking either rigorous oversight or a check-and-balance system for those the organization had hired. ACORN had in its ranks several employees who, wanting a paycheck but not willing to do the hard work of registering voters, chose the path of least effort and faked voter registration cards. The law nonetheless requires that all cards be submitted to local election officials, which meant that even those obviously bogus ones could not be thrown in the trash. Hence, Mickey Mouse apparently wanted to vote, as did Jive Turkey. This debacle was tailor-made to fuel the narrative of widespread voter ID fraud. Stoking the flames further yet was Obama's previous work, years earlier, with an affiliate of ACORN.[23]

Oddly enough, ACORN had already been investigated extensively by the George W. Bush administration, which had pressured U.S. attorneys to find evidence of fraud. No matter how hard they tried, though, they simply couldn't. And when some of the attorneys in the Department of Justice refused to throw suspicion on Democratic candidates by filing half-baked or trumped-up charges of voter registration fraud, especially before an election, they were summarily fired.[24]

There have been proven instances of vote fraud in the past, but those cases involved election officials' wrongdoing or the manipulation of absentee ballots. The kind of voter registration fraud that seized the imagination of GOP activists, on the other hand, which is based on stealing someone's identity or creating a fake persona to cast a ballot, thus altering the results of an election, is in fact very rare. The convoluted scheme is not used because "it is an exceedingly dumb strategy."[25] To have real impact would require an improbable conspiracy involving millions of people. Robert Brandon, president of the Fair Elections Legal Network, notes, "You can't steal an election one person at a time. You can by stuffing ballot boxes—but voter I.D.s won't stop that."[26]

Protecting the integrity of the ballot box, however, is not nor has it ever been the issue. Rather, the goal has been to intimidate and harass key populations to keep them away from the polls. It is a bit more sophisticated than in the days of Mississippi senator Theodore Bilbo's 1946 call to arms to get a rope and a match to keep blacks away from the voting booth, but the intent is the same.[27]

Over time, disfranchisement has become more subtle, more palatable, and more sophisticated. In 1962, while in Arizona, William Rehnquist, who was subsequently appointed by Nixon to the Supreme Court and, under Ronald Reagan, elevated to chief justice, had begun to perfect new methods of voter intimidation—elements of which gained widespread usage in the twenty-first century. First, Rehnquist's group of Republican stalwarts sent "do not forward" mail to residents in Democratic strongholds. Then, based on the faulty premise that returned cards meant the person was no longer in the district, on Election Day his troops questioned the legitimacy of the voter based on nothing more substantial than returned mail, and demanded that the mostly black and Hispanic population prove that they could read and write by interpreting portions of the Constitution.[28]

Obama's election sent similar efforts into overdrive. The pillorying of ACORN, in particular, allowed the fearful specter of voter fraud to be raised, leading to a bevy of "protect the ballot box" initiatives. In Wisconsin, for instance, a rigorous voter ID law was passed in the wake of charges of rampant fraud at the polls. But in a state with more than 3.4 million registered voters, the 10 to 12 people convicted of voter fraud each year were usually ex-felons, who simply sought to cast a ballot before their voting rights had been restored.[29] Even the Bush campaign's concerted drive to find rampant voter fraud throughout the nation uncovered that out of the 197 million votes cast for federal candidates between 2002 and 2005, all of 26 convictions or guilty pleas were registered—roughly .00000013 percent of the tallied ballots.[30]

Each restriction and requirement crafted and pushed through Republican-dominated state legislatures and signed off by Republican governors was carefully aimed at the population of voters who had helped put a black man in the White House. The goal, as one Mitt Romney supporter expressed in 2012, was to "Put the White Back in the White House."[31] And those efforts turned poor whites, students, and the elderly into collateral damage that got caught in the blowback.

One of the most onerous if innocuous-sounding changes is the requirement for government-issued photo IDs in order to vote. In Texas, that makes more than one million student IDs ineligible while concealed weapons permits are valid. Missouri congressman Emanuel Cleaver could only say in disgust, "You have to be a very mean-spirited and ideologically warped person to believe that this is right and that this is fair." The Brennan Center for Justice estimates that as "many as 12 percent of eligible voters nationwide may not have government-issued photo ID," and that "percentage is likely even higher for students, seniors and people of color."[32] In fact, a joint report by the NAACP and the NAACP Legal Defense and Educational Fund emphasized the "alarming" impact of the law. The ID requirement would eliminate more than six million African American voters and nearly three million Latinos. And while that is roughly 25 percent of black and 16 percent of Latino voters, "only 8% of whites are without a current government-issued photo ID."[33]

Nor is the obvious solution of securing an ID that simple. Georgia's laws, for instance, are instructive about the economic impact of proving one's right to vote. The state requires three separate categories of documentation to secure a government-issued photo ID. The first is proof of citizenship, which overwhelmingly requires either a birth certificate or a passport, but the cost of the latter (which for the working poor is roughly 10 percent of one month's take-home pay) puts that out of reach for many.[34] Up to 13 million American citizens do not have ready access to citizenship documents, the Brennan Center reports, and this phenomenon is highly correlated with minorities, the poor, and the elderly.[35]

Second, Georgia requires documentation of the prospective voter's social security number, which is either the card itself or a W-2, the latter of which requires a job. In 2011, black unemployment in Georgia was 16.4 percent. In the capital city of Atlanta, nearly one fourth of all African Americans were unemployed, compared with just 3.1 percent of whites.[36] Access to a W-2, then, bears strong and fairly obvious racial implications.

Finally, Georgia requires for proof of residence two addressed items of mail, generally, a bank statement and a utility bill. More than 20 percent of African Americans, as compared with 3 percent of whites, do not have a bank account.[37] Due to the changes in the economy and the need to pool limited resources, almost 6 percent of all families in the United States are in multigenerational households. African Americans, those younger than thirty-five years old, as well as Asians and Latinos, are overly represented in this type of living arrangement.[38] Regardless of the number of adults in a home, only one name appears on the utility bills, making it difficult for the others to prove they actually live there.

Wisconsin took another tack when Republican governor Scott Walker championed a bill requiring a government-issued photo ID to vote, and then proceeded to close the Department of Motor Vehicles in areas with Democratic voters while simultaneously extending the hours in Republican strongholds. And "this in a state in which half of blacks and Hispanics are estimated to lack a driver's license and a quarter of its DMV offices are open less than one day per month." In Texas, there are no ID-issuing offices in fully a third of its counties.[39] Alabama, while enacting a voter ID law in 2011, subsequently shut down DMV offices in its Black Belt counties, the very ones that overwhelmingly voted for Obama in the 2012 election. Facing a national uproar after announcing the closures, Governor Robert Bentley backtracked, but ever so slightly. Alabama agreed to allow the DMV offices in the Black Belt counties to be open at least one day a month.[40]

The Republicans in Pennsylvania pushed through a rigorous voter ID law and then failed to follow through on a pledge to provide free IDs for those who couldn't afford them. Nor did Pennsylvania establish enough mobile units to get to residents, particularly those in rural areas. Issuing a stinging rebuke, state judge Bernard McGinley declared that since Pennsylvania required the IDs, it now needed to provide the means for the state's citizens to obtain what had essentially become the passport to the vote. The judge noted the scarcity of mobile units and the fact that many of the license offices were open only a few days a week, which had created lengthy wait times and virtual inaccessibility and, therefore, placed "an unreasonable burden on people trying to exercise their right to vote."[41]

In another ploy toward disfranchisement, efforts were made to eliminate or greatly curtail early voting, essential for those unable to leave work on a Tuesday to vote. This has created significant difficulties for people who have jobs where one must punch the clock, take no more than an hour for lunch, and travel miles away from where one resides, and where one's polling place is therefore located. On Election Day, moreover, the lines at the voting precincts in key neighborhoods have been notoriously long. Six- to twelve-hour waits in line were reported in the 2008 election, and, as a recent Brennan Center study found, predominately African American and Latino precincts experienced longer wait times because the government allocated fewer operable machines and staff to those polling places.[42]

Early voting had provided one important and demonstrably successful solution—and that was the problem.

Once Florida governor Rick Scott took office in 2011, he and a group of GOP consultants discerned the pathways African Americans used to exercise the right to vote and promptly set out to shut those routes down. In Atwater-esque language, Scott explained that this was about protecting the integrity of the ballot box and democracy by making it more difficult to commit "voter fraud." Scott not only slashed early voting from two weeks to eight days; he also eliminated the opportunity to vote the Sunday immediately before Election Day. This was a calculated hit. Statewide in 2008, blacks made up more than one third of those who voted on the preceding Sunday. And, in Palm Beach County, more than 60 percent of those voting early were African Americans, many of whom had boarded buses right after church to cast their ballots. Eliminating that pathway to the polls was high on the priority hit list, one Republican remarked: "I know that the cutting out of the Sunday before Election Day was one of their targets only because that's a big day when the black churches organize themselves," he said, giving lie to Scott's insistence that this was about eliminating "voter fraud."[43]

Another device in the disfranchisement tool kit was a tactic that Rehnquist had used years earlier in Arizona: sending out mass mailings to minority neighborhoods, waiting for the "return to sender" cards to come back, then checking those names against public voting rolls in order to demand a purge of those names. Florida has been one of the most aggressive states to adopt this procedure, using records from the Department of Motor Vehicles to identify and scrub 180,000 names from the voter rolls. More important, it began this purge just months before the upcoming 2012 presidential election, limiting the opportunity for individuals to verify the reliability of the redacted list. Voters showed up at the polls only to find that their names were nowhere to be found. They had been disfranchised. Indeed, after the election, Florida's secretary of state identified only 85 names (out of the original 180,000) that should have been removed from the list.[44]

Such voter-roll purges were fully supported by the updated version of Rehnquist's Army of Challengers. The modern incarnation, True the Vote, was founded in Texas—born of the Tea Party—and defines itself as a citizen-based group committed to "free and fair elections for all Americans."[45] Using a flawed database and even Facebook, True the Vote members pore over public lists of registered voters, identify those whose names or addresses don't match up perfectly with their own records, and then set out to challenge those marked on their list as frauds to cast a ballot. They often target the multigenerational households that are more common in African American, Hispanic, and Asian families, arguing that an address with a number of adults who have registered to vote has to be bogus. True the Vote poll watchers have been conspicuously present in black precincts on Election Day, taking notes, ruffling feathers, challenging voters, clogging the lines, causing delays, frustrating voters who then leave without casting a ballot, ignoring warnings from election officials, and looking for any evidence of supposed ACORN-like fraud.[46]

Barack Obama's election was a catalyst for a level of voter suppression activities that had not been seen so clearly or disturbingly in decades. Nowhere was this more apparent than in the Supreme Court's 2013 gutting of the Voting Rights Act. The case began in 2008. Shelby County, Alabama commissioners, though required by Section 5 preclearance of the VRA to receive approval from the U.S. Department of Justice before making any changes in election procedures, voting qualifications, or district boundaries, annexed several subdivisions to the city of Calera, and then, in direct violation of the VRA, redrew the district boundaries of the lone black councilman, Ernest Montgomery, reducing the percentage of African Americans in his precinct from 69 to 29 percent. He lost the election. Attorneys from the NAACP Legal Defense Fund alerted the Department of Justice, which then required Shelby County to hold another election using the original district boundaries. The commissioners balked. "Federal oversight was no longer needed," they asserted. "We've made progress."[47]

In 2010, Shelby County filed suit in federal district court, charging that Section 5 of the Voting Rights Act was unconstitutional because Congress did not have the authority to reauthorize the act in 2006. The district court disagreed, as did the U.S. Court of Appeals in 2011. The judges were unequivocal:

> *Congress drew reasonable conclusions from the extensive evidence it gathered and acted pursuant to the Fourteenth and Fifteenth Amendments, which entrust Congress with ensuring that the right to vote—surely among the most important guarantees of political liberty in the Constitution—is not abridged on account of race. In this context, we owe much deference to the considered judgment of the People's elected representatives.*[48]

The U.S. Supreme Court looked at Shelby County's clear violation of the law and, in a 5–4 decision penned by Chief Justice John Roberts, came down squarely on the side of the commissioners. In *Shelby County v. Holder* (2013), Roberts and four other justices treated the rationale for the Voting Rights Act as now obsolete. They conceded the past terror and the pernicious laws that had resulted in millions of African Americans being disfranchised. But it was a new day in the South, Roberts wrote confidently. "Largely because of the Voting Rights Act, voting tests were abolished, disparities in voter registration and turnout due to race were erased, and African Americans attained political office in record numbers." Although that success should have led the court to conclude that, without the protections of the VRA, those changes could easily be erased, that success instead led Roberts and four of his colleagues, including the lone black justice on the court, Clarence Thomas, to veer in the opposite direction, asserting that because the law has worked so well, and because other states aren't held to the same scrutiny, the act, as reauthorized by Congress in 2006, was out of sync with modern times. With that, the justices kept Section 5 but declared unconstitutional Section 4 of the act, which provides the conditions under which the Department of Justice may place a jurisdiction under the oversight stipulated by the statute.[49]

How the court arrived at that decision is a testament to twisted facts and ignored evidence. Roberts, for example, contended that the VRA placed burdens on jurisdictions because of past misdeeds that could not be justified by "current needs." The so-called burdens he alluded to, however, were borne only by those jurisdictions with a long, well-documented history of discrimination and a systematic pattern, after the initial passage of the Voting Rights Act in 1965, of trying to craft laws that violated the basic right to vote for all citizens. Locales that required Department of Justice scrutiny had a nearly fifty-year history after the VRA of continued attempts to discriminate. In fact, the act contains a "bail out" provision, wherein the federal government no longer needs to monitor what a jurisdiction does; indeed, the bar to achieve "bail out" status is not all that high, requiring a jurisdiction to abide by the law for an appreciable length of time, following which the extra scrutiny of the Voting Rights Act no longer applies. Numerous counties in Virginia, as well as North Carolina's Wake County, Georgia's Sandy Springs, Texas's North Austin, and Alabama's Pinson, having met the standard, have been thus "bailed out." The fact that the majority of other locales in the old Confederacy, in the heart of what is now GOP country, have not says more about the tenuousness of the right to vote than it does about the rigors of the Voting Rights Act.[50]

Moreover, the court's depiction of the Voting Rights Act as unduly discriminatory against the South and static is wrong on both counts. First, over the years the Department of Justice has had to "bail in" other districts throughout the United States because of racially discriminatory laws and policies that have blocked equal access to the ballot box. This includes eight counties in Arizona, one in Idaho, four jurisdictions in Alaska, two in California, three counties in New York, and one in Wyoming, as well as towns in Connecticut, Massachusetts, Maine, and New Hampshire.[51] Discrimination has never been just a Southern phenomenon, and the VRA has recognized that. In short, the vigorous use of bail-in and bail-out provisions utterly undercut Roberts's contention that the law is an ancient artifact that somehow does not address "current needs."

Moreover, the court's overriding concern that the law is somehow anti-South, while sounding strangely similar to John Mitchell's argument in 1970, willfully overlooks the region's continuing attempts to silence black voters. Discrimination did not stop in 1965, nor in 1975, nor in 2005. Since 2011, nine out of the twelve states of the old Confederacy, according to the NAACP, have adopted or proposed two or more requirements to tighten access to the polls, such as placing restrictions on voter registration drives and requiring a government-issued photo ID to vote.[52] The only thing keeping the wolves at bay during that time was the Voting Rights Act's preclearance provision. The Supreme Court's ruling in *Shelby County v. Holder*, however, turned the dogs loose.

Immediately following the ruling, Arizona, Arkansas, Florida, Iowa, Kansas, Mississippi, North Carolina, Texas, and Virginia all passed a compendium of voter suppression laws. By the following year, right before the 2014 midterm elections, thirteen additional states had passed voter restriction statutes. All were under the guise of protecting the "integrity" of the ballot box, but all had the intent of limiting and frustrating voting by African Americans and, now, Latinos too.[53] The only recourse available was to take these states to court and demonstrate the discriminatory intent and effect of their electoral policies. This is exactly how Richard Nixon and his attorney general had hoped to gut the VRA in 1970. The long, litigious delays meant that, unlike the days of a robust and fully functioning Voting Rights Act, which prevented discrimination before it could do damage, the courts would now come in only after the fact.

Texas is a case in point. Almost the moment *Shelby County v. Holder* was announced, the Republican legislature put through a highly restrictive voter ID law, S.B. 14. A phalanx of civil rights organizations, including the NAACP and the League of United Latin American Citizens, minority voters, and Mexican American legislative and Hispanic judges associations, immediately sued the state of Texas. During the two-week trial in the fall of 2014, the attorney general of Texas, Greg Abbott, argued that the law was necessary to stop and prevent rampant voter-identification fraud. Yet, out of ten million votes, he could produce only two documented cases of voter impersonation. On the other hand, it became clear that nearly six hundred thousand Texans, mainly poor, black, and Hispanic, didn't have the newly required IDs and often faced financial and bureaucratic obstacles in obtaining them. Thus, in September 2014, in a stinging dressing-down of the state, district court judge Nelva Gonzales Ramos ruled that Texas's voter-ID law "creates an unconstitutional burden on the right to vote, has an impermissible discriminatory effect against Hispanics and African-Americans, and was imposed with an unconstitutional discriminatory purpose." Texas, she emphasized, had levied "an unconstitutional poll tax" on its citizens.[54]

Ramos's ruling, which declared that Texas had deliberately created discriminatory voting requirements, was a trip wire to reinstate the Voting Rights Act's Section 5 preclearance statute in Texas. The state, therefore, intended to fight the decision. The first order of business, though, was to seek immediately a judicial delay to allow the voter ID law to remain in place during the upcoming midterm election. Chaos would reign at the polls, argued Texas attorney general Abbott before the Fifth Circuit Court of Appeals, were the law changed this close to an election. He also assured the court that keeping the voter ID law in place would not "substantially injure" the plaintiffs.[55]

On October 14, 2014, the Fifth Circuit judges agreed and granted Texas's request to allow a deliberately discriminatory law to operate during the all-important midterm election. As the judges saw it, "This is not a run-of-the-mill case" and Ramos's ruling "substantially disturbs the election process of the State of Texas just nine days before early voting begins. Thus, the value of preserving the status quo here is much higher than in most other contexts."[56]

The U.S. Department of Justice, civil rights groups, and individual voters then joined together and raced to the U.S. Supreme Court, seeking to overturn the Fifth Circuit's ruling. While the U.S. Supreme Court, led by Justice Antonin Scalia, ruled in favor of the state without any comment on the merits of S.B. 14, Justice Ruth Bader Ginsburg's dissent was incisive, tearing away at the supposed chaos that might occur in the election if the discredited voter-ID law was suddenly jettisoned. There "is little risk," she wrote, of disrupting the election process. All Texas needed to do was "reinstate the voter identification process it employed for ten years (from 2003 to 2013) and in five federal general elections." After all, she observed, the new requirements for voter ID had only been used in three state elections where the voter turnout ranged from 1.48 percent to 9.98 percent. While those Texas primaries were relatively low stakes, Ginsburg noted, the November 2014 election "would be the very first federal general election conducted" under the new voter-ID regime. And that was the problem. The Supreme Court, she wrote, could not allow a "purposefully discriminatory law, one that likely imposes an unconstitutional poll tax and risks denying the right to vote to hundreds of thousands of eligible voters" to be used in a federal election. But that is precisely what the U.S. Supreme Court did.[57]

After the election, the case went back to the Fifth Circuit Court of Appeals, as the U.S. Department of Justice, civil rights groups, and a number of voters sought to invalidate S.B. 14 once and for all. In August 2015, the federal appeals court panel's deliberations focused on whether the legislature had actually intended to create a statute so blatantly discriminatory. The question of intent was central in determining whether Texas would have to undergo Section 5 preclearance scrutiny again. In a decision that fully satisfied neither of the parties, the panel of federal judges ruled that the Texas legislature had not set out, in fact, to write a law that discriminated so clearly against Hispanics and African Americans. However, the jurists continued, S.B. 14, the state's voter ID law, did violate what was left of the Voting Rights Act.[58]

Confronted with being chastised for massive disfranchisement, Greg Abbott, the newly elected governor and former attorney general, continued the fiction that this law was about the sanctity of the ballot box. "Texas will continue to fight for its voter ID requirement to ensure the integrity of elections in the Lone Star State," he declared. Attorney General Ken Paxton, for his part, defiantly stated that the ruling would not undermine the "fundamental question of Texas' right to protect the integrity of our elections," adding that "our state's common-sense voter ID law remains in effect." Despite all this bluster about the "integrity of elections," however, there wasn't any. It was clear that between Judge Ramos's decision and the Fifth Circuit's ruling, as one civil rights advocate noted, "we've now gone through a federal election with this discriminatory voting law in place."[59]

In addition to blocking access to the polls, the GOP's strategy is to make the very function of government so distasteful and haphazard that only the most diehard idealists or craven partisans would even bother to vote. Congressional Tea Party members have bottled up legislation, confirmation hearings, and deliberations on pressing issues such as the economy—all to demonstrate how government does not and cannot function.[60] Casting Obama as uncompromising and irrational, a Republican Congress shut down the federal government at a cost to the nation of $24 billion.[61] They then blamed the president.[62] Obama, one pundit declared, "is betting that the Republicans will have to fold under the pressure that he creates. He is betting that they have picked the wrong issue, and that he will win by holding his breath. Understand the terms of the president's bet: Americans lose until he wins."[63] These "public servants" seemed not to care what damage they did—even to their own reputations. Indeed, that was just the point: Government—least of all under a black president—just does not function. As public approval of Congress plummeted to the single digits—indeed, one survey found that "Congress is less popular than hemorrhoids, jury duty and toenail fungus"—the result was that in the 2014 midterm elections, the United States had the lowest voter turnout since 1942.[64] So many of those who had been mobilized and energized in 2008 were now disillusioned, demoralized, and, in many cases, disfranchised, and most simply stayed home.

The vitriol heaped on Obama was simply unprecedented—not least given the sheer scale of challenges he found himself confronting, and the measurable success he achieved in doing so. Obama came to office with the nation perched on the edge of a financial abyss as foreclosures and the subprime mortgage crisis consumed twenty-two trillion dollars in net wealth; the nation engaged in two endless, futile wars that had already caused thousands of American deaths (let alone the hundreds of thousands of Iraqi and Afghani ones), and even more injuries, and were running up a four- to six-trillion-dollar price tag; and the nation having 16 percent of its population lacking health insurance.[65] Obama's centrist solutions and utter lack of radicalism in the face of a recalcitrant and obstructionist Congress should have made him a hero to traditional Republicans. But just the opposite happened; by the end of his first term, the president had an 85.7 percent disapproval rating among the GOP.[66] One progressive wrote, "You hate Obama with a passion, despite the fact that he is a tax cutting, deficit reducing war President who undermines civil rights and delivers corporate friendly watered down reforms that benefit special interests just like a Republican. You call him a Kenyan. You call him a socialist. You dance with your hatred, singing it proudly in the rain like it was a 1950's musical."[67]

That hatred started early. When Obama was just a candidate, the racially motivated threats to his life led to Secret Service protection well before he was even a front-runner for the nomination.[68] After he became the Democratic nominee, "there was a sharp and very disturbing increase in threats to Obama in September and early October, at the same time that the crowds at [GOP vice presidential candidate Sarah] Palin rallies became more frenzied." The heated, virulent rhetoric led Michelle Obama to ask, "Why would they try to make people hate us?"[69]

In Obama's first year in office alone, there was a 400 percent increase in death threats, as compared to those received by one of the least popular presidents in American history, George W. Bush.[70] Facebook eventually shut down a page where hundreds answered yes to the question "Should Obama be killed?"[71] The president's Twitter account was inundated with death threats such as "Kill yourself you tree swinging nigger" and "POTUS you can count on me waiting for you in the parking lot."[72]

Nor was it just the "crazies." Respectable elements in American society actively tilled the hate-filled ground, lending an aura of authority to this campaign of terror. During the 2008 campaign, John McCain's strategists deliberately demonized not just Obama's policies but also the man himself, who mystically morphed into this Muslim, black nationalist, socialist, foreign, Arab, Kenyan, un-American immigrant monstrosity straight out of *The Manchurian Candidate*.[73] So vilified was Obama that the very office of the president ensured no respect. Breaking every rule of decorum and receiving millions of kudos for doing so, South Carolina congressman Joe Wilson shouted at Obama, "You lie!" during a 2009 joint session of Congress.[74] In another unceremonious and unprecedented slap in the face, Speaker of the House John Boehner (R-OH) invited Israeli prime minister Benjamin Netanyahu, who has had a contentious relationship with the president, to address Congress but didn't inform the White House until hours before the speech. Boehner admitted "keeping President Obama in the dark": "I frankly didn't want them [the Obama administration/White House] getting in the way and quashing what I thought was a real opportunity," he explained.[75]

Somehow many have convinced themselves that the man who pulled the United States back into some semblance of financial health, reduced unemployment to its lowest level in decades, secured health insurance for millions of citizens, ended one of our recent, all-too-intractable wars in the Middle East, reduced the staggering deficit he inherited from George W. Bush, and masterminded the takedown of Osama bin Laden actually hates America.[76] One woman noted that there was a billboard on the interstate near her town that read, "The U.S. Seals took out one threat to America, let's vote out the other in November."[77] Former New York mayor Rudy Giuliani told an audience, "I do not believe, and I know this is a horrible thing to say, but I do not believe that the president loves America . . . He wasn't brought up the way you were brought up and I was brought up through the love of this country."[78] Similarly, John Sununu, the former New Hampshire governor and an ally of Obama's 2012 presidential opponent, Mitt Romney, declared that he wished that "this president would learn to be an American."[79]

The hatred of Obama even seeped into those sworn to serve and protect. One white Florida police chief joked, "At first, I felt a swell of pride and patriotism while Barack Obama took his oath of office.

However, all that pride quickly vanished as I later watched 21 Marines, in full dress uniform with rifles, fire a 21-gun salute to the President. It was then that I realized how far America's military had deteriorated. Every damn one of them missed the bastard."[80] One New Hampshire police commissioner was observed sitting in the local diner glaring at the TV as he kept calling Obama a "fucking nigger."[81] A dispatcher in Ohio proudly sent e-mails that Air Force One's new call letters were NI66ER.[82] And in response to a friend's text that "all niggers must fucking hang," a San Francisco police officer replied, "Ask my 6 year old what he thinks about Obama."[83] Then there's Ferguson, Missouri, where the second in command of the police force exchanged a series of e-mails with his lieutenant and a court official in which one "depicted Barack Obama as a chimpanzee, another doubted his ability as a black man to hold a job for four years, while a third labeled a photograph of a black tribal gathering 'Michelle Obama's high school reunion.'"[84]

Jelani Cobb wrote poignantly about the "paradox of progress."[85] Sadly, the ascent of a black man to the presidency of the United States did not, despite all the talk of hope and a post-racial society, signal progress. Instead, it has led to a situation, not so unlike the era of Jim Crow, where a sense of physical vulnerability is shared across classes in the black community.[86]

A woman driving to her new job at a Texas college is pulled over for not using a turn signal, jailed, and then found dead in her cell.[87] A former college football player is injured in a car accident, seeks help, and is shot dead by the police.[88] A high school boy goes out of his house to purchase Skittles and iced tea, only to be stalked through the neighborhood by a man with a criminal record who is carrying a loaded weapon. The unarmed child ends up dead, while the grown man is acquitted.[89] A twelve-year-old is playing in the park with a toy gun; police kill him within two seconds of their arrival.[90] A man merely makes eye contact with a police officer, and by the time he arrives at the jail, is nearly dead, neck broken.[91] A twenty-two-year-old woman is out with some friends when an off-duty police officer, thinking he sees something suspicious, fires into the crowd. The bullet slams into her skull and she dies. He is later acquitted.[92]

Even where the wound is not fatal, it is grievous. An endowed professor at Harvard is arrested for being in his own house.[93] New York attorney and author Lawrence Otis Graham thought that teaching his children all the rules of respectability—dress, clothes, hair, behavior in public places—and showering them with all the education, vacations, and stable home life that money could afford would provide protection. He was wrong. His son's routine walk to class at a boarding school in New England became something much more as a carload of whites drove by and sliced through the child with the epithet "nigger" as if it were a machete.[94]

Black respectability or "appropriate" behavior doesn't seem to matter. If anything, black achievement, black aspirations, and black success are construed as direct threats. Obama's presidency made that clear. Aspirations and the achievement of these aspirations provide no protection. Not even to the God-fearing.

On June 17, 2015, South Carolinian Dylann Roof, a white, unemployed twenty-one-year-old high school dropout, was on a mission to "take his country back." Ever since George Zimmerman had walked out of the courthouse a free man after killing Trayvon Martin, and a racially polarized nation debated the verdict, Roof had looked to understand the history of America. Trolling through the Internet, he stumbled across the Council of Conservative Citizens (CCC), the progeny of the 1950s White Citizens' Council that had terrorized black people, closed schools, and worked hand in hand with state governments to defy federal civil rights laws. Its intentions on the web were cleverly masked, skewing the facts, rewriting history, and draped in the flag to lend an aura of authority and respectability.[95]

The White Citizens' Council had tapered off during the late 1950s, but it had a rebirth in the 1980s and, in its new incarnation, became one of the go-to destinations for ambitious Republicans. The CCC's core values center on a Christianity that justifies slavery, embraces racially homogenous societies, and emphasizes blacks as a "retrograde species of humanity." But despite the group's avowed racist belief system, in the mid to late 1990s, as the Southern Poverty Law Center reports, "the group boasted of having 34 members who were in the Mississippi legislature and had powerful Republican Party allies, including then-Senate Majority Leader Trent Lott of Mississippi." By 2004, Mississippi governor Haley Barbour, the chair of the Republican National Committee, and thirty-seven other powerful politicians had all attended CCC events in the twenty-first century. In 2013, it was discovered that Roan Garcia-Quintana, a Tea Party stalwart on South Carolina governor Nikki Haley's reelection steering committee, was a CCC board member. Moreover, the Council of Conservative Citizens' webmaster, Kyle Rogers, was a member of the GOP executive committee in Dorchester County, South Carolina, as recently as 2013. In addition, the Council of Conservative Citizens' chair, Earl Holt III, gave "$65,000 to Republican campaign funds in recent years," including donations to the 2016 presidential campaigns of Rand Paul (R-KY), Rick Santorum (R-PA), and Ted Cruz (R-TX).[96]

The CCC, then, enjoyed precisely the cachet of respectability that racism requires to achieve its own goals within American society. And its website of hatred and lies provided the self-serving education Dylann Roof so desperately craved. He drank in the poison of its message, got into his car, drove to Charleston, entered Emanuel AME Church, and landed in a Bible study with a group of African Americans who were the very model of respectability. Roof prayed with them. Read the Bible with them. Thought they were "so nice." Then he shot them dead, leaving just one woman alive so that she could tell the world what he had done and why.[97]

"You're taking over our country," he said, and he knew this to be true.[98]

Afterword to the Paperback Edition

After the Election: Imagining

Not even eighty thousand votes. It wasn't much out of 136 million ballots. Still, that "infinitesimal 0.0006% of the national vote" gave Donald Trump just enough to cross the Electoral College's threshold and claim victory.[1] *Whose* victory, however, was the big question. Aleksandr Dugin, ideological mentor to Russian dictator Vladimir Putin, seemed clear as he exclaimed "Washington is ours!"[2] Indeed, the mood in Moscow was "ebullient."[3]

Rumblings about the Republican nominee's compromised ties to the Kremlin had, in fact, bubbled up during the campaign, erupting finally in a searing charge by Hillary Clinton during the third debate that Trump would be "Putin's puppet."[4] Already, by July 2016, a former British intelligence officer, Christopher Steele, had uncovered a far too cozy and mutually beneficial relationship of information swapping "between the Trump campaign and the Kremlin." Moreover, as Steele dug deeper, he found that the "Russian regime has been cultivating, supporting and assisting TRUMP for at least 5 years." Steele added that the "aim, endorsed by PUTIN, has been to encourage splits and divisions in [the] western alliance." If the scheme worked, the bedrock of U.S. national security policy would lay in shambles. Breaking apart NATO and causing massive rifts between the United States and its European allies would, as South Carolina Senator Lindsey Graham intoned, advance Putin's overarching goal to "destroy democracy around the world."[5]

Prominent Republicans, therefore, had strong doubts about Trump's fitness for office. Florida Senator Marco Rubio charged that the real estate mogul was a "con man who was dangerous and unqualified to control the nation's nuclear codes."[6] A number of Republican foreign policy experts blasted Trump as "utterly unfit" and a "Frankenstein Monster" whose "demagoguery" was an "appeal for a certain kind of dictatorship."[7] Mitt Romney pilloried Trump as "a fraud and a phony who would drive the country to the point of collapse." John McCain echoed that assessment, labeling the Republican nominee a threat to U.S. national security. The message was clear: The real estate developer's "election could put the United States and its democratic system in peril."[8]

Yet despite the unmistakable warning signs, including the Republican nominee's consistent fawning over Putin and cavalier pronouncements about carrying out the dictator's foreign policy agenda, including dismantling NATO; despite an October briefing based on the findings of seventeen U.S. intelligence agencies about Russian interference in the 2016 election; and despite Trump's apparent inability to "pivot" toward anything presidential, Republicans simply refused to do the one thing that would have stopped the mogul's destructive ascent to the White House cold: put an end to voter suppression.[9]

While the polls seesawed back and forth from one candidate to the other—depending upon which scandal or faux pas had most recently occurred—African Americans consistently opposed Trump with an intensity equaled by no other demographic. Their opposition was long, hard, and deep. It was resolute, built upon years of knowing Trump's history of racial discrimination in housing and employment.[10] It was steeped in his infuriating birther-movement attacks against Obama, and laced with his calls to execute the Central Park Five and, then, his utter disgust with the accused's exoneration after DNA and a confession by the actual rapist freed the four imprisoned African Americans and one Latino.[11] Not surprisingly, the antipathy blacks had for Trump was palpable. At one point, in August 2016, he actually placed fourth in the polls for African Americans behind Democrat Hillary Clinton, Libertarian Gary Johnson, and the Green Party's Jill Stein.[12] As journalist Joan Walsh noted in a later instance when prominent African Americans rejected the legitimacy of Trump's presidency, "Or maybe it means that people who've seen the worst of American injustice are trying to warn the rest of us when it's coming for us again."[13]

Comprising 13 percent of the electorate, African Americans stood as the firewall between a democracy continuing to evolve and one threatened by the corrosion of a Trump presidency tainted with the "drip, drip, drip of scandal," ethics violations, foreign intrigue, and authoritarianism.[14] Although the Republicans clearly knew the threat that Trump posed to American democracy, the party had already zeroed in on the power of the black vote and was clear on where the greater danger lay. Ever since Obama's election and the subsequent *Shelby County v. Holder* decision, the GOP, controlling the majority of state governments, had worked assiduously to close off African Americans' access to the ballot box. In Ohio, the GOP instituted a series of voter suppression laws, including literacy tests that led Secretary of State Jon Husted to discard no fewer than 12 percent of absentee ballots for spelling errors. Moreover, his top aide, Matthew Damschroder, acknowledged in a deposition that while the state enforced a range of voter suppression laws in counties like Cuyahoga, home to major cities such as Cleveland, white rural counties went nearly untouched.[15] Indeed, this disparate treatment carried through to mass purging of voter registration lists: "In the state's three largest counties that include Cleveland, Cincinnati and Columbus, voters have been struck from the rolls in Democratic-leaning neighborhoods at roughly twice the rate as in Republican neighborhoods." Those three counties alone absorbed a loss of 144,000 voters.[16] Ohio also curtailed the number of polling places available for early voting. Cincinnati, with hundreds of thousands of residents, had only one designated spot and, as expected, a line out the building that stretched for half a mile.[17]

All of this voter suppression occurred while Ohio governor John Kasich established himself as a fierce critic of Donald Trump.[18] Yet the governor, while making symbolic gestures of defiance—for example, refusing to attend the Republican National Convention in his own state, or responding "Why would I?" to a reporter asking if he would endorse Trump—did nothing to remove the barriers his administration had put in place to make it doubly difficult for blacks to vote in the state of Ohio.[19]

This scenario played out over and over, especially in "swing states with high non-white populations."[20] With its coveted twenty-nine Electoral College votes, Marco Rubio's Florida had for all intents and purposes permanently disfranchised 1.7 million residents because of felony convictions—one of only three states in America to block access to the voting booth even after all elements of the sentence were completed. Yet, in neither of the other two states, Kentucky and Iowa, was electoral punishment of convicted felons as draconian. Indeed, Florida's efforts to disfranchise African Americans reads like a primer in white rage. During Reconstruction, the Sunshine state first cast a shadow over blacks' voting rights using felony disfranchisement, Black Codes, and vagrancy laws to undermine African Americans' citizenship. Later, after the Voting Rights Act of 1965, Florida doubled down using an all-white commission with a large contingent of right-wing John Birch Society members to craft a series of statutes to keep as many black people as possible away from the polls. Then, after Obama's election, Governor Rick Scott welded together a series of guidelines that required a fourteen-year waiting period after sentencing requirements were completed before a person could even petition the governor to restore his or her voting rights. The process, by design, is cumbersome, unduly harsh, and, not surprisingly, since Scott's tenure in office, led to only 8 percent of the requests gaining approval—as compared to 93 percent in Iowa and 86 percent in Kentucky.[21]

Florida's supposedly race-neutral (but obviously racially targeted) law fell disproportionately on the black community. Twenty-three percent of all age-eligible African Americans in the state, although they had already served their time, were banned from participating in one of the most fundamental rights in a democracy. In Florida, stunningly, felonies are not confined to burglaries and robberies but include offenses such as letting a helium balloon float up in the air, walking through a construction zone, or "catching lobsters with tails too short."[22] Using the targeted power of the criminal justice system as a tool of voter suppression meant that five times as many registered Democrats as Republicans were disfranchised. And for that, the nation paid dearly. Refusal to honor the voting rights of American citizens allowed Trump to win Florida by more than 100,000 votes.[23]

In Wisconsin, 300,000 residents lacked the government-issued photo ID required to vote and Governor Scott Walker was determined to keep it that way.[24] Although a firestorm of protests led him to back off his plan to close or significantly reduce the operating hours of the Department of Motor Vehicles in "low-income" areas, such as parts of Milwaukee, the intent was clear.[25] The state's largest city accounted for 70 percent of all African Americans in Wisconsin. The GOP, therefore, sowed confusion, even in defiance of a federal court order, about what IDs were permissible and how and where to vote with or without one. The ploy paid off: 60,000 fewer people cast a ballot in 2016 than in the previous presidential election, with Milwaukee alone accounting for 68 percent of that attrition.[26] Trump won Wisconsin by 27,000 votes.[27]

Some of the most aggressive efforts to put as many obstacles in the way of African American voters as possible occurred in North Carolina. The Electoral Integrity Project, in fact, would label the state a "pseudo-democracy" somewhere between Iran and Venezuela because of the vicious voter suppression laws and ruthless GOP government officials whose quest for control was shameless and relentless.[28] The Republicans' new law, HB 589, cut early voting, eliminated same-day registration, and imposed stringent ID requirements that affected 1.2 million citizens.[29] Even when the Fourth Circuit intervened and slammed HB 589 as a racially discriminatory law that targeted blacks with "almost surgical precision," North Carolina's GOP countered with local measures to bear down and strangle African Americans' right to vote.[30] In Mecklenburg County, which includes the city of Charlotte and more than 15 percent of the state's African American voters, GOP-controlled local election boards eliminated eighteen polling places and left 750,000 age-eligible citizens with only four sites for early voting. In eighteen other counties, including Guilford with more than 350,000 registered voters, the Republicans decided that providing one polling place per county was more than sufficient.[31] By design, wait times inched up to four hours, while the lines wrapped around the buildings.[32]

In addition, the Republicans reached into an old bag of tried-and-true tools of disfranchisement. In Guilford as well as two other counties with sizeable African American populations, the GOP election board authorized a massive voter purge using the same methods employed in the 1960s by eventual Supreme Court Justice William Rehnquist and decades later by the Tea Party: "a single piece of returned mail."[33] The plan worked, and GOP stalwarts bragged that their efforts were bearing fruit. The North Carolina Republican Party issued a press release boasting that "African American Early Voting is down 8.5% from this time in 2012 . . . As a share of Early Voters, African Americans are down 6.0%."[34] Guilford County alone, with only one polling station, witnessed a 9 percent drop in black voter turnout.[35] So effective was the GOP's voter suppression that a greater percentage of African American voters cast a ballot in counties hit by Hurricane Matthew and under a state of emergency than in those counties "under the new voter suppression rules."[36]

Gerrymandering was another shopworn but effective device. Shortly after coming to power in 2011, the North Carolina legislature redrew district boundaries to dilute the voting power of more than 2.2 million African Americans.[37] In this blatant display of rigging an election, the GOP crammed the bulk of the state's black population into a few bizarrely drawn precincts, thereby artificially capping the size of the delegation representing African Americans in the legislature while simultaneously carving out a number of districts for suburban and rural whites to ensure the lion's share of seats for the GOP in the General Assembly. In its August 2016 ruling, the federal court blasted the gerrymandered districts, but just like the voter ID case in Texas two years earlier, the judges were reluctant to dismantle immediately the racially discriminatory districts, especially with the election just a few months away.[38]

The unfortunate source of this chaos was the Republican-appointed members of the U.S. Supreme Court who gutted the Voting Rights Act in the *Shelby County v. Holder* decision. Now, the federal court, just as in the days of the Civil Rights Act of 1957, only had jurisdiction after the racially discriminatory and unconstitutional voting restrictions had snaked their way onto the books and coiled like a python around an election or two. Gerrymandered districts, not only in North Carolina but also in Wisconsin and Alabama, therefore, remained in place during the 2016 election.[39] State defiance of federal courts, reminiscent of the contempt shown the *Brown* decision, became the operating principle for Wisconsin, Ohio, Kansas, Florida, and more as voter IDs, purged voter rolls, and curtailed early voting hours undercut blacks' citizenship rights.[40]

Donald Trump thanked African Americans for not showing up at the polls to vote, which he knew had helped secure his victory, but the real assist came from the Republican Party.[41] Kansas Secretary of State Kris Kobach, a Trump adviser, had spent nearly a decade developing a database, Crosscheck, that ostensibly prevented electoral fraud by identifying individuals registered to vote in multiple states. The program, used in more than half the nation, however, fails miserably at its stated purpose but has proved remarkably adept at flagging racially identifiable surnames to launch a purge of minorities from voter rolls. Indeed, up to one million black, Hispanic, and Asian American voters were subject to disfranchisement without any viable notice based solely on a flawed database and the lie of rampant voter fraud.[42] Moreover, 43 percent of counties in the United States previously covered by the Voting Rights Act, now freed from preclearance requirements because of the *Shelby County v. Holder* decision, closed 868 polling locations before the 2016 election. In other words, while the U.S. population grew, especially as minority communities became a larger share of the voting age electorate, Republican regimes cut nearly 900 polling places where American citizens could cast a ballot. This was a particularly "pernicious tactic for disenfranchising voters of color" because it was "often done quietly, late in the election season, making pre-election intervention or litigation virtually impossible."[43] The reduction in polling places carried another benefit for voter suppression advocates. A recent Harvard study found that the long lines with voters waiting hours to cast a ballot "not only disenfranchise working-class voters who can't afford to wait, but also discourage voters from participating in future elections."[44] A Pew Research report thus noted that demography was not electoral destiny, turnout was—a message the GOP took to heart.[45]

As the possibility of a Trump presidency went from comical to actual, despite the Republican leadership learning firsthand about the mogul's unseemly ties with Vladimir Putin, key members of the GOP made a conscious decision to ignore those mounting national security concerns to advance what was to them a more important agenda.[46] In fact, in a June 2016 meeting of the GOP, party leaders Kevin McCarthy and Paul Ryan remarked how "maniacal" Russian propaganda was, how it was designed to turn a nation against itself, and then noted, amid laughter, that the Kremlin had already hacked the Democratic National Committee. McCarthy then alerted the group that the links between the GOP frontrunner and the nation's adversary were clear. "Putin pays . . . Trump . . . Swear to God." And Ryan responded not with alarm about a foreign menace tampering with U.S. national security but with a *Godfather*-like warning that it was important to keep that bit of information "in the family." "No Leaks."[47] Although jarring, we have seen this before. When sheriffs in Mississippi, in the midst of World War I, stopped trains for days on end to prevent African Americans from leaving the state, U.S. national security, even with the *Lusitania* at the bottom of the Atlantic, was not the top priority. When the Soviets launched Sputnik and signaled the technological ability to strike the United States with their nuclear arsenal, the congressional Democrats' response was not to mobilize and invest in the education of all Americans to meet the U.S.'s desperate need for scientists and engineers. Instead, Congress ensured that Jim Crow remained sacred; that whites-only universities, in defiance of *Brown*, had access to hundreds of millions of dollars in federal aid; and that we, as a nation, would leave black children with underfunded schools and America unable to fully tap all of the brainpower at its disposal.

The motivation in 2016 was equally nefarious and destructive. Trump tapped into an increasingly powerful conservative base that had been nurtured for decades on the Southern Strategy's politics of anti-black resentment.[48] Similar to George Wallace's run for the presidency in 1968, Trump's supporters bristled at the thought that public policies would provide any help to African Americans and were certain that blacks were getting much more than they deserved from the government while the "average American" was getting much less. The message was clear: They weren't deserving and weren't really even Americans.[49]

Policies like the Affordable Care Act (ACA), which provided health insurance to millions of uninsured and previously uninsurable Americans, should have been one of those race-neutral programs that did not engender this depth of anger—especially because one of Trump's primary constituencies benefited substantially from it. A Gallup poll showed that "the uninsured population among low-income white people without a college degree . . . dropped from 25% in 2013 to 15%" just three years later.[50] As much as Trump voters valued finally having access to health care to deal with chronic illnesses like diabetes, to get screenings for cancer, and to make possible a liver transplant, those benefits came with a bitter and unforgivable downside. ACA was Obamacare, which was bad enough in itself.[51] But there was also the "anger . . . that other people were getting even better, even cheaper benefits—and those other people did not deserve the help."[52] In vintage dog-whistle language, Trump supporters explained that Obamacare was proof that "Americans have grown too lazy and entitled," that these "other people are getting health care for free," and that "the economy is rigged for people who receive government assistance."[53]

Trump supporters, therefore, saw their candidate as "America's last chance" to recreate a nation that reminded them of the good ol' days.[54] The country's growing diversity, Obama's very existence in the White House, and the ever-increasing visibility of African Americans in colleges and corporations had fueled a sense that these gains were "likely to reduce the influence of white Americans in society."[55] Trump's win exposed in frightening ways the "ethnonationalist rage centered around a black president" and the fear that all of the resources and wealth accumulated through centuries of public policy would be subject to "redistribution from older, white America to its younger, more diverse" population.[56]

The ubiquitous campaign slogan "Make America Great Again" (MAGA) was, therefore, freighted with heavy racial baggage.[57] Some 20 percent of Trump supporters believed the Emancipation

Proclamation had been bad public policy and that the enslaved should have never been freed.[58] And, while hurling the United States back to the 1850s seemed far-fetched, the Republican nominee's campaign and rallies conjured up the whitewashed images—pre-*Brown*, pre–Civil Rights Movement, and pre–Voting Rights Act—of the 1950s. Boldly and ruthlessly implemented, MAGA would freeze racial inequality in place, create apartheid in the United States, and secure white political, economic, and cultural domination. Hillary Clinton, for all of her skills and all of her whiteness, offered a different vision and simply could not resonate with a large body of American voters. She spoke forcefully and often about economic anxiety, education, and creating living-wage jobs for a nonindustrial economy. But she spoke of a society where all would benefit and have access, not just whites.[59] Trump, on the other hand, dangled a vision before his constituency where the vast resources of the nation would flow to whites, who in a few years would be a numerical minority, but whose comfortable lifestyle would be supported by a large but virtually rightless body of workers, cowed by threats of deportation and virtually unchecked police power in black and brown neighborhoods.

Despite all of the groans about Trump's ideological heresy, the GOP embraced this horrific agenda because many of its pet projects required dismantling a state apparatus that focused (no matter how flawed) on advancing and protecting rights, equality, and justice.[60] The Republican leadership in Congress chose to overlook Trump's purported coziness with the Russians and the strong possibility that the Kremlin has damaging, extortionist evidence against the next president of the United States, in order to seize the opportunity presented by a Trump administration to legislatively hurl the civil rights world back to the early 1950s and plunge the financial regulatory sector into the 1920s.[61] Visions of dismantling laws to curb the fevered excesses of capitalism while drastically reducing federal support for education, Medicare, and Medicaid had long danced like sugar plum fairies on the GOP's congressional agenda.[62] Such a neo-apartheid world would include heightening voter suppression, legalizing racial profiling in policing underpinned by a nationwide stop-and-frisk program, weakening laws that protect labor, stopping cities from raising the minimum wage in their locales, defunding "nutritional assistance for hungry children," and ensuring that the Electoral College continues to insulate "the white establishment" against the changing demographic of America.[63] This is the recipe to Make America Great Again.

It is, of course, a macabre fantasy. The political, moral, and legal costs required to construct and sustain an apartheid regime—to create the full-blown security apparatus to suppress what will eventually be the bulk of a nation's population and to find a continuous substantial flow of foreign capital to offset the inordinate expense—means that it is destined to fail. Previous attempts at a herrenvolk democracy have collapsed under the financial and moral weight that no society can bear for long. But as sociologist Tressie McMillan Cottom observed, "Whiteness defends itself. Against change, against progress, against hope, against black dignity, against black lives, against reason, against truth, against facts, against native claims, and against its own laws and customs."[64] This is what allowed flag-waving, patriotic Republicans to overwhelmingly prefer Russian dictator Vladimir Putin to U.S. President Barack Obama.[65] This is what allowed Trump supporters to acknowledge how ill-suited the mogul was to be president even as they were drawn to his coarse, horrific language about Mexican rapists, Muslim terrorists, and black hellholes.[66] This is what allowed Trump supporters who are dependent upon the Affordable Care Act to nevertheless elect politicians who had tried nearly sixty times to repeal the ACA but who also espouse racially tinged lies about voter fraud and the need for voter suppression laws.[67]

The Russian roulette Trump supporters played with their own economic and political viability was due, as well, to a bad case of historical amnesia, which erased the role government played in lifting their own standard of living while leaving intact pleasing fables of rugged individualism and bootstrap grit. In this fairy tale, government only fostered dependency and helped those who were lazy and undeserving. Yet, as Obama noted, "if somebody didn't have a problem with their daddy being employed by the federal government, and didn't have a problem with the Tennessee Valley Authority electrifying certain communities, and didn't have a problem with the interstate highway system being built, and didn't have a problem with the [Federal Housing Administration] subsidizing the suburbanization of America, and that all helped you build wealth and create a middle class—and then suddenly as soon as African Americans or Latinos are interested in availing themselves of the same mechanisms as ladders into the middle class, you now have a violent opposition to them—then I think you at least have to ask yourself the question of how consistent you are, and what's different, and what's changed."[68]

Having ridden a wave of racial resentment into the White House, Donald Trump now threatens to imperil the institutions upon which the United States has been built.[69] The unbridled anger at Obama for having had the audacity to become president and the subsequent Republican insistence on bogus voter fraud claims to justify disfranchising millions of voters, especially African Americans and Latinos, cracked the firewall that would have kept the most suspect and unpopular incoming president in recorded history from gaining access to the nuclear codes.[70]

That is the bad news. But it is not the only news. First, we can never forget that most Americans who voted were repulsed by Trump's racism, xenophobia, and misogyny. He lost the popular vote by more than 2.8 million ballots—greater than the combined total populations of Wyoming, Vermont, Alaska, and North Dakota.[71]

Nor can we forget that when confronted with the reality of a Trump presidency, white racial resentment, and GOP perfidy, millions of Americans began advocating, organizing, arguing, and fighting for a nation that would be more inclusive, humane, and rights based. The Women's March stretched from sea to shining sea the day after the inauguration in the largest civil rights protest in the nation's history.[72] Neighbors, strangers, allies, and ideological opposites flooded airports, parks, and even Pennsylvania Avenue for days on end chanting "no hate, no fear, refugees are welcomed here" to protest Trump's travel ban against Muslims, whose visas and even green cards suddenly became irrelevant while their religion was the only evidence necessary to detain them. Immigration lawyers also dared imagine a very different kind of nation as they swooped in, camped out on the floors of O'Hare, Dulles, and JFK airports, and drafted writs of habeas corpus while demanding to see and provide counsel to those whom Customs and Border Protection had detained and blocked from entering the United States because their god's name was Allah.[73] The ACLU, which usually brings in $3–4 million in donations a year, received $24 million in one weekend to fight against the racism and Islamophobia inherent in Trump's Muslim ban.[74] Senators and representatives, who were prepared to rubber stamp Trump's appointees and policies, faced a mobilized, energized constituency flooding congressional phone lines and packing town halls demanding accountability, competency, democracy, and decency.[75] Grizzled New Yorkers refused to ignore the swastikas scrawled on a subway car, and, instead, went to work: "Hand sanitizer gets rid of Sharpie pen. We need alcohol," one man said. Soon passengers, determined to "do the right thing," began passing around tissues and hand sanitizer to remove the hate-filled messages plastered along the signs and walls of the train.[76]

Americans, shaken out of their complacency that democracy will just run on its very own, are now taking ownership of this nation, of what it means—inclusively—to be in the United States. Trump's actions, including installing a white supremacist as his chief strategist, have compelled activists and everyday Americans to confront what is at stake, to contemplate what kind of nation they stand to lose, and to "imagine" what kind of nation they want and are willing to fight for.[77] As thousands take to the streets to march, as lawsuit after lawsuit rains down on the courts, as boycott after boycott sends the economic and cultural message of an empowered and unbowed people, and as honest, fact-based dialogues about race and racism converge with those on class, sexual orientation, and gender, they say "we are one."

This is how we begin to defuse the power of white rage. It is time to move into that future. It is a future where the right to vote is unfettered by discriminatory restrictions that prevent millions of American citizens from having any say in their own government. A poll tax in 1942 that led to only 3 percent of the voting-age population in seven Southern states choosing elected officials was never a democracy. And neither, in this decade, is a voter turnout of 1.48 percent in Texas's statewide election. Moreover, the millions of dollars that Republican governors and legislators have spent on new voter suppression laws—purportedly to stop a voter fraud problem that never existed—while gutting health care, mental health, and education funding in already strained state budgets, suggests that the cost of subverting democracy extends far beyond the ballot box.[78]

The future is one that invests in our children by making access to good schools the norm, not the exception, and certainly not dependent on zip code. We know the consequences of dysfunctional school systems. We see the wasted lives, just as clearly as Eisenhower and Congressman Carl Elliott saw them during the Sputnik crisis. At that time, the political leaders chose to look away, to avert their eyes, as if leaving millions of children in segregated, decrepit schools did not undermine the hopes of America's smallest citizens while also undercutting the strength of the nation as a whole. We can choose not to listen to the rage and, instead, craft a stronger, more viable future for this nation. We can ask tough questions such as: Why use property taxes as the basis for funding schools when that method rewards discriminatory public policy and perpetuates the inequalities that undermine our society?

The future is one that takes seriously a justice system whose enormous powers are actually used to serve and protect. The misuse is storied—from the convict-lease labor system, to one that allowed known murderers to walk around scot-free, to one that is now employed to undercut the gains of the Civil Rights Movement.[79] A program that stops and frisks predominantly those who are the least likely to have illegal contraband is not law enforcement.[80] A war on drugs that uses race and ethnicity as the litmus test for crime is not justice.[81] Millions of black citizens recognize this and, therefore, question the very legitimacy of this key pillar in American democracy.[82] Meanwhile, state budgets have cracked under the strain of bloated, unsustainable prison systems.[83] Mayors worry that their cities will ignite when yet another black person, who is more likely than not unarmed, is killed by police.[84] The costs of the continued misuse of the criminal justice system are more than the United States can bear—morally, politically, and financially.

It is time to rethink America.

Imagine if Reconstruction had actually honored the citizenship of four million freed people—provided the education, political autonomy, and economic wherewithal warranted by their and their ancestors' hundreds of years of free labor. If, instead of continually refighting the Civil War, we had actually moved on to rebuilding a strong, viable South, a South where poor whites, too—for they had been left out as well—could gain access to proper education.

Imagine the educational prowess our population might now boast had *Brown* actually been implemented. What a very different nation we would be if all the enormous legal and political efforts that went into subverting and undermining the right to education had actually been used to uphold and ensure that right. If all those hundreds upon hundreds of millions of federal dollars poured into science education had actually rained down on those hungry for education, regardless of race, ethnicity, or income. Think about what a different national conversation we might be having, even as the economy turns ever more surely to knowledge-based, rather than watching our share of the world's scientists and engineers dwindle.

Imagine if the Civil Rights Movement had really resulted in Martin Luther King's "Beloved Community," instead of in a society that, to this day, willfully celebrates the very presidential administration that launched a war on drugs against its own people, who were neither mobilized nor addicted to begin with—a war on drugs that was manufactured out of whole cloth for devious and self-serving ends. Think about how different our cities and our rural areas would be without the scourge of drugs that has decimated families and communities. What if all the billions of dollars that have been diverted into militarizing police for a phony war and building prison after prison had been devoted instead to education, to housing, to health care?

Imagine if, instead of launching into spurious attacks about his citizenship and filling the blogosphere with racist simian depictions, the United States had been able to harness the awe-inspiring symbolism of our first black president, which had already led an Iranian and a Russian, among others, to see something in the spirit of America that surpassed even its material wealth.

We shouldn't have to imagine.

Full voting rights for American citizens, funding and additional resources for quality schools, and policing and court systems in which racial bias is not sanctioned by law—all these are well within our grasp. Visionaries, activists, judges, and politicians before us saw what America could be and fought hard for that kind of nation.

This is the moment now when all of us—black, white, Latino, Native American, Asian American—must step out of the shadow of white rage, deny its power, understand its unseemly goals, and refuse to be seduced by its buzzwords, dog whistles, and sophistry. This is when we choose a different future.

Acknowledgments

Thank you doesn't even come close. So please accept the power and gratitude behind the words for making this book possible. Thank you to the Op-Ed Project for helping me hone my voice, especially Chloe Angyal. In life there are game changers: Jelani Cobb and Carlos Lozada, you opened the door to the *Washington Post*. Thank you. Then came Rob McQuilkin, who saw what the article could become. Thank you for your insight, support, brilliance, and humor all along the way. You are the sine qua non. Claire Mao, you are indispensable. Susan Whitlock, once again, you jumped in with a keen, masterful eye. Wow! George Gibson, an editor like no other. You are simply amazing. What a gift you have and are.

At Emory University, I thank Robin Forman, who helped in more ways than he can know to make this book a reality. Nathan McCall, thank you for providing great insight on how "to write to the front page." Natasha Trethewey, thank you for the priceless advice. I was blessed with a cadre of research assistants who knocked it out of the park! Thank you, Teresa Green, Erica Sterling, and Timothy Rainey II. Thank you, Dianne Stewart, who encouraged me above and beyond the call of friendship; there's a special place in the universe for you. La Shanda Perryman, I remain in awe. You took care of business so that I could do the same. How you helped me keep every last one of those balls in the air, I'll never know, but I'm so glad you did.

And most of all, I thank a wonderful group of friends and colleagues who read every single word, provided insightful feedback, and did so quickly even when their own research agendas, administrative responsibilities, and teaching loads were overflowing. Your generosity is incomparable. Thank you, thank you, thank you, Dorothy Brown, Sherman James, and Brett Gadsden. Dorothy, in particular, I have to single out and give my heartfelt gratitude. You persuaded me, in your distinct South Bronx way, to apply to the Op-Ed Project; you read proposals and chapters; you listened and then asked the most powerful frame-changing questions; and you directed me to salient and timely resources, especially concerning the law, the justice system, tax policy, and the Supreme Court. Maya Angelou has a poem with your name all over it: "Phenomenal Woman"—that's you.

Finally, I have a family that is wild, unruly, fun, smart, irreverent, and politically contentious and that has my back at all times. Earl, David, and Wendell, thank you. Barry, Rhea, Lisa, Monica, Shirley, and Uncle Sam, Aunt Barbara, and Aunt Lennie, your love and patience are priceless. And to the two most wonderful sons, Aaron and Drew, who help me keep everything in perspective, I love you.

Notes

Prologue Kindling

1. Carol Anderson, "Ferguson Isn't About Black Rage Against Cops. It's White Rage Against Progress," *Washington Post*, August 29, 2014, http://www.washingtonpost.com/opinions/ferguson-wasnt-black-rage-against-cops-it-was-white-rage-against-progress/2014/08/29/3055e3f4-2d75-11e4-bb9b-997ae96fad33_story.html.
2. Michael Cooper, "Officers in Bronx Fire 41 Shots, and an Unarmed Man Is Killed," *New York Times*, February 5, 1999, http://www.nytimes.com/1999/02/05/nyregion/officers-in-bronx-fire-41-shots-and-an-unarmed-man-is-killed.html, accessed September 9, 2015.
3. *Nightline*, "America in Black and White: The Shooting of Amadou Diallo," ABC, February 26, 1999.
4. Andrew Gelman, Jeffrey Fagan, and Alex Kiss, "An Analysis of the New York City Police Department's 'Stop-and-Frisk' Policy in the Context of Claims of Racial Bias," *Journal of the American Statistical Association* (September 2007): 813–23; New York City Department of Planning, "2000 Census Summary," http://www.nyc.gov/html/dcp/html/census/pop2000.shtml#population, accessed November 22, 2015.
5. Melissa V. Harris-Perry, *Barbershops, Bibles, and BET: Everyday Talk and Black Political Thought* (Princeton, NJ: Princeton University Press, 2004).
6. *Missouri v. Jenkins*, 495 U.S. 33 (1990); *Missouri v. Jenkins*, 515 U.S. 70 (1995).

7. *This American Life*, "The Problem We All Live With," July 31, 2015, http://www.thisamericanlife.org/radio-archives/episode/562/transcript, accessed November 19, 2015.
8. Gary R. Kremer, Antonio F. Holland, and Lorenzo J. Greene, *Missouri's Black Heritage*, rev. ed. (Columbia: University of Missouri Press, 1993); Greg Gordon, "2006 Missouri's Election Was Ground Zero for GOP," *Common Dreams*, May 3, 2007, http://www.commondreams.org/news/2007/05/03/2006-missouris-election-was-ground-zero-gop, accessed November 19, 2015; U.S. Department of Justice, "Investigation of the Ferguson Police Department," March 4, 2015, http://www.justice.gov/sites/default/files/opa/press-releases/attachments/2015/03/04/ferguson_police_department_report.pdf, accessed November 19, 2015.
9. For the health consequences of black resilience, resolve, and success, see Sherman A. James, "John Henryism and the Health of African Americans," *Culture, Medicine and Psychiatry* 18 (1994): 163–82.
10. Jo Jones and William D. Mosher, "Fathers' Involvement with Their Children: United States, 2006–2010," National Health Statistics Report, no. 71 (December 20, 2013): 1–21, http://www.cdc.gov/nchs/data/nhsr/nhsr071.pdf, accessed September 7, 2015; Frank Vyan Walton, "The Absent Black Father Myth—Debunked by CDC," *Daily Kos*, May 13, 2015, http://www.dailykos.com/story/2015/05/13/1383179/-The-absent-black-father-myth-debunked-by-CDC, accessed July 28, 2015; Christopher Mathias, "NYPD Stop and Frisks: 15 Shocking Facts About a Controversial Program," *Huffington Post*, May 15, 2012, http://www.huffingtonpost.com/2012/05/13/nypd-stop-and-frisks-15-shocking-facts_n_1513362.html, accessed September 8, 2015; "White and Hispanic Teens More Likely to Abuse Drugs Than African Americans," *Duke Medicine*, November 7, 2011, http://corporate.dukemedicine.org/news_and_publications/news_office/news/white-and-hispanic-teens-more-likely-to-abuse-drugs-than-african-americans/view, accessed September 8, 2015; Karolyn Tyson, William Darity Jr., and Domini R. Castellino, "It's Not

'A Black Thing': Understanding the Burden of Acting White and Other Dilemmas of High Achievement," *American Sociological Review* 70, no. 4 (August 2005): 582–605.

One Reconstructing Reconstruction

1. Alexander Tsesis, ed., *The Promises of Liberty: The History and Contemporary Relevance of the Thirteenth Amendment* (New York: Columbia University Press, 2010), xviii.
2. A. J. Langguth, *After Lincoln: How the North Won the Civil War and Lost the Peace* (New York: Simon and Schuster, 2014), 59; "Personal Freedom," PBS, http://www.pbs.org/jefferson/enlight/person.htm, accessed January 16, 2015.
3. "Personal Freedom," PBS.
4. James M. McPherson, "In Pursuit of Constitutional Abolitionism," in *The Promises of Liberty*, ed. Tsesis, 27; "Civil War Casualties. The Cost of War: Killed, Captured, Wounded, and Missing," http://www.civilwar.org/education/civil-war-casualties.html, accessed January 25, 2015.
5. "Second Inaugural Address of Abraham Lincoln," Saturday, March 4, 1865, http://avalon.law.yale.edu/19th_century/lincoln2.asp, accessed November 6, 2015.
6. Theda Skocpol, "America's First Social Security System: The Expansion of Benefits for Civil War Veterans," *Political Science Quarterly* 108 (Spring 1993): 85–116; Megan J. McClintock, "Civil War Pensions and the Reconstruction of Union Families," *Journal of American History* 83 (September 1996): 456–80; Donald R. Shaffer, "'I Do Not Suppose That Uncle Sam Looks at the Shin': African Americans and the Civil War Pension System," *Civil War History* 46 (June 2000): 132–47.
7. David Brion Davis, "The Rocky Road to Freedom: Crucial Barriers to Abolition in the Antebellum Years," in *The Promises of Liberty*, ed. Tsesis, xiii.
8. Alexander Tsesis, "The Thirteenth Amendment's Revolutionary

Aims," in *The Promises of Liberty*, 10, 11; Davis, "The Rocky Road to Freedom," xii; Langguth, *After Lincoln*, 23.

9. William M. Wiecek, "Emancipation and Civic Status: The American Experience, 1865–1915," in *The Promises of Liberty*, ed. Tsesis, 87.
10. Michael Vorenberg, "Abraham Lincoln and the Politics of Black Colonization," *Journal of the Abraham Lincoln Association* 14, no. 2 (Summer 1993): 33; Rick Beard, "Lincoln's Panama Plan," *New York Times*, August 16, 2012, http://opinionator.blogs.nytimes.com/2012/08/16/lincolns-panama-plan/?_r=0, accessed November 22, 2015.
11. "Black Residents of Nashville to the Union Convention," January 9, 1865, http://www.freedmen.umd.edu/tenncon.htm, accessed February 25, 2015.
12. Frank L. Owsley, *King Cotton Diplomacy: The Foreign Relations of the Confederate States of America* (Chicago: University of Chicago Press, 1931, 1959).
13. Langguth, *After Lincoln*, 61.
14. Confederate States of America—Mississippi Secession: "A Declaration of the Immediate Causes Which Induce and Justify the Secession of the State of Mississippi from the Federal Union," Avalon Project, Lillian Goldman Law Library, Yale Law School, http://avalon.law.yale.edu/19th_century/csa_missec.asp, accessed January 27, 2015.
15. Davis, "The Rocky Road to Freedom," xvi.
16. "The Condition of Affairs in South Carolina," *Liberator*, June 23, 1865.
17. Davis, "The Rocky Road to Freedom," xvii.
18. Frederick Douglass, "The Serfs of Russia . . . Were Given Three Acres of Land," in *Life and Times of Frederick Douglass* (Boston, 1892), https://chnm.gmu.edu/courses/122/recon/douglass.htm, accessed January 13, 2015.
19. Davis, "The Rocky Road to Freedom," xvi.
20. "Black Residents of Nashville to the Union Convention," January

9, 1865, http://www.freedmen.umd.edu/tenncon.htm, accessed February 25, 2015.

21. "The Fight for Equal Rights: Black Soldiers in the Civil War," http://www.archives.gov/education/lessons/blacks-civil-war, accessed February 18, 2015; Annette Gordon-Reed, *Andrew Johnson*, American Presidents Series, ed. Arthur M. Schlesinger Jr. and Sean Wilentz (New York: Times Books, 2011), 98.
22. Leslie M. Harris, "The New York City Draft Riots of 1863," excerpt from *In the Shadow of Slavery: African Americans in New York City, 1626–1863*, http://www.press.uchicago.edu/Misc/Chicago/317749.html, accessed February 19, 2015.
23. Davis, "The Rocky Road to Freedom," xviii.
24. Langguth, *After Lincoln*, 87.
25. "The Condition of Affairs in South Carolina," *Liberator*, June 23, 1865.
26. Samuel Thomas: Testimony before Congress (1865), Col. Samuel Thomas, Assistant Commissioner, Bureau of Refugees, *Freedmen and Abandoned Lands* in 39th Cong., 1st Sess., Senate Exec. Doc. 2 (1865).
27. Michael A. Ross, *Justice of Shattered Dreams: Samuel Freeman Miller and the Supreme Court During the Civil War Era* (Baton Rouge: Louisiana State University Press, 2003), 148.
28. Langguth, *After Lincoln*, 39–40, 74.
29. Ibid., 39–40.
30. Mark O. Hatfield, with the Senate Historical Office, *Andrew Johnson (1865): Vice Presidents of the United States, 1789–1993* (Washington, D.C.: Government Printing Office, 1997), www.senate.gov.
31. Gordon-Reed, *Andrew Johnson*, 113; Ross, *Justice of Shattered Dreams*, 105–6.
32. St. George L. Sioussat, "Andrew Johnson and the Early Phases of the Homestead Bill," *Mississippi Valley Historical Association* 5, no. 3 (December 1918): 273.
33. Langguth, *After Lincoln*, 134.

34. Gordon-Reed, *Andrew Johnson*, 115; Richard B. McCaslin, "Reconstructing a Frontier Oligarchy: Andrew Johnson's Amnesty Proclamation and Arkansas," *Arkansas Historical Quarterly* 49, no. 4 (Winter 1990): 313; W.E.B. Du Bois, *Black Reconstruction in America: 1865–1880*, introduction by David Levering Lewis (New York: Touchstone, 1995), 246.
35. Du Bois, *Black Reconstruction*, 245.
36. "Forty Acres and a Mule," BlackPast.org, http://www.blackpast.org/aah/forty-acres-and-mule, accessed February 19, 2015.
37. Du Bois, *Black Reconstruction*, 223.
38. Langguth, *After Lincoln*, 106, 115.
39. Eric Foner, *Reconstruction: America's Unfinished Revolution, 1863–1877* (New York: Harper and Row Publishers, 1988), 159–61.
40. Langguth, *After Lincoln*, 83; Peter Dreier, "The Status of Tenants in the United States," *Social Problems* 30, no. 2 (December 1982): 181; Hannah L. Anderson, "That Settles It: The Debate and Consequences of the Homestead Act of 1862," *History Teacher* 45, no. 1 (November 2011): 118.
41. Sioussat, "Andrew Johnson and the Early Phases of the Homestead Bill," 276–80; Gordon-Reed, *Andrew Johnson*, 115, 121.
42. Du Bois, *Black Reconstruction*, 245; Brooks D. Simpson, review of Hans Trefousse, *Andrew Johnson: A Biography*, in *Pennsylvania Magazine of History and Biography* 114, no. 3 (July 1990): 446–48; David W. Bowen, *Andrew Johnson and the Negro* (Knoxville: University of Tennessee Press, 1989).
43. Sioussat, "Andrew Johnson and the Early Phases of the Homestead Bill," 276.
44. Ross, *Justice of Shattered Dreams*, 112–13; Langguth, *After Lincoln*, 121.
45. Gordon-Reed, *Andrew Johnson*, 100.
46. "Report on the Condition of the South by Carl Schurz," first published 1865, 39th Congress, Senate, 1st Session, Ex. Doc. No. 2, 89–91, http://www.wwnorton.com/college/history/give-me-liberty4/docs/

CSchurz-South_Report-1865.pdf, accessed February 19, 2015; Langguth, *After Lincoln*, 111.

47. Ibid.; Gordon-Reed, *Andrew Johnson*, 117.
48. Gordon-Reed, *Andrew Johnson*, 118.
49. Hatfield, "Andrew Johnson."
50. Gordon-Reed, *Andrew Johnson*, 118–19.
51. "Radical Politics in Virginia (May 1866)," in *Documentary History of Reconstruction*, vol. 1, ed. Walter Lynwood Fleming (Cleveland, OH: A. H. Clark, 1906), 230, 231.
52. Ross, *Justice of Shattered Dreams*, 111.
53. Louisiana Democratic Platform, October 2, 1865, in *Documentary History of Reconstruction*, ed. Fleming, 229; *Dred Scott v. Sandford*, 60 U.S. 393 (1856).
54. Gordon-Reed, *Andrew Johnson*, 112.
55. Quoted in Foner, *Reconstruction*, 199.
56. Du Bois, *Black Reconstruction*, 167.
57. Mississippi Black Code, *Laws of the State of Mississippi, Passed at a Regular Session of the Mississippi Legislature, Held in Jackson, October, November, and December, 1865* (Jackson, 1866), 82–93, 165–67; Leon F. Litwack, *Been in the Storm So Long: The Aftermath of Slavery* (New York: Random House, 1980), 368; David M. Oshinsky, *"Worse Than Slavery": Parchman Farm and the Ordeal of Jim Crow Justice* (New York: Free Press, 1996), 21.
58. Foner, *Reconstruction*, 209, 215.
59. Langguth, *After Lincoln*, 108–9.
60. "Labor in the Rebel States," *North American and United States Gazette*, November 18, 1865.
61. "What the South Has Done," *North American and United States Gazette*, November 18, 1865.
62. Andrew Johnson, "First Annual Message," December 4, 1865, online by Gerhard Peters and John T. Woolley, American Presidency Project, http://www.presidency.ucsb.edu/ws/?pid=29506, accessed February 21, 2015.
63. Jennifer Mason McAward, "*McCulloch* and the Thirteenth

Amendment," *Columbia Law Review* 112, no. 7, Symposium: The Thirteenth Amendment—Meaning, Enforcement, and Contemporary Implications (November 2012), 1786–87; Francis Newton Thorpe, *The Constitutional History of the United States* (Chicago: Callaghan and Co., 1901), 200–201, 209–10, 220.

64. Langguth, *After Lincoln*, 132.
65. Stephanie Condon, "After 148 Years, Mississippi Finally Ratifies 13th Amendment, Which Banned Slavery," CBS News, February 18, 2013, http://www.cbsnews.com/news/after-148-years-mississippi-finally-ratifies-13th-amendment-which-banned-slavery, accessed February 22, 2015.
66. Foner, *Reconstruction*, 226.
67. Litwack, *Been in the Storm So Long*, 368, 370.
68. Gordon-Reed, *Andrew Johnson*, 107.
69. Ibid., 128; Langguth, *After Lincoln*, 113.
70. Veto of the Freedmen's Bureau Bill, Andrew Johnson, February 19, 1866, http://teachingamericanhistory.org/library/document/veto-of-the-freedmens-bureau-bill, accessed February 24, 2015.
71. Ibid.; Langguth, *After Lincoln*, 135.
72. Confederate States of America—Mississippi Secession: "A Declaration of the Immediate Causes."
73. Langguth, *After Lincoln*, 55.
74. "Labor in the Rebel States," *North American and United States Gazette*.
75. Langguth, *After Lincoln*, 110.
76. Ross, *Justice of Shattered Dreams*, 115.
77. Douglas A. Blackmon, *Slavery by Another Name: The Re-Enslavement of Black Americans from the Civil War to World War II* (New York: Anchor Books, 2009), 107.
78. Ross, *Justice of Shattered Dreams*, 114.
79. Oshinksy, "*Worse Than Slavery*"; Blackmon, *Slavery by Another Name*.
80. Christopher Waldrep, "Substituting Law for the Lash: Emancipation and Legal Formalism in a Mississippi County

Court," *Journal of American History* 82, no. 4 (March 1996): 1435–37.

81. Mark T. Carleton, *Politics and Punishment: The History of the Louisiana State Penal System* (Baton Rouge: Louisiana State University Press, 1971), 13, 31.
82. Donald H. Zeigler, "A Reassessment of the Younger Doctrine in Light of the Legislative History of Reconstruction," *Duke Law Journal* 1983, no. 5 (November 1983): 994; Blackmon, *Slavery by Another Name*, 108–10.
83. James D. Anderson, *The Education of Blacks in the South, 1860–1935* (Chapel Hill: University of North Carolina Press, 1988), 4, 17.
84. Langguth, *After Lincoln*, 113–14.
85. Ibid., 113.
86. Anderson, *The Education of Blacks in the South*, 5, 6, 7, 11.
87. Ibid., 17; Wayne Flynt, *Dixie's Forgotten People: The South's Poor Whites* (Bloomington: Indiana University Press, 2004), 35.
88. John H. Abel Jr. and LaWanda Cox, "Andrew Johnson and His Ghost Writers: An Analysis of the Freedmen's Bureau and Civil Rights Veto Messages," *Mississippi Valley Historical Review* 48, no. 3 (December 1961): 469.
89. *President Johnson's Veto of the Civil Rights Act 1866*, http://teachingamericanhistory.org/library/document/veto-of-the-civil-rights-bill, accessed February 24, 2015.
90. Ibid.
91. Gordon-Reed, *Andrew Johnson*, 130.
92. Langguth, *After Lincoln*, 148.
93. Bobby L. Lovett, "Memphis Riots: White Reaction to Blacks in Memphis, May 1865–July 1866," *Tennessee Historical Quarterly* 38, no. 1 (Spring 1979): 9–33.
94. Barry A. Crouch, "Spirit of Lawlessness: White Violence; Texas Blacks, 1865–1868," *Journal of Social History* 18, no. 2 (Winter 1984): 218.
95. Ibid., 217, 218, 221; Ross, *Justice of Shattered Dreams*, 147.

96. Gordon-Reed, *Andrew Johnson*, 128–29; Foner, *Reconstruction*, 264–65.
97. Langguth, *After Lincoln*, 170, 171, 172, 182; Gordon-Reed, *Andrew Johnson*, 112.
98. Douglass, "The Serfs of Russia . . . Were Given Three Acres of Land."
99. Michael Les Benedict, "New Perspectives on the Waite Court," *Tulsa Law Review* 47, no. 109 (2011): 116.
100. Wiecek, "Emancipation and Civic Status," 92.
101. See the headnote in *Santa Clara County v. Southern Pacific Railroad Company*, 118 U.S. 394 (1886).
102. "The Supreme Court: The First One Hundred Years, Landmark Cases—*Slaughterhouse*," http://www.pbs.org/wnet/supremecourt/antebellum/landmark_slaughterhouse.html, accessed March 5, 2015; *The Slaughterhouse Cases*, 83 U.S. 36 (1873).
103. Ross, *Justice of Shattered Dreams*, 200.
104. "Virginia Minor Case Trial," www.nps.gov/archive/jeff/minor_case_trial.html, accessed August 30, 2006; *Minor v. Happersett*, 88 U.S. 162 (1874).
105. Bruce R. Trimble, *Chief Justice Waite: Defender of the Public Interest* (Princeton, NJ: Princeton University Press, 1938), 162; *United States v. Reese et al.*, 92 US 214 (1876).
106. Foner, *Reconstruction*, 437.
107. Trimble, *Chief Justice Waite*, 168; *United States v. Cruikshank*, 92 U.S. 542 (1876).
108. *The Civil Rights Cases*, 109 U.S. 3 (1883).
109. Wiecek, "Emancipation and Civic Status," 93, 94, 95.
110. *Hall v. DeCuir*, 95 U.S. 485 (1877).
111. Wiecek, "Emancipation and Civic Status," 92.
112. *Plessy v. Ferguson* 163 U.S. 537 (1896).
113. *Cumming v. Richmond County Board of Education*, 175 U.S. 528 (1899).
114. "Disenfranchisement by Means of the Poll Tax," *Harvard Law Review* 53, no. 4 (February 1940): 645–52.
115. *Williams v. Mississippi*, 170 U.S. 213 (1898).

116. Manfred Berg, *"The Ticket to Freedom": The NAACP and the Struggle for Black Political Integration* (Gainesville: University of Florida Press, 2005), 105.
117. Wiecek, "Emancipation and Civic Status," 89–90.
118. Ibid., 93–94; *Giles v. Harris*, 189 U.S. 475 (1903).
119. Equal Justice Initiative, "Lynching in America: Confronting the Legacy of Racial Terror," (2015), 8.
120. Wiecek, "Emancipation and Civic Status," 80.

Two Derailing the Great Migration

1. "Making the World 'Safe for Democracy': Woodrow Wilson Asks for War," http://historymatters.gmu.edu/d/4943, accessed November 7, 2015.
2. Walter White to Governor Dorsey, July 10, 1918, http://www.maryturner.org/images/memorandum.pdf, accessed October 25, 2015.
3. "11 Lynched Instead of 6 as First Reported in Georgia: Names of Ringleaders Known," *Philadelphia Tribune*, September 7, 1918.
4. Walter White to Governor Dorsey, July 10, 1918; C. Tyrone Forehand, "A Place to Lay Their Heads: Mary Turner and the Rampage of 1918," http://www.maryturner.org/images/place.pdf, accessed October 25, 2015.
5. Philip Dray, *At the Hands of Persons Unknown: The Lynching of Black America* (New York: Random House, 2002), 245; Forehand, "A Place to Lay Their Heads"; Walter White to Governor Dorsey, July 10, 1918.
6. James Allen et al., *Without Sanctuary: Lynching Photography in America* (Santa Fe, NM: Twin Palms Publishers, 2000), 8–35.
7. Walter White to Governor Dorsey, July 10, 1918.
8. James R. Grossman, *Land of Hope: Chicago, Black Southerners, and the Great Migration* (Chicago: University of Chicago, 1991), 16.

9. Quoted in Isabel Wilkerson, *The Warmth of Other Suns: The Epic Story of America's Great Migration* (New York: Vintage Books, 2011), 165.
10. "The Truth About the North," Chicago Commission on Race Relations, *The Arrival in Chicago, 1922*, in *Black Protest and the Great Migration: A Brief History with Documents*, ed. Eric Arnesen (Boston: Bedford St. Martin's 2003), 67–68; Grossman, *Land of Hope*, 16, 18.
11. Ethan Michaeli, *Defender: How the Legendary Black Newspaper Changed America: From the Age of the Pullman Porters to the Age of Obama* (Boston and New York: Houghton Mifflin Harcourt, 2016), 62.
12. "Great Migration: The African-American Exodus North," NPR, September 13, 2010, http://www.npr.org/templates/story/story.php?storyId=129827444, accessed May 14, 2015; Earl Lewis, "Expectations, Economic Opportunities, and Life in the Industrial Age: Black Migration to Norfolk, Virginia, 1910–1945," in *The Great Migration in Historical Perspective: New Dimensions of Race, Class, and Gender*, ed. Joe William Trotter Jr. (Bloomington: Indiana University Press, 1991), 23.
13. Grossman, *Land of Hope*, 49.
14. Michaeli, *Defender*, 63.
15. Roi Ottley, *The Lonely Warrior: The Life and Times of Robert S. Abbott* (Chicago: H. Regnery Co., 1955), 160.
16. Grossman, *Land of Hope*, 60.
17. Brian Kelly, *Race, Class, and Power in the Alabama Coalfields, 1908–1921* (Urbana and Chicago: University of Illinois Press, 2001), 150.
18. Dray, *At the Hands of Persons Unknown*; "Lynchings by State and Race: 1882–1968," http://law2.umkc.edu/faculty/projects/ftrials/shipp/lynchingsstate.html, accessed November 8, 2015; Amy Louise Wood, *Lynching and Spectacle: Witnessing Racial Violence in America, 1890–1940* (Chapel Hill: University of North Carolina Press, 2011); William H. Chafe, Raymond Gavins, and

Robert Korstad, ed., *Remembering Jim Crow: African Americans Tell About Life in the Segregated South* (New York: New Press, 2001), 206–7, 211–16; Danielle McGuire, *At the Dark End of the Street: Black Women, Rape and Resistance—a New History of the Civil Rights Movement from Rosa Parks to the Rise of Black Power* (New York: Knopf, 2010).

19. Grossman, *Land of Hope*, 34; Leon F. Litwack, *Trouble in Mind: Black Southerners in the Age of Jim Crow* (New York: Vintage Books, 1998), 159; Editor's Mail, Anonymous letter from Georgia, *Chicago Defender* April 28, 1917.
20. Grossman, *Land of Hope*, 17; Litwack, *Trouble in Mind*, 157–58.
21. Pete R. Daniel, *The Shadow of Slavery: Peonage in the South, 1901–1969* (Chicago and Urbana: University of Illinois Press, 1990).
22. Wilkerson, *The Warmth of Other Suns*, 166, 167; *Oh Freedom After While*, directed by Steven John Ross and narrated by Julian Bond (California Newsreel, 1999), 56 minutes, DVD.
23. Wilkerson, *The Warmth of Other Suns*, 170.
24. "Better Reasons for Going North," *Chicago Defender*, March 31, 1917; Michaelis, *Defender*, 64.
25. Chafe, *Remembering Jim Crow*, 207.
26. "Sharecropper Migration," *American Experience*, PBS, http://www.pbs.org/wgbh/americanexperience/features/general-article/flood-sharecroppers, accessed June 21, 2015; Litwack, *Trouble in Mind*, 37.
27. Grossman, *The Land of Hope*, 36; Emmett J. Scott, *Negro Migration During the War*, Carnegie Endowment for International Peace: Preliminary Economic Studies of the War, no. 16, ed. David Kinley (New York: Oxford University Press, 1920), 82.
28. Wilkerson, *The Warmth of Other Suns*, 164; John A. Farrell, *Clarence Darrow: Attorney for the Damned* (New York: Vintage Books, 2012), 402; Joe William Trotter Jr., "Introduction: Black Migration in Historical Perspective, a Review of the Literature," in

The Great Migration in Historical Perspective, 13; Scott, *Negro Migration During the War*, 77.

29. Ottley, *The Lonely Warrior*, 161, 164.
30. Grossman, *Land of Hope*, 40; Frank Alexander Ross and Louise Venable Kennedy, *A Bibliography of Negro Migration* (New York: Columbia University Press, 1934), 48, https://archive.org/stream/bibliographynegr00rossmiss/bibliographynegr00rossmiss_djvu.txt, accessed November 8, 2015.
31. Grace Elizabeth Hale, *Making Whiteness: The Culture of Segregation in the South, 1890–1940* (New York: Vintage Books, 1998).
32. Grossman, *The Land of Hope*, 52, 53, 64.
33. Ibid., 39.
34. "Luring Labor North," *New Orleans Times-Picayune*, August 22, 1916, in *Black Protest and the Great Migration*, ed. Arnesen, 59–60.
35. Ottley, *The Lonely Warrior*, 165.
36. http://www.measuringworth.com/uscompare/relativevalue.php.
37. Scott, *Negro Migration During the War*, 73.
38. "South Hurt by Labor Shortage," *Chicago Defender*, August 4, 1923.
39. Scott, *Negro Migration During the War*, 76. Emphasis in original.
40. "Arrest White Man for Enticing Men North," *Chicago Defender*, May 19, 1917; "1100 Negroes Desert Savannah, Georgia," *McDowell Times*, August 11, 1916, in *Black Protest and the Great Migration*, 59; "Workmen Kept from Leaving: Southerners like Pharaoh Loathe to Let Colored Folk Go, Agents Arrested, Workmen Jailed for Attempting to Come North," *Afro-American*, August 19, 1916; "White Men and Party Held," *Chicago Defender*, March 24, 1917; "Labor Agents Held as Race Deserts South," *Chicago Defender*, January 31, 1920.
41. Spencer R. Crew, *Field to Factory: Afro-American Migration, 1915–1940* (Washington, D.C.: National Museum of American History, 1987), 6–7.

42. Grossman, *Land of Hope*, 75.
43. Kevin Boyle, *Arc of Justice: A Saga of Race, Civil Rights, and Murder in the Jazz Age* (New York: Owl Books, 2004), 1–2; James R. Grossman, "The White Man's Union: The Great Migration and the Resonance of Race and Class in Chicago, 1916–1922," in *The Great Migration in Historical Perspective*, 88.
44. Louis R. Harlan, *Booker T. Washington: The Making of a Black Leader, 1856–1901*, vol. 1 (New York: Oxford University Press 1972); Pero Gaglo Dagbovie, "Exploring a Century of Historical Scholarship on Booker T. Washington," *Journal of African American History* 92, no. 2 (Spring 2007): 239–64.
45. Ottley, *The Lonely Warrior*, 163. Emphasis added.
46. Ibid., 163.
47. Ibid., 165–66.
48. Ibid., 170.
49. Grossman, *Land of Hope*, 44.
50. Scott, *Negro Migration During the War*, 76.
51. "Bars Chicago Defender from Arkansas County," *Chicago Daily Tribune*, February 16, 1920.
52. Grossman, *Land of Hope*, 44.
53. Grossman, "The White Man's Union," 91.
54. Ottley, *The Lonely Warrior*, 167.
55. Grossman, *Land of Hope*, 44.
56. Scott, *Negro Migration During the War*, 77; Ottley, *The Lonely Warrior*, 165.
57. Scott, *Negro Migration During the War*, 78.
58. Ibid., 77.
59. Wilkerson, *The Warmth of Other Suns*, 163.
60. "Workmen Kept from Leaving," *Afro-American*, August 19, 1916.
61. "Arrest Workers Who Flee from Southern Farms," *Chicago Defender*, May 5, 1923.
62. Scott, *Negro Migration During the War*, 77.
63. Ottley, *The Lonely Warrior*, 165.
64. Scott, *Negro Migration During the War*, 74.

65. Grossman, *Land of Hope*, 50.
66. Wilkerson, *The Warmth of Other Suns*, 163; Scott, *Negro Migration During the War*, 77.
67. Scott, *Negro Migration During the War*, 78.
68. Kelly, *Race, Class, and Power in the Alabama Coalfields*, 149.
69. Grossman, *Land of Hope*, 49.
70. Kelly, *Race, Class, and Power in the Alabama Coalfields*, 150.
71. Judith Stein, *The World of Marcus Garvey: Race and Class in Modern Society* (Baton Rouge: Louisiana State University Press, 1991), 40.
72. Grossman, *Land of Hope*, 34; Linda McMurry Edwards, *To Keep the Waters Troubled: The Life of Ida B. Wells* (New York: Oxford University Press 1998), 144.
73. "More Thousands Kiss the South a Last Good-By," *Chicago Defender*, December 30, 1922.
74. Grossman, *Land of Hope*, 60.
75. Farrell, *Clarence Darrow*, 404.
76. "Jim Crow Stories: Red Summer 1919," https://www.pbs.org/wnet/jimcrow/stories_events_red.html, accessed November 8, 2015.
77. Cameron McWhirter, *Red Summer: The Summer of 1919 and the Awakening of Black America* (New York: Henry Holt and Co., 2011); Michaeli, *Defender*, 110–14.
78. "The Truth About the North," in *Black Protest and the Great Migration*, 68.
79. N. Caroline Harney and James Charlton, "The Siege on South Peoria Street," *Chicago Reader*, January 13, 2000, http://www.chicagoreader.com/chicago/the-siege-on-south-peoria-street/Content?oid=901207, accessed June 20, 2015.
80. Whet Moser, "How White Housing Riots Shaped Chicago: Over Two Decades, the City Was Wracked by Violence. The Policies That Fed Attacks, and Those That Resulted from It, Changed the Landscape of Chicago—and Baltimore," *Chicago Magazine*, April 29, 2015, http://www.chicagomag.com/city-life/April-

2015/How-White-Housing-Riots-Shaped-Chicago, accessed June 20, 2015.

81. George Edmund Haynes, "Negroes Move North: Their Departure from the South," *Survey* 40, no. 5 (May 4, 1918): 116.
82. Steven Watts, *The People's Tycoon: Henry Ford and the American Century* (New York: Knopf, 2005), 178–87.
83. Scott Martelle, *Detroit: A Biography* (Chicago: Chicago Review Press, 2012), 85; Boyle, *Arc of Justice*, 7.
84. Boyle, *Arc of Justice*, 9.
85. Walter White, *A Man Called White: The Autobiography of Walter White*, foreword by Andrew Young (New York: Viking Press, 1948; Athens: Brown Thraser of the University of Georgia, 1995), 73.
86. Martelle, *Detroit*, 90–91.
87. Beth Tompkins Bates, *The Making of Black Detroit in the Age of Henry Ford* (Chapel Hill: University of North Carolina Press, 2012), 105; *Michigan Reports: Cases Decided in the Michigan Supreme Court*, from March 30–June 5, 1922, no. 218 (Chicago: Callaghan and Company, 1922): 625–32.
88. Bates, *The Making of Black Detroit*, 105; Farrell, *Clarence Darrow*, 400; Roneisha Mullen and Dale Rich, "Black History Month: Doctor Barred from Home, an Angry Mob Greets Physician in All-White Neighborhood in 1925," *Detroit News* February 17, 2011, http://www.detroitnews.com/article/20110217/METRO/102170372#ixzz3diiHp7Z0, accessed June 21, 2015.
89. Boyle, *Arc of Justice*, 20, 22.
90. Thomas Dyja, *The Dilemma of Black Identity in America: Walter White* (Chicago: Ivan R. Dee, 2008), 90.
91. Boyle, *Arc of Justice*, 16.
92. Farrell, *Clarence Darrow*, 404.
93. McWhirter, *Red Summer*, 98–110; Rawn James Jr., "The Forgotten Washington Race War of 1919," *History News Network*, February 28, 2010, http://historynewsnetwork.org/article/123811, accessed November 8, 2015.

94. Farrell, *Clarence Darrow*, 404; Paul Ortiz, "Ocoee, Florida: Remembering the Single Bloodiest Day in American Political History," *Facing South*, http://www.southernstudies.org/2010/05/ocoee-florida-remembering-the-single-bloodiest-day-in-modern-us-political-history.html, accessed November 8, 2015.
95. Farrell, *Clarence Darrow*, 400.
96. Ibid., 413.
97. Boyle, *Arc of Justice*, 170.
98. Ibid., 133–35.
99. Phyllis Vine, *One Man's Castle: Clarence Darrow in Defense of the American Dream* (New York: Amistad, 2004), 118.
100. Boyle, *Arc of Justice*, 19.
101. Ibid., 182–84.
102. Ibid., 184.
103. Ibid., 184–85.
104. Bates, *The Making of Black Detroit*, 110.
105. Boyle, *Arc of Justice*, 195–96.
106. Ibid., 185–86.
107. Ibid., 187–90.
108. Vine, *One Man's Castle*, 137; Boyle, *Arc of Justice*, 186.
109. Boyle, *Arc of Justice*, 194–195, 300, 304.
110. Vine, *One Man's Castle*, 164.
111. Boyle, *Arc of Justice*, 174.
112. Thomas Sugrue, *Origins of the Urban Crisis: Race and Inequality in Postwar Detroit* (Princeton, NJ: Princeton University Press, 1996, 2005), 24.
113. Boyle, *Arc of Justice*, 178–79.
114. Farrell, *Clarence Darrow*, 417.
115. White, *A Man Called White*, 74–75.
116. Martelle, *Detroit*, 111.
117. Farrell, *Clarence Darrow*, 412.
118. Ibid., 406.
119. Ibid., 409–410; White, *A Man Called White*, 77–78.
120. Farrell, *Clarence Darrow*, 413, 415.

121. Ibid., 418.
122. Ibid., 399.
123. Sondra Kathyrn Wilson, *In Search of Democracy: The NAACP and the Writings of James Weldon Johnson, Walter White and Roy Wilkins, 1920–1977* (New York: Oxford University Press, 1999), 73.
124. Farrell, *Clarence Darrow*, 423.
125. Ibid., 425.
126. Trial Transcript, Monday, May 10, 1926, 9:30 A.M., 10.
127. Farrell, *Clarence Darrow*, 425.
128. Ibid., 423–25.
129. Trial Transcript, Monday, May 10, 1926, 9:30 A.M., 11.
130. Farrell, *Clarence Darrow*, 426.
131. Trial Transcript, Monday, May 10, 1926, 9:30 A.M., 7.
132. Boyle, *Arc of Justice*, 190, 246, 344–346.

Three Burning *Brown* to the Ground

1. C. Vann Woodward, *The Strange Career of Jim Crow*, 3d ed. (New York: Oxford University Press, 1974), 97–102; No. 76–811, *Regents of the University of California v. Bakke* Opinion Drafts—Marshall (1 of 2), p. 11, *Lewis Powell Papers*, Washington and Lee School of Law, http://law2.wlu.edu/powellarchives/page.asp?pageid=1322, accessed July 7, 2015.
2. *Sweatt v. Painter*, 339 U.S. 629 (1950).
3. *Missouri ex rel. Gaines v. Canada*, 305 U.S. 337 (1938).
4. *McLaurin v. Oklahoma State Regents*, 339 U.S. 637 (1950).
5. Genna Rae McNeil, *Groundwork: Charles Hamilton Houston and the Struggle for Civil Rights*, foreword by Judge A. Leon Higginbotham Jr. (Philadelphia: University of Pennsylvania Press, 1983); Richard Kluger, *Simple Justice: The History of* Brown v. Board of Education *and Black America's Struggle for Equality* (New York: Vintage Books, 2004); Mark Tushnet, *Making Civil Rights Law: Thurgood Marshall and the Supreme Court, 1936–1961* (New York: Oxford University Press, 1994).

6. Brett Gadsden, *Between North and South: Delaware, Desegregation, and the Myth of American Sectionalism* (Philadelphia: University of Pennsylvania Press, 2013), 111.
7. Peter Irons, *Jim Crow's Children: The Broken Promise of the* Brown *Decision* (New York: Penguin Books, 2002), 108–9.
8. Jill Ogline Titus, *Brown's Battleground: Students, Segregationists and the Struggle for Justice in Prince Edward County, Virginia* (Chapel Hill: University of North Carolina Press, 2011), 15.
9. Irons, *Jim Crow's Children*, 80–81; Titus, *Brown's Battleground*, 3.
10. Titus, *Brown's Battleground*, 4.
11. I use the term "Deep South" to refer to Alabama, Georgia, Louisiana, Mississippi, and South Carolina.
12. Tomiko Brown-Nagin, *Courage to Dissent: Atlanta and the Long History of the Civil Rights Movement* (New York: Oxford University Press, 2011), 95–96, 445.
13. State Department of Education of Louisiana, "Ninety-Fifth Annual Report for the Session 1943–44," Bulletin No. 543 (December 1944), 170–71.
14. Carol Anderson, *Bourgeois Radicals: The NAACP and the Struggle for Colonial Liberation, 1941–1960* (New York: Cambridge University Press, 2014), 292.
15. Kluger, *Simple Justice*, 3, 8.
16. Jessie Parkhurst Guzman, ed., *Negro Year Book: A Review of Events Affecting Negro Life, 1941–1946* (Tuskegee, AL: Tuskegee Institute, 1947), 70; U.S. Department of Commerce, Bureau of the Census, *1950 United States Census of Population*, Series PC-14 (Washington, D.C.: Government Printing Office, 1953), 4.
17. *Morris v. Williams* 59 F. Supp. 508 (1944).
18. Numan V. Bartley, *The Rise of Massive Resistance: Race and Politics in the South During the 1950s* (Baton Rouge: Louisiana State University Press, 1969, 1997), 5, 9.
19. Bartley, *The Rise of Massive Resistance*, 26.
20. Roy Wilkins, *Standing Fast: The Autobiography of Roy Wilkins* (New York: Da Capo Press, 1994), 218.

21. Stephen E. Ambrose, *Eisenhower: The President*, vol. 2 (New York: Simon and Schuster, 1984), 190.
22. Ambrose, *Eisenhower*, 143; Carol Anderson, *Eyes off the Prize: The United Nations and the African American Struggle for Human Rights, 1944–1955* (New York: Cambridge University Press, 2003), 214.
23. Anderson, *Eyes off the Prize*, 12. The initial calculation was the equivalent in 1998 of $632 million, which in 2014 is comparable to $1.2 trillion. See http://www.measuringworth.com/uscompare/relativevalue.php.
24. Sarah Caroline Thuesen, *Greater Than Equal: African American Struggles for Schools and Citizenship in North Carolina, 1919–1965* (Chapel Hill: University of North Carolina Press, 2013), 204; Bartley, *The Rise of Massive Resistance*, 55, 57; Wilkins, *Standing Fast*, 218.
25. Anderson, *Eyes off the Prize*, 214.
26. Wilkins, *Standing Fast*, 218.
27. Irons, *Jim Crow's Children*, 87.
28. Barbara Barksdale Clowse, *Brainpower for the Cold War: The Sputnik Crisis and National Defense Education Act of 1958* (Westport, CT: Greenwood Press, 1981), 43.
29. Bartley, *The Rise of Massive Resistance*, 80.
30. Wilkins, *Standing Fast*, 233–34.
31. Bartley, *The Rise of Massive Resistance*, 45–46.
32. Ibid., 41; U.S. Department of Commerce, Bureau of the Census, *Census Population: 1950*, pt. 11, vol. 2, by Howard G. Brunsman (Washington, D.C.: Government Printing Office, 1952), 214.
33. Bartley, *The Rise of Massive Resistance*, 46; U.S. Department of Commerce, *Census of Population*, 124.
34. Bartley, *The Rise of Massive Resistance*, 54–56.
35. Wilkins, *Standing Fast*, 214.
36. Angie Maxwell, *The Indicted South: Public Criticism, Southern Inferiority, and the Politics of Whiteness* (Chapel Hill: University of North Carolina Press, 2014), 194.

37. Ibid., 193; John Kyle Day, *The Southern Manifesto: Massive Resistance and the Fight to Preserve Segregation* (Jackson: University of Mississippi Press, 2014), 7.
38. Wilkins, *Standing Fast*, 215; Titus, *Brown's Battleground*, 27.
39. Jack Dougherty, *More Than One Struggle: The Evolution of Black School Reform in Milwaukee* (Chapel Hill: University of North Carolina Press, 2004).
40. Ronald P. Formisano, *Boston Against Busing: Race, Class, and Ethnicity in the 1960s and 1970s*, 2d ed. (Chapel Hill: University of North Carolina Press, 2004).
41. Berg, *Ticket to Freedom*, 156.
42. Bartley, *The Rise of Massive Resistance*, 7.
43. Berg, *Ticket to Freedom*, 156; Michael J. Klarman, Brown v. Board of Education *and the Civil Rights Movement* (New York: Oxford University Press, 2007), 180; Wilkins, *Standing Fast*, 223.
44. Bartley, *The Rise of Massive Resistance*, 30.
45. Guzman, *Negro Yearbook*, 70; David C. Colby, "The Voting Rights Act and Black Registration in Mississippi," *Publius* 16, no. 4, Assessing the Effects of the U.S. Voting Rights Act (Autumn 1986): 127.
46. Berg, *Ticket to Freedom*, 156; Day, *The Southern Manifesto*, 17.
47. William Bradford Huie, "The Shocking Story of Approved Killing in Mississippi," *The Murder of Emmett Till*, American Experience, PBS, http://www.pbs.org/wgbh/amex/till/sfeature/sf_look_confession.html, accessed June 25, 2015.
48. Klarman, Brown v. Board of Education, 180.
49. Charles M. Payne, *I've Got the Light of Freedom: The Organizing Tradition and the Mississippi Freedom Struggle* (Berkeley: University of California Press, 1995, 2007), 1.
50. Berg, *Ticket to Freedom*, 155.
51. Bartley, *The Rise of Massive Resistance*, 30.
52. Guzman, *The Negro Yearbook*, 70.
53. Alabama Black Belt Counties Registered Voters in 1960, Table 6, from the records of Assistant U.S. Attorney General for Civil

Rights Burke Marshall, http://www.teachingforchange.org/wp-content/uploads/2014/12/1960registeredvoters.pdf, accessed July 3, 2015.

54. Klarman, Brown v. Board, 181; *Reynolds v. Sims*, 377 U.S. 533 (1964).
55. *Brown v. Board of Education*, 349 U.S. 294 (1955).
56. Day, *The Southern Manifesto*, 14–15; Bartley, *The Rise of Massive Resistance*, 127.
57. Anderson, *Bourgeois Radicals*, 304.
58. Alexander Azarian and Eden Fesshazion, "The State Flag of Georgia: The 1956 Change in Its Historical Context," Senate Research Office, State of Georgia; Donald Lee Grant, *The Way It Was in the South: The Black Experience in Georgia* (Athens: University of Georgia, 2001), 378.
59. Day, *The Southern Manifesto*, 9–10.
60. Ibid., 9, 11.
61. Klarman, Brown v. Board of Education, 169.
62. Day, *The Southern Manifesto*; Titus, *Brown's Battleground*, 14–15; "The Southern Manifesto of 1956, March 12, 1956," http://history.house.gov/Historical-Highlights/1951-2000/The-Southern-Manifesto-of-1956, accessed June 28, 2015.
63. Jack W. Peltason, *Fifty-eight Lonely Men: Southern Federal Judges and School Desegregation* (Urbana: University of Illinois Press, 1971), 93.
64. Charles J. Ogletree Jr., *All Deliberate Speed: Reflections on the First Half-Century of* Brown v. Board of Education (New York: W. W. Norton, 2004), 130–31.
65. Erwin Chemerinsky, *The Case Against the Supreme Court* (New York: Viking, 2014), 139.
66. Thuesen, *Greater Than Equal*, 202; William H. Chafe, *Civilities and Civil Rights: Greensboro, North Carolina, and the Black Struggle for Freedom* (New York: Oxford University Press 1981).
67. Thuesen, *Greater Than Equal*, 205; U.S. Department of

Commerce, *Census of Population: 1950*, 109, 122, 125, 129, 130, 137, 154, 165, 169, 214, 353.

68. Irons, *Jim Crow's Children*, 186.
69. Gadsden, *Between North and South*, 147; Tony Allan Freyer, *Little Rock on Trial:* Cooper v. Aaron *and School Desegregation* (Lawrence: University Press of Kansas, 2007).
70. *Cooper v. Aaron*, 358 U.S. 1 (1958); Ogletree, *All Deliberate Speed*, 129.
71. Wilkins, *Standing Fast*, 249.
72. Irons, *Jim Crow's Children*, 185–87.
73. About fifty white students ended up going to a neighboring school about forty miles away. Transportation costs were covered by the state.
74. Sondra Gordy, *Finding the Lost Year: What Happened When Little Rock Closed Its Public Schools* (Fayetteville: University of Arkansas Press, 2009), 71.
75. Wilkins, *Standing Fast*, 258.
76. Gadsden, *Between North and South*, 147.
77. Bob Smith, *They Closed Their Schools: Prince Edward County, Virginia, 1951–64* (Chapel Hill: University of North Carolina Press, 1965), 151–52; Bartley, *The Rise of Massive Resistance*, 275.
78. Titus, *Brown's Battleground*, 19.
79. Maxwell, *The Indicted South*, 179–80.
80. Titus, *Brown's Battleground*, 22.
81. Day, *The Southern Manifesto*, 12.
82. Titus, *Brown's Battleground*, 31.
83. Irons, *Jim Crow's Children*, 190–91.
84. Titus, *Brown's Battleground*, 10.
85. Christopher Bonastia, *Southern Stalemate: Five Years Without Public Education in Prince Edward County, Virginia* (Chicago: University of Chicago Press, 2012), 2; "Study of Prince Edward Shows Closed Schools Hurt Negroes," *New York Times*, October 18, 1964.

86. Irons, *Jim Crow's Children*, 192.
87. "The Forgotten Children of the 'New Frontier': Prince Edward County," *Afro-American*, April 8, 1961.
88. "Prince Edward Says Schools Not Required," *Washington Post*, July 7, 1961.
89. *Griffin et al. v. County School Board of Prince Edward County et al.*, 375 U.S. 391 (1964); *Griffin v. County School Board of Prince Edward County*, 377 U.S. 218 (1964).
90. Titus, *Brown's Battleground*, 10.
91. Bartley, *The Rise of Massive Resistance*, 135; Klarman, Brown v. Board of Education, 165.
92. "Prince Edward County Schools Again Closed by County," *Washington Post*, April 25, 1969.
93. Ogletree, *All Deliberate Speed*, 128.
94. Smith, *They Closed Their Schools*, 147.
95. Lisa A. Hohl, "Open the Doors: An Analysis of the Prince Edward County, Virginia Free School Association" (master's thesis, University of Richmond, 1993).
96. Bonastia, *Southern Stalemate*, 157.
97. Liza Mundy, "Making Up for Lost Time: Virginia Has Created a Scholarship Program to Give African American Adults from Prince Edward County Something They Were Denied as Children: An Education," *Washington Post*, November 5, 2006.
98. Bonastia, *Southern Stalemate*, 157.
99. See, for example, *Struggles in Steel*, produced by Ray Henderson and Tony Buba (California Newsreel, 1996), 58 minutes, DVD.
100. U.S. Department of Commerce, Census Bureau, "1940–2010: How Has America Changed?," http://www.census.gov/library/infographics/1940_census_change.html, accessed July 1, 2015.
101. Martin Chancey, "The Relative Decline of the United States Economy," *Science and Society* 26, no. 4 (Fall 1962): 385–99.
102. Jefferson Cowie and Joseph Heathcott, ed., *Beyond the Ruins: The Meanings of Deindustrialization*, foreword by Barry Bluestone (Ithaca, NY: ILR Press, 2003); Derek Thompson,

"Where Did All the Workers Go? 60 Years of Economic Change in 1 Graph," *Atlantic* January 26, 2012, http://www.theatlantic.com/business/archive/2012/01/where-did-all-the-workers-go-60-years-of-economic-change-in-1-graph/252018, accessed June 30, 2015; Organization for Economic Development and Cooperation, "The Knowledge-Based Economy" (Paris, 1996): 1–46.

103. Joe Weisenthal, "Here's the New Ranking of Top Countries in Reading, Science, and Math," *Business Insider*, December 3, 2013, http://www.businessinsider.com/pisa-rankings-2013-12, accessed July 4, 2015; Stephanie Banchero, "U.S. High-School Students Slip in Global Rankings," *Wall Street Journal*, December 3, 2013, http://www.wsj.com/news/articles/SB10001424052702304579404579234511824563116?mod=djemalertNEWS, accessed July 4, 2015.
104. Bonastia, *Southern Stalemate*, 7; Titus, *Brown's Battleground*, 32–33.
105. Bartley, *The Rise of Massive Resistance*, 213.
106. Wilkins, *Standing Fast*, 222.
107. Ibid., 241–42.
108. Ibid., 238–39; Bartley, *The Rise of Massive Resistance*, 213–17; Berg, *Ticket to Freedom*, 157.
109. Bartley, *The Rise of Massive Resistance*, 216–17; Wilkins, *Standing Fast*, 241–42.
110. George Lewis, "White South, Red Nation: Massive Resistance and the Cold War," in Clive Webb, ed., *Massive Resistance: Southern Opposition to the Second Reconstruction* (New York: Oxford University Press, 2005), 127.
111. Bartley, *The Rise of Massive Resistance*, 221.
112. Ibid., 120, 186–87; Charles C. Bolton, "Mississippi's School Equalization Program, 1945–1954: 'A Last Gasp to Try to Maintain a Segregated Educational System,'" *Journal of Southern History* 66, no. 4 (November 2000): 790.
113. Robert Divine, *The Sputnik Challenge: Eisenhower's Response*

to the Soviet Satellite (New York: Oxford University Press, 1993), xiv–xv.

114. John Finney, "U.S. Missile Experts Shaken by Sputnik: Weight of Satellite Seen as Evidence of Soviet Superiority in Rocketry," *New York Times*, October 13, 1957.
115. "The Military Meaning," *Washington Post*, October 8, 1957.
116. Matthew Brzenzinski, *Red Moon Rising: Sputnik and the Hidden Rivalries That Ignited the Space Age* (New York: Times Books, 2007), 221.
117. Brzenzinski, *Red Moon Rising*, 222.
118. Clowse, *Brainpower for the Cold War*, 3.
119. Ibid., 102.
120. Divine, *The Sputnik Challenge*, 52, 54–55, 57.
121. Clowse, *Brainpower for the Cold War*, 37–38, 50, 52–53, 102.
122. Day, *The Southern Manifesto*, 6.
123. Clowse, *Brainpower for the Cold War*, 4.
124. Anderson, *Eyes off the Prize*, 214–15.
125. Dwight D. Eisenhower to Swede Hazlett, October 23, 1954, http://www.eisenhower.archives.gov/research/online_documents/civil_rights_brown_v_boe/1954_10_23_DDE_to_Hazlett.pdf, accessed November 14, 2015.
126. Dwight D. Eisenhower to Swede Hazlett, July 27, 1957, http://www.eisenhower.archives.gov/research/online_documents/civil_rights_brown_v_boe/1957_07_22_DDE_to_Hazlett.pdf, accessed November 14, 2015.
127. Clowse, *Brainpower for the Cold War*, 43, 67, 119.
128. Wilkins, *Standing Fast*, 255.
129. Clowse, *Brainpower for the Cold War*, 119–21.
130. Ibid., 47, 104, 138.
131. Robert A. Margo, *Race and Schooling in the South, 1880–1950: An Economic History* (Chicago: University of Chicago Press, 1990), 15, http://www.nber.org/books/marg90-1, accessed July 14, 2015.
132. "Doctoral Degree Awards to African Americans Reach Another

All-Time High," *Journal of Blacks in Higher Education*, 2006, http://www.jbhe.com/news_views/50_black_doctoraldegrees.html, accessed July 11, 2015. (Note that the growth cited in this article is driven overwhelmingly by doctorates in education.)

133. Rodney C. Adkins, "America Desperately Needs More STEM Students. Here's How to Get Them," *Forbes* July 9, 2012, http://www.forbes.com/sites/forbesleadershipforum/2012/07/09/america-desperately-needs-more-stem-students-heres-how-to-get-them, accessed July 11, 2015.
134. Kluger, *Simple Justice*, 3.
135. Susan Egerter, Paula Braveman, et al., "Issue Brief No. 5, Exploring the Social Determinants of Health: Education and Health," Robert Wood Johnson Foundation (April 2011): 1–17; "Is this Representative Government? Voting Rates by Educational Attainment," *Postsecondary Education Opportunity*, no. 48 (June 1996), http://www.postsecondary.org/last12/48696Voting.pdf, accessed July 4, 2015.
136. Klarman, Brown v. Board, 165, 182, 185; Gary Orfield, Susan E. Eaton, and the Harvard Project on School Desegregation, *Dismantling Desegregation: The Quiet Reversal of* Brown v. Board of Education (New York: New Press 1996); Erica Frankenberg and Gary Orfield, ed., *The Resegregation of Suburban Schools: A Hidden Crisis in American Education* (Cambridge, MA: Harvard Education, 2012).
137. Gordy, *Finding the Lost Year*, 170, 171.
138. Irons, *Jim Crow's Children*, 177.
139. "Table 233: Educational Attainment by State," U.S. Census Bureau, 2011 http://www.census.gov/compendia/statab/2012/tables/12s0233.xls, accessed July 3, 2015; U.S. Census Bureau, "State Rankings—Statistical Abstract of the United States: Personal Income Per Capita in Current Dollars, 2007," http://www.census.gov/statab/ranks/rank29.html, accessed July 3, 2015; Miranda Hitti, "How States Rank on Health Care: Hawaii Is First, Oklahoma and Mississippi Are Last on Foundation's First

State Scorecard on Health Care," WebMD, http://www.webmd.com/news/20070613/how-states-rank-on-health-care, accessed July 3, 2015.

140. "Farmville, VA: Income Map, Earnings Map, and Wages Data," http://www.city-data.com/income/income-Farmville-Virginia.html, accessed June 7, 2015.

141. "Secretary Arne Duncan's Remarks at OECD's Release of the Program for International Student Assessment (PISA) 2009 Results," December 7, 2010, http://www.ed.gov/news/speeches/secretary-arne-duncans-remarks-oecds-release-program-international-student-assessment-pisa-2009-results, accessed July 4, 2015.

Four **Rolling Back Civil Rights**

1. Gene Roberts and Hank Klibanoff, *The Race Beat: The Press, the Civil Rights Struggle, and the Awakening of a Nation* (New York: Knopf, 2006); J. Mills Thornton III, *Dividing Lines: Municipal Politics and the Struggle for Civil Rights in Montgomery, Birmingham, and Selma* (Tuscaloosa: University of Alabama Press, 2002), 291, 309, 311, 355; Taylor Branch, *Pillar of Fire: America in the King Years, 1963–65* (New York: Simon and Schuster, 1998), 562; Diane McWhorter, *Carry Me Home: Birmingham, Alabama the Climactic Battle of the Civil Rights Revolution* (New York: Touchstone Book, 2001), 370–74, 520–30.
2. Adam Fairclough, *To Redeem the Soul of America: The Southern Christian Leadership Conference and Martin Luther King, Jr.* (Athens: University of Georgia Press, 2001).
3. Dan T. Carter, *From George Wallace to Newt Gingrich: Race in the Conservative Revolution* (Baton Rouge: Louisiana State University Press, 1996), 29; Richard Nixon, *RN: The Memoirs of Richard Nixon* (New York: Touchstone Books, 1978, 1990), 435; Jill Lepore, "Richer and Poorer: Accounting for Inequality," *New*

Yorker, March 16, 2015, http://www.newyorker.com/magazine/2015/03/16/richer-and-poorer, accessed August 4, 2015.

4. Michelle Alexander, *The New Jim Crow: Mass Incarceration in the Age of Colorblindness*, foreword by Cornel West (New York: New Press, 2010, 2012), 6.
5. James W. Loewen, "The Last Innocents: The Civil Rights Movement and the Teaching of High School History," *Southern Changes* 17, no. 2 (1995): 14–17; Derrick P. Aldridge, "The Limits of Master Narratives in History Textbooks: An Analysis of Representations of Martin Luther King, Jr.," *Teachers College Record* 104, no. 4 (April 2006): 662–86; William Brink and Louis Harris, *Black and White: A Study of U.S. Racial Attitudes Today* (New York: Simon and Schuster, 1966), 121; Jim Tankersley, Peyton Craighill, and Scott Clement, "Half of American Whites See No Racism Around Them," *Washington Post*, June 18, 2015; Lepore, "Richer and Poorer."
6. Nixon, *RN*, 435. Also see *Shelby County v. Holder*, 570 U.S. ____ (2013) http://www.supremecourt.gov/opinions/12pdf/12-96_6k47.pdf, accessed August 15, 2015.
7. Danny Vinik, "The Economics of Reparations: Why Congress Should Meet Ta-Nehisi Coates's Modest Demand," *New Republic*, May 21, 2014, http://www.newrepublic.com/article/117856/academic-evidence-reparations-costs-are-limited, accessed July 26, 2015; Joe R. Feagin, "Documenting the Costs of Slavery, Segregation, and Contemporary Racism: Why Reparations Are in Order for African Americans," *Harvard BlackLetter Law Journal* 20 (2004), 53–55.
8. Patrick J. Buchanan, "A Brief for Whitey," March 21, 2008, http://buchanan.org/blog/pjb-a-brief-for-whitey-969, accessed July 31, 2015.
9. Edward E. Baptist, *The Half Has Never Been Told: Slavery and the Making of American Capitalism* (New York: Basic Books, 2014); Matthew Yglesias, "America's Slaves Were More Valuable Than All Its Industrial Capital Combined," *Slate*, July 18, 2013,

http://www.slate.com/blogs/moneybox/2013/07/18/america_s_slave_wealth.html, accessed July 27, 2015; L. Todd Wood, "No Oprah, I've Never Owned A Slave . . . Am I Supposed to Feel Guilty About Something I Didn't Do?" *Western Journalism*, April 8, 2014, http://www.westernjournalism.com/news-flash-left-living-american-ever-owned-slave, accessed July 26, 2015; Sarita Choury, "S.C. Rep. Supports Flag: 'We Didn't All Come from White, Plantation Homes,'" *Savannah Morning News*, June 25, 2015, http://savannahnow.com/news/2015-06-25/sc-rep-supports-flag-we-didnt-all-come-white-plantation-homes, accessed July 26, 2015; John Foster, *White Race Discourse: Preserving Racial Privilege in a Post-Racial Society* (Lanham, MD: Lexington Books, 2013), 97.

10. Raymond Wolters, *Right Turn: William Bradford Reynolds, the Reagan Administration, and Black Civil Rights* (New Brunswick, NJ: Transaction Publishers, 1996); Ira Katznelson, *When Affirmative Action Was White: An Untold History of Racial Inequality in Twentieth-Century America* (New York: W. W. Norton, 2005); Stephanie Greco Larson, *Media and Minorities: The Politics of Race in News and Entertainment* (Lanham, MD: Rowman and Littlefield, 2006), 90–91. For the rationale behind affirmative action, see "President Lyndon B. Johnson's Commencement Address at Howard University: 'To Fulfill These Rights,'" June 4, 1965, http://www.lbjlib.utexas.edu/johnson/archives.hom/speeches.hom/650604.asp, accessed July 29, 2015.
11. Alexander, *The New Jim Crow*, 54; Brink and Harris, *Black and White*, 129; Joshua L. Rabinowitz, David O. Sears, Jim Sidanius, and Jon A. Krosnick, "Why Do White Americans Oppose Race-Targeted Policies? Clarifying the Impact of Symbolic Racism," *Political Psychology* 30, no. 5 (2009): 805–28.
12. See, for example, Ben Shapiro, "Dylann Roof Was Ultimate Lone Wolf, Left Blames Right Anyway," Breitbart, June 22, 2015, http://www.breitbart.com/big-journalism/2015/06/22/dylann-roof-was-ultimate-lone-wolf-left-blames-right-anyway, accessed

August 3, 2015; John Blake, CNN, "The New Threat: 'Racism Without Racists,'" November 27, 2014, http://www.cnn.com/2014/11/26/us/ferguson-racism-or-racial-bias, accessed August 15, 2015.

13. Jesse Curtis, "Awakening the Nation: Mississippi Senator John C. Stennis, the White Countermovement, and the Rise of Colorblind Conservatism, 1947–1964" (master's thesis, Kent State University, 2014), 149.
14. Mark Green and Gail MacColl, *There He Goes Again: Ronald Reagan's Reign of Error* (New York: Pantheon Books, 1983), 85–86, 90, 91; Ian Haney López, *Dog Whistle Politics: How Coded Racial Appeals Have Reinvented Racism and Wrecked the Middle Class* (New York: Oxford University Press, 2014), 59.
15. Brink and Harris, *Black and White*, 106, 129.
16. Curtis, "Awakening the Nation," 147.
17. Carter, *From George Wallace to Newt Gingrich*, 5–6.
18. Kenneth O'Reilly, *Nixon's Piano: Presidents and Racial Politics from Washington to Clinton* (New York: Free Press, 1995), 290.
19. Carter, *From George Wallace to Newt Gingrich*, 15, 19; O'Reilly, *Nixon's Piano*, 280–81.
20. Robert M. Collins, *More: The Politics of Economic Growth in Postwar America* (New York: Oxford University Press, 2000), 68–97.
21. David O. Sears and Tom Jessor, "Whites' Racial Policy Attitudes: The Role of White Racism," *Social Science Quarterly* 77, no. 4 (December 1996): 756.
22. Brink and Harris, *Black and White*, 100, 120.
23. Ibid., 104; "Indicator 16: Median Family Income," 44, National Center for Education Statistics, http://nces.ed.gov/pubs98/yi/yi16.pdf, accessed July 26, 2015. Table B–42: Civilian Unemployment Rate, 1965–2011, *Economic Report of the President*, http://www.gpo.gov/fdsys/pkg/ERP-2012/pdf/ERP-2012-table42.pdf, accessed July 26, 2015.
24. No. 263. Educational Attainment, by Race and Hispanic Origin: 1960 to 1998, U.S. Census Bureau, Statistical Abstract of the

United States: 1999, 169, https://www.census.gov/prod/99pubs/99statab/sec04.pdf, accessed July 26, 2015.

25. *Green v. County School Board of New Kent County*, 391 U.S. 430 (1968); *Swann v. Charlotte-Mecklenburg Board of Education*, 402 US 1 (1971); *Penick v. Columbus Board of Education*, 583 F.2d 787 (1978).
26. Herbert Hill, "Race and the Steelworkers Union: White Privilege and Black Struggles," review of Judith Stein, *Running Steel, Running America*, in *New Politics* 8, no. 4 (new series), whole no. 32, Winter 2002, http://nova.wpunj.edu/newpolitics/issue32/hill32.htm#r15, accessed November 15, 2015; *Griggs v. Duke Power Co.*, 401 U.S. 424 (1971).
27. Rosemary Stevenson, "Black Politics in the U.S.: A Survey of Recent Literature," *Black Scholar* 19, no. 2 (March–April 1988): 58–61.
28. Brink and Harris, *Black and White*, 120.
29. Carter, *From George Wallace to Newt Gingrich*, 29; Thomas J. Sugrue, "Crabgrass-Roots Politics: Race, Rights, and the Reaction Against Liberalism in the Urban North, 1940–1964," *Journal of American History* 82, no. 2 (September 1995): 551–78.
30. O'Reilly, *Nixon's Piano*, 361.
31. Alexander, *The New Jim Crow*, 44.
32. O'Reilly, *Nixon's Piano*, 281.
33. Ari Berman, *Give Us the Ballot: The Modern Struggle for Voting Rights in America* (New York: Farrar, Straus and Giroux, 2015), 74.
34. Jaclyn Ronquillo, Thomas F. Denson, Brian Lickel, Zhong-Lin Lu, Anirvan Nandy, and Keith B. Maddox, "The Effects of Skin Tone on Race-Related Amygdala Activity: An fMRI Investigation," *Social Cognitive and Affective Neuroscience* 2, no. 1 (2007): 39–44.
35. "The First Civil Right," Nixon campaign ad, 1968, http://www.livingroomcandidate.org/commercials/1968, accessed August 8, 2015.

36. Carter, *From George Wallace to Newt Gingrich*, 30; Alexander, *The New Jim Crow*, 44, 46–47.
37. Carter, *From George Wallace to Newt Gingrich*, 30.
38. For the history of linking African Americans with crime, see Khalil Gibran Muhammad, *The Condemnation of Blackness: Race, Crime, and the Making of Modern Urban America* (Cambridge, MA: Harvard University Press 2010); Naomi Murakawa, *The First Civil Right: How Liberals Built Prison America* (New York: Oxford University Press, 2014).
39. O'Reilly, *Nixon's Piano*, 296.
40. Haney López, *Dog Whistle Politics*.
41. Berman, *Give Us the Ballot*, 74.
42. Ibid., 76; *Allen v. State Board of Elections*, 393 U.S. 544 (1969). Also see Todd S. Purdum, "The Republican Who Saved Civil Rights," *Politico Magazine*, March 31, 2014, http://www.politico.com/magazine/story/2014/03/the-movers-behind-the-civil-rights-act-105216, accessed August 8, 2015.
43. Berman, *Give Us the Ballot*, 77.
44. *ABC News Turning Point*, "Murder in Mississippi: The Price of Freedom," Anthony Ross Potter (producer), (New York: ABC News, 1994), VHS.
45. Thornton, *Dividing Lines*, 487–89.
46. John Dittmer, *Local People: The Struggle for Civil Rights in Mississippi* (Urbana and Chicago: University of Illinois Press, 1995), 109–110, 215.
47. Department of Justice, "History of Federal Voting Rights Laws: The Voting Rights Act of 1965, the 1965 Enactment," http://www.justice.gov/crt/about/vot/intro/intro_b.php, accessed July 30, 2015.
48. *South Carolina v. Katzenbach*, 383 U.S. 301, 327–28 (1966).
49. Colby, "The Voting Rights Act and Black Registration in Mississippi," 130; Dean J. Kotlowski, "Unhappily Yoked? Hugh Scott and Richard Nixon," *Pennsylvania Magazine of History and Biography* 125, no. 3 (July 2001): 247.

50. Berman, *Give Us the Ballot*, 77.
51. Kotlowski, "Unhappily Yoked," 247–49.
52. Berman, *Give Us the Ballot*, 78.
53. Ibid., 83; *South Carolina v. Katzenbach*, 383 U.S. 301; Lawrence Edward Carter, *Walking Integrity: Benjamin Elijah Mays, Mentor to Martin Luther King Jr.* (Macon, GA: Mercer University Press, 1998), 43–44.
54. Department of Justice, "The Effect of the Voting Rights Act," http://www.justice.gov/crt/about/vot/intro/intro_c.php, accessed July 30, 2015.
55. *Alexander v. Holmes County Board of Education*, 396 U.S. 1218 (1969) https://supreme.justia.com/cases/federal/us/396/1218/case.html, accessed July 30, 2015.
56. Nixon, *RN*, 418–24; Alfonso A. Narvaez, "Clement Haynsworth Dies at 77; Lost Struggle for High Court Seat," *New York Times*, November 23, 1989.
57. Robert D. Bullard, "The Mountains of Houston: Environmental Justice and the Politics of Garbage," *Cite* (Winter 2014), 28–33; Christopher Silver, "The Racial Origins of Zoning in American Cities," in *Urban Planning and the African American Community: In the Shadows*, ed. June Manning Thomas and Marsha Ritzdorf (Thousand Oaks, CA: Sage Publications, 1997), http://www.asu.edu/courses/aph294/total-readings/silver%20–%20racialoriginsofzoning.pdf, accessed August 4, 2015.
58. Chemerinsky, *The Case Against the Supreme Court*, 141.
59. Ibid.; *Rodriguez v. San Antonio Independent School District*, 337 F. Supp. 280 (1971).
60. *Rodriguez v. San Antonio Independent School District*.
61. *San Antonio Independent School District v. Rodriguez*, 411 U.S. 1 (1973); Chemerinsky, *The Case Against the Supreme Court*, 141.
62. Catherine S. Chilman, "Families in Poverty in the Early 1970's: Rates, Associated Factors, Some Implications," *Journal of Marriage and Family* 37, no. 1 (February 1975); 51, 53.
63. *San Antonio Independent School District v. Rodriguez*.

64. Ibid.
65. Cherminsky, *The Case Against the Supreme Court*, 143; Samantha Meinke, "Milliken v Bradley: The Northern Battle for Desegregation," *Michigan Bar Journal* (September 2011), 20.
66. *Milliken v. Bradley*, 418 U.S. 717 (1974).
67. Ibid.
68. Cornell University Law School, Legal Information Institute, "Regents of the Univ. of Cal. v. Bakke," https://www.law.cornell.edu/supremecourt/text/438/265, accessed August 16, 2015; William Trombley, "Bending of Medical School Admission Rules Rapped: UC President, Regents' Chairman Upset over Davis Dean's Favors for Powerful and Wealthy," *Los Angeles Times*, July 14, 1976.
69. *Regents of the University of California v. Bakke*, 438 U.S. 265 (1978); Lewis Powell to William Brennan, memo, July 23, 1978, Bakke 76-811, Folder 10, *Lewis Powell Papers*, Washington and Lee School of Law, http://law2.wlu.edu/powellarchives/page.asp?pageid=1322, accessed July 7, 2015; Memorandum to the Conference from Mr. Justice Powell, 1st Draft, November 1977, 23, *Powell Papers*; Justice Byron R. White, Memorandum for the Conference, October 13, 1977, *Powell Papers*; William G. Bowen and Derek Bok, *The Shape of the River: Long-term Consequences of Considering Race in College and University Admissions* (Princeton, NJ: Princeton University Press, 1998), 8.
70. Scott Jaschik, "Affirmative Action for White C+ Guys," *Inside Higher Ed*, November 2, 2006, https://www.insidehighered.com/news/2006/11/02/towson, accessed August 8, 2015; Rob Mank, "Men Far More Likely to Benefit from Affirmative Action in College Admissions," CBS NEWS, September 26, 2011, http://www.cbsnews.com/news/men-far-more-likely-to-benefit-from-affirmative-action-in-college-admissions, accessed August 8, 2015. Administrators struggle to create gender balance on campuses because men's entrance qualifications are far below women applicants.

71. Justice Marshall dissent, First Printed Draft, June 28, 1978 (2 of 2), Bakke 76-811, *Powell Papers*, Washington and Lee School of Law, http://law2.wlu.edu/powellarchives/page.asp?pageid=1322, accessed July 7, 2015.
72. Joseph L. Naar, "Blacks in College Doubled Since 1970," *American Journal of Economics and Sociology* 37, no. 3 (July 1978): 239–40.
73. Bowen and Bok, *The Shape of the River*, 1–11.
74. Frank Newport, "Americans Say Reagan Is the Greatest U.S. President," *Gallup*, February 18, 2011, http://www.gallup.com/poll/146183/Americans-Say-Reagan-Greatest-President.aspx, accessed August 7, 2015.
75. O'Reilly, *Nixon's Piano*, 355.
76. *Neshoba: The Price of Freedom*, produced by Pro Bono and Pagano, produce and directed by Micki Dickoff and Tony Pagano (New York: First Run Features, 2010), 88 minutes, DVD; Alexander, *The New Jim Crow*, 48; Carter, *From George Wallace to Newt Gingrich*, 66.
77. Comment by Hugh Jim Bissell on August 13, 2015, at 07:01:07 A.M. PDT, https://www.dailykos.com/story/2015/08/11/1411087/-Head-of-Dept-of-History-at-West-Point-destroys-argument-that-Civil-War-wasnt-fought-over-slavery?detail=emailclassic, accessed August 15, 2015.
78. Bob Herbert, "Impossible, Ridiculous, Repugnant," *New York Times*, October 6, 2005.
79. Michael Schaller, *Ronald Reagan* (New York: Oxford University Press, 2011), 3, 35; George Lipsitz, *The Possessive Investment in Whiteness: How White People Profit from Identity Politics* (Philadelphia: Temple University Press, 1998), 5; Michael K. Brown, *Race, Money, and the American Welfare State* (Ithaca, NY: Cornell University Press, 1999), 323, 326–32, 334, 341–44; Jill S. Quadagno, *The Color of Welfare: How Racism Undermined the War on Poverty* (New York: Oxford University Press, 1994).
80. Pearl T. Robinson, "Black Political Power—Upward or Downward,"

The State of Black America, 1982 (New York: National Urban League, 1982), 83; Ellen Warren, "Reagan Urges 'Colorblind' Society," *Philadelphia Inquirer*, February 12, 1986, http://articles.philly.com/1986-02-12/news/26089072_1_soviet-nuclear-secrets-illegal-quotas-colorblind-society, accessed November 16, 2015; Peter Grier, "Reagan and Civil Rights: Building Just Society; Affirmative Action v. Colorblindness," *Christian Science Monitor*, May 26, 1983, http://www.csmonitor.com/1983/0526/052641.html, accessed November 16, 2015.

81. O'Reilly, *Nixon's Piano*, 370; Green and MacColl, *There He Goes Again*, 89; Niara Sudarkasa, "Black Enrollment in Higher Education: The Unfulfilled Promise of Equality," National Urban League, *The State of Black America, 1988* (New York: National Urban League, 1988), 8, 10, 11–12.
82. Green and MacColl, *There He Goes Again*, 116.
83. O'Reilly, *Nixon's Piano*, 370.
84. Anne C. Lewis, "Administration Seems Willing to Turn Back Both the Clock and the Constitution on Civil Rights," *Phi Delta Kappan* 64, no. 8 (April 1983): 523–24; Wolters, *Right Turn*, 335–58.
85. William Bradford Reynolds, "Individualism vs. Group Rights: The Legacy of Brown," *Yale Law Journal* 93, no. 6 (May 1984): 1002–3; Mary C. Doyle, "From Desegregation to Resegregation: Public Schools in Norfolk, Virginia 1954–2002," *Journal of African American History* 90, no. 1–2 (Winter 2005): 73–76; John E. Jacob, "Black America, 1987: An Overview," *The State of Black America, 1988*, 2; Anne C. Lewis "With Liberty and Justice: For Whom?" *Phi Delta Kappan* 67, no. 3 (November 1985): 179–80.
86. Jacob, "Black America, 1987," 1.
87. Jonathan Harsch, "Reagan Cuts Eat into School Lunches," *Christian Science Monitor* September 17, 1981, http://www.csmonitor.com/1981/0917/091746.html, accessed August 14, 2015.

88. David H. Swinton, "Economic Status of Blacks, 1987," *The State of Black America, 1988* (New York: National Urban League, 1988), 136.
89. Robert W. Fairlie and William A. Sundstrom, "The Emergence, Persistence, and Recent Widening of the Racial Unemployment Gap," *Industrial and Labor Relations Review* 52, no. 2 (January 1999): 255, 257.
90. Bernard E. Anderson, "Economic Patterns in Black America," *The State of Black America, 1982*, 3–4; O'Reilly, *Nixon's Piano*, 369–70; Green and MacColl, *There He Goes Again*, 92; Jacob, "Black America, 1987: An Overview," 1.
91. Peter Dreier, "Reagan's Legacy: Homelessness in America," National Homelessness Institute, *Shelter Online*, no. 135 (May–June 2004), http://www.nhi.org/online/issues/135/reagan.html, accessed January 12, 2010.
92. David Cooper, Mary Gable, and Algernon Austin, "The Public-Sector Jobs Crisis: Women and African Americans Hit Hardest by Job Losses in State and Local Governments," *Economic Policy Institute*, May 2, 2012, http://www.epi.org/publication/bp339-public-sector-jobs-crisis, accessed August 11, 2015.
93. Bernard E. Anderson, "Economic Patterns in Black America," *The State of Black America* (New York: National Urban League, 1982), 7; Howell Raines, "Reagan Aims to Cut 37,000 Federal Jobs, Saving $1.3 Billion," *New York Times*, March 7, 1981.
94. Jane Mayer and Jill Abramson, *Strange Justice: The Selling of Clarence Thomas* (Boston and New York: Houghton Mifflin, 1994), 116.
95. William Raspberry, "A Double Disaster for EEOC," *Washington Post*, November 18, 1981; Hanes Walton, *African American Power and Politics: The Political Context Variable* (New York: Columbia University Press, 1997), 25; Vernon E. Jordan Jr. and John E. Jacob, "Introduction," *The State of Black America, 1982* (New York: National Urban League, 1982), vii; John Hope Franklin, *The Color Line: Legacy for the Twenty-first Century* (Columbia: University of Missouri Press, 1993), 14.

96. Douglas Frantz, "Thomas Seems Sure to Face Criticism on EEOC Policies," *Los Angeles Times*, July 3, 1991; O'Reilly, *Nixon's Piano*, 366; Mayer and Abramson, *Strange Justice*, 129–30, 143.
97. Jordan and Jacob, "Introduction," *The State of Black America, 1982* (New York: National Urban League, 1982), vii.
98. U.S. Census Bureau, Indicator 16, Median Family Income, http://nces.ed.gov/pubs98/yi/yi16.pdf; David H. Swinton, "Economic Status of Blacks, 1987," *The State of Black America, 1988*, 130, 132; Carter, *From George Wallace to Newt Gingrich*, 63.
99. Walton, *African American Power and Politics*, 26.
100. Raines, "Reagan Aims to Cut 37,000 Federal Jobs."
101. Ronald Reagan, "Radio Address to the Nation on Federal Drug Policy," October 2, 1982, *The American Presidency Project*, www.ucsb.edu/ws/?pid=43085, accessed July 6, 2015.
102. Andrew B. Whitford and Jeff Yates, *Presidential Rhetoric and the Public Agenda: Constructing the War on Drugs* (Baltimore: Johns Hopkins University Press, 2009), 75.
103. "Backyard 1954–1990," *The Cold War* 6, Jeremy Isaacs Production for Turner Original Productions, series producer Martin Smith (Warner Home Video, 1998), VHS.
104. Schaller, *Ronald Reagan*, 39; Richard H. Ullman, "At War with Nicaragua," *Foreign Affairs* 62, no. 1 (Fall 1983): 39–40.
105. Alexander Cockburn and Jeffrey St. Clair, *Whiteout: The* CIA, *Drugs, and the Press* (London and New York: Verso, 1998), 5; Ullman, "At War with Nicaragua," 41.
106. Schaller, *Ronald Reagan*, 75.
107. Cockburn and St. Clair, *Whiteout*, 8.
108. Schaller, *Ronald Reagan*, 40; Cockburn and St. Clair, *Whiteout*, 23, 297.
109. Cockburn and St. Clair, *Whiteout*, 2, 5–6, 24; "Key Figures in CIA-Crack Cocaine Scandal Begin to Come Forward," *Huffington Post*, October 10, 2014, http://www.huffingtonpost.com/2014/10/10/gary-webb-dark-alliance_n_5961748.html, accessed August 13, 2015.

110. "The Drug Gangs," *Newsweek*, March 28, 1988, found in "The FBI File on Crips and Bloods: Drug Gangs"; Matt Lait, "The Battle to Control 50,000 Gang Members on the Streets of Los Angeles," *Washington Post*, April 26, 1983, found in "The FBI File on Crips and Bloods: Drug Gangs."
111. Daniel Ryan Davis, "The Charisma of Crack Cocaine: The Impact of Crack on Black America, 1984–2010" (Ph.D. dissertation, Michigan State University, 2012), 56, 80.
112. Howard Kohn and Vicki Monks, "The Dirty Secrets of George Bush: The Vice President's Illegal Operations," *Rolling Stone*, November 3, 1988, http://www.rollingstone.com/politics/news/the-dirty-secrets-of-george-bush-19881103, accessed August 29, 2015.
113. Kohn and Monks, "The Dirty Secrets of George Bush"; U.S. Senate, Committee on Foreign Relations, Subcommittee on Terrorism, Narcotics and International Operations, "Drugs, Law Enforcement and Foreign Policy," 100th Cong., 2d. Sess., December 1988, 96–97; Ronald Reagan, "Radio Address to the Nation on Federal Drug Policy," October 2, 1982, *The American Presidency Project*, www.ucsb.edu/ws/?pid=43085, accessed July 6, 2015.
114. Reagan, "Radio Address to the Nation on Federal Drug Policy"; Cockburn and St. Clair, *Whiteout*, 308–9.
115. CIA, "The Contra Story: Introduction," https://www.cia.gov/library/reports/general-reports-1/cocaine/contra-story/intro.html, accessed August 29, 2015; Cockburn and St. Clair, *Whiteout*, 49.
116. Schaller, *Ronald Reagan*, 75–76.
117. Another stream of revenue was illegal arms sales to Iran, see Malcolm Byrne, *Iran-Contra: Reagan's Scandal and the Unchecked Abuse of Presidential Power* (Lawrence, KS: University Press of Kansas, 2014).
118. David Brock, *Blinded by the Right: The Conscience of an Ex-Conservative* (New York: Crown, 2002), 43.

119. "High Crimes and Misdemeanors: The Iran-Contra Scandal," *Frontline*, November 27, 1990, http://billmoyers.com/content/high-crimes-misdemeanors-reagan-iran-contra-scandal, accessed August, 29, 2015.
120. Kerry Committee, 146, "The Contras, Cocaine, and Covert Operations," National Security Archive Electronic Briefing Book No. 2, National Security Archive, http://nsarchive.gwu.edu/NSAEBB/NSAEBB113/north06.pdf, accessed January 25, 2016; Michael Palmer to Phil Buechler, invoice, February 25, 1986, National Security Archive, http://nsarchive.gwu.edu/NSAEBB/NSAEBB2/docs/doc05.pdf, accessed February 11, 2016; Oliver North Meeting with Rob Owen, minutes, August 9, 1985, National Security Archive Electronic Briefing Book No. 2, National Security Archive, http://nsarchive.gwu.edu/NSAEBB/NSAEBB2/docs/doc01.pdf, accessed November 28, 2014; T.C. [Robert Owen] to The Hammer [Oliver North], memo, April 1, 1985, National Security Archive, http://nsarchive.gwu.edu/NSAEBB/NSAEBB2/docs/doc03.pdf, accessed November 28, 2014; T.C. [Robert Owen] to BG [Oliver North] February 10, 1986, National Security Archive, http://nsarchive.gwu.edu/NSAEBB/NSAEBB2/docs/doc04.pdf, accessed November 28, 2014; Cockburn and St. Clair, *Whiteout*, 35.
121. Oliver North, notepad, July 12, 1985, National Security Archive, http://nsarchive.gwu.edu/NSAEBB/NSAEBB2/docs/doc02.pdf, accessed November 28, 2014; Union Nicaraguense Opositora (UNO), September 26, 1986, Luis Posada Carriles, "The Declassified Record: CIA and FBI Documents Detail Career in International Terrorism; Connection to U.S.," National Security Archive, http://nsarchive.gwu.edu/NSAEBB/NSAEBB153/19860902.pdf, accessed August 29, 2015.
122. FBI interview with Dennis Ainsworth, January 21, 1987, SF 211-11, National Security Archive, http://nsarchive.gwu.edu/NSAEBB/NSAEBB2/docs/doc15.pdf, accessed November 28, 2014; Cockburn and St. Clair, *Whiteout*, 9, 40.

123. Alan D. Fiers, Government Witness, *United States of America vs Clair Elroy George*, July 29, 1992, National Security Archive, http://nsarchive.gwu.edu/NSAEBB/NSAEBB2/docs/doc10.pdf, accessed February 11, 2016; Seymour Hersh, "Panama Strongman Said to Trade in Drugs, Arms and Illicit Money," *New York Times*, June 12, 1986; John Herbers, "Panama General Accused by Helms," *New York Times*, June 22, 1986; "Alarm About Panama," *New York Times*, June 24, 1986; James LeMoyne, "Panama's Strongman Tries to Ride out the Storm," *New York Times*, June 25, 1986; Oliver North to NSJMP [John Poindexter], memo, August 23, 1986, National Security Archive, http://nsarchive.gwu.edu/NSAEBB/NSAEBB2/docs/doc07.pdf, accessed February 11, 2016; NSJMP [John Poindexter] to NSOLN [Oliver North], August 23, 1986, National Security Archive, http://nsarchive.gwu.edu/NSAEBB/NSAEBB2/docs/doc08.pdf, accessed February 11, 2016; NSOLN [Oliver North] to NSJMP [John Poindexter], September 20, 1986, National Security Archive, http://nsarchive.gwu.edu/NSAEBB/NSAEBB2/docs/doc11.pdf, accessed February 12, 2016; Oliver North notebook, meeting with Noriega, September 22, 1986, National Security Archive, http://nsarchive.gwu.edu/NSAEBB/NSAEBB2/docs/doc12.pdf, accessed February 12, 2016; Kerry Committee excerpt, p. 76, National Security Archive, http://nsarchive.gwu.edu/NSAEBB/NSAEBB2/docs/doc14.pdf, accessed November 28, 2014; Oliver North to John Poindexter, September 17, 1986, memo, National Security Archive, http://nsarchive.gwu.edu/NSAEBB/NSAEBB2/docs/doc13.pdf, accessed November 28, 2014; Note From: Oliver North, memo, September 18, 1986, ibid; Peter Kornbluh, testimony, "Congressional Inquiry into Alleged Central Intelligence Agency Involvement in the South Central Los Angeles Crack Cocaine Drug Trade," National Security Archive, http://nsarchive.gwu.edu/NSAEBB/NSAEBB2/pktstmny.htm, accessed November 28, 2014.

124. Todd R. Clear, *Imprisoning Communities: How Mass Incarceration Makes Disadvantaged Neighborhoods Worse* (New York: Oxford University Press, 2007).
125. Whitford and Yates, *Presidential Rhetoric and the Public Agenda*, 63.
126. Ibid., 97.
127. J. J. Mahoney, T. F. Newton, Y. Omar, E. L. Ross, and R. De La Garza, "The Relationship Between Lifetime Stress and Addiction Severity in Cocaine-Dependent Participants," *European Neuropsychopharmacology* 23, no. 5 (May 2013): 351–57, doi:10.1016/j.euroneuro.2012.05.016, Epub June 28, 2012.
128. Ronald Reagan, "Speech to the Nation on the Campaign Against Drug Abuse," September 14, 1986, http://millercenter.org/president/reagan/speeches/speech-5465, accessed November 16, 2015.
129. Whitford and Yates, *Presidential Rhetoric and the Public Agenda*, 89–90.
130. Craig Reinarman and Harry G. Levine, "Crack in the Rearview Mirror: Deconstructing Drug War Mythology," *Social Justice* 31, no. 1–2 (95–96), Resisting Militarism and Globalized Punishment (2004): 187.
131. Jennifer E. Cobbina, "Race and Class Differences in Print Media Portrayals of Crack Cocaine and Methamphetamine," *Journal of Criminal Justice and Popular Culture* 15, no. 2 (2008): 152.
132. Reinarman and Levine, "Crack in the Rearview Mirror,"187.
133. Albert Samaha, "Cheaper, More Addictive, and Highly Profitable: How Crack Cocaine Took Over NYC in the 1980s," *Village Voice*, August 12, 2014, http://www.villagevoice.com/news/cheaper-more-addictive-and-highly-profitable-how-crack-took-over-nyc-in-the-80s-6664480, accessed November 16, 2015.
134. Gary Webb and Pamela Kramer, "Waters Calls on Reno, CIA and Congress for Investigation," *San Jose Mercury News*, September 4, 1996, http://www.narconews.com/darkalliance/drugs/scrip905.htm, accessed August 17, 2015; Cockburn and St. Clair, *Whiteout*, 65.

135. Lee P. Brown, "Crime in the Black Community," *The State of Black America, 1988* (New York: National Urban League, 1988), 102.
136. Roland G. Fryer Jr., Paul S. Heaton, Steven D. Levitt, and Kevin M. Murphy, "Measuring Crack Cocaine and Its Impact," *Economic Inquiry* 51, no. 3 (July 2013): 1651–52.
137. George Davey Smith, Sam Harper, John Lynch, and Scott Burris, "Trends in the Black-White Life Expectancy Gap in the United States, 1983–2003," *JAMA* 297, no. 11 (March 21, 2007): 1224–32, doi:10.1001/jama.297.11.1224.
138. Fryer Jr., "Measuring Crack Cocaine and Its Impact," 1651–52.
139. NAACP, "Bill to End 100:1 Crack/Powder Cocaine Sentencing Disparity Will Soon Go Before the Full House of Representatives," http://www.naacp.org/action-alerts/entry/bill-to-end-100-1-crack---powder-cocaine-sentencing-disparity-will-soon-go-, accessed November 16, 2015.
140. Brown, "Crime in the Black Community," 102.
141. Clear, *Imprisoning Communities*, 55; H.R. 5484—Anti-Drug Abuse Act of 1986, https://www.congress.gov/bill/99th-congress/house-bill/5484, accessed August 16, 2015; H.R.5210—Anti-Drug Abuse Act of 1988, https://www.congress.gov/bill/100th-congress/house-bill/5210, accessed August 16, 2015; *Department of Housing and Urban Development v. Rucker*, 535 U.S. 125 (2002); Alexander, *The New Jim Crow*, 145–47.
142. Alexander, *The New Jim Crow*, 61.
143. Ibid., 63; *Terry v. Ohio*, 392 U.S. 1 (1968); Joshua Correll, Bernadette Park, Charles M. Judd, Bernd Wittenbrink, Melody S. Sadler, and Tracie Keesee, "Across the Thin Blue Line: Police Officers and Racial Bias in the Decision to Shoot," *Journal of Personality and Social Psychology* 92, no. 6 (June 2007): 1006–23, http://dx.doi.org/10.1037/0022-3514.92.6.1006; Larry K. Gaines, *An Analysis of Traffic Stop Data in the City of Riverside* (Riverside, CA: City of Riverside, 2002).
144. *United States v. Brignoni-Ponce*, 422 U.S. 873 (1975); Alexander, *The New Jim Crow*, 131.

145. *Hutto v. Davis*, 454 U.S. 370 (1982); Alexander, *The New Jim Crow*, 90.
146. *McClesky v. Kemp* 481 U.S. 279 (1987); Alexander, *The New Jim Crow*, 109–11.
147. *Purkett v. Elem*, 514 U.S. 765 (1995); Alexander, *The New Jim Crow*, 119, 122–23.
148. *Armstrong v. United States*, 517 U.S. 456 (1996); Alexander, *The New Jim Crow*, 115–17.
149. *Whren v. United States*, 517 U.S. 806 (1996); Alexander, *The New Jim Crow*, 108–9.
150. *Alexander v. Sandoval*, 532 U.S. 275 (2001); Alexander, *The New Jim Crow*, 137, 139.
151. *Atwater v. City of Lago Vista*, 532 U.S. 318 (2001); Alexander, *The New Jim Crow*, 67, 69.
152. Andrew Gumbel, "American Travesty," *Independent*, August 20, 2002.
153. Thom Marshall, "Tulia Farmer Dug in Heels for Justice," *Houston Chronicle*, April 23, 2003; Gumbel, "American Travesty."
154. Bob Herbert, "Kafka in Tulia," *New York Times*, July 29, 2002.
155. NAACP-LDF, "Bad Times in Tulia, Texas," September 29, 2000, http://www.naacpldf.org/case-issue/bad-times-tulia-texas, accessed November 17, 2015.
156. Jim Henderson, "Tulia Lawyer's Long Struggle to be Rewarded Today," *Houston Chronicle*, June 16, 2003; Gumbel, "American Travesty"; NAACP-LDF, "Bad Times in Tulia, Texas."
157. Herbert, "Kafka in Tulia."
158. Gumbel, "American Travesty."
159. Jim Henderson, "Tulia Residents Uncertain About Return to Normalcy," *Houston Chronicle*, June 18, 2003.
160. Gumbel, "American Travesty."
161. Morgan Whittaker, "Criminal Injustice: The Percentage of African-Americans in Prison," MSNBC, September 23, 2013.

162. Clear, *Imprisoning Communities*, 4, 49.
163. Human Rights Watch, "Incarcerated America," http://www.hrw.org/legacy/backgrounder/usa/incarceration/us042903.pdf, accessed August 17, 2015.
164. Duke Medicine and News Communication, "White and Hispanic Teens More Likely to Abuse Drugs Than African Americans," November 7, 2011, http://corporate.dukemedicine.org/news_and_publications/news_office/news/white-and-hispanic-teens-more-likely-to-abuse-drugs-than-african-americans, accessed November 17, 2015; Maia Szalavitz, "Study: Whites More Likely to Abuse Drugs Than Blacks," *Time*, November 7, 2011, http://healthland.time.com/2011/11/07/study-whites-more-likely-to-abuse-drugs-than-blacks, accessed August 17, 2015.
165. Alexander, *The New Jim Crow*, 126–27.
166. Murakawa, *The First Civil Right*, 3.

Five How to Unelect a Black President

1. "Reactions from Around the World," *New York Times*, November 5, 2008, http://thecaucus.blogs.nytimes.com/2008/11/05/reactions-from-around-the-world/?_r=0, accessed September 1, 2015.
2. "Reaction to Obama Elected 1st Black US President," *USA Today*, November 5, 2008, posted November 5, 2008, http://usatoday30.usatoday.com/news/world/2008-11-05-1271317715_x.htm, accessed September 1, 2015.
3. "Obama's Victory on Newspaper Front Pages" slideshows, *Huffington Post*, December 6, 2008, http://www.huffingtonpost.com/2008/11/05/obamas-victory-on-newspap_n_141311.html, accessed September 1, 2015.
4. Claire Cohen, "Breakdown of Demographics Reveals How Black Voters Swept Obama into White House," *Daily Mail*, November 5, 2008; "How Groups Voted in 2008," *Roper Center.*
5. Sam Roberts, "2008 Surge in Black Voters Nearly Erased Racial Gap," *New York Times*, July 20, 2009.

6. "How Groups Voted in 2008," *Roper Center*; Fred Lucas, "Romney Polls Better Among White Evangelicals Than Bush, McCain," *CNS News*, October 23, 2012, http://cnsnews.com/news/article/romney-polls-better-among-white-evangelicals-bush-mccain, accessed September 7, 2015.
7. Rosalind S. Helderman and Jon Cohen, "As Republican Convention Emphasizes Diversity, Racial Incidents Intrude," *Washington Post*, August 29, 2012, http://www.washingtonpost.com/politics/2012/08/29/b9023a52-f1ec-11e1-892d-bc92fee603a7_story.html, accessed September 4, 2015.
8. "2008 Voter Turnout," Factcheck.org, January 8, 2009, http://www.factcheck.org/2009/01/2008-voter-turnout/, accessed September 4, 2015.
9. Andrew O'Hehir, "I Watched Fox News for Five Hours Last Night," *Salon*, November 6, 2008, www.salon.com/2008/11/06/watching_fox, accessed September 3, 2015.
10. Frank Newport, "Democrats Racially Diverse; Republicans Mostly White: Democrats and Independents Grow More Diverse Since 2008," *Gallup*, February 8, 2013, http://www.gallup.com/poll/160373/democrats-racially-diverse-republicans-mostly-white.aspx, accessed September 4, 2015.
11. Roberts, "2008 Surge in Black Voters Nearly Erased Racial Gap."
12. Lorraine C. Minnite, "Research Memo: First-Time Voters in the 2008 Election," Project Vote, April 2011, http://www.projectvote.org/images/publications/Reports%20on%20the%20Electorate/FINAL%20First-Time-Voters-in-2008-Election.pdf, accessed September 4, 2015.
13. Stephanie Siek and Joe Sterling, "Census: Fewer White Babies Being Born," CNN, May 17, 2012, http://inamerica.blogs.cnn.com/2012/05/17/census-2011-data-confirm-trend-of-population-diversity, accessed September 4, 2015; "U.S. Public Becoming Less Religious: Modest Drop in Overall Rates of Belief and Practice, but Religiously Affiliated Americans Are as Observant as Before," Pew Research Center, November 3, 2015, http://www.pewforum.

org/2015/11/03/u-s-public-becoming-less-religious/, accessed December 29, 2015.

14. Thomas E. Mann and Norman J. Ornstein, *It's Even Worse Than It Looks: How the American Constitutional System Collided with the New Politics of Extremism* (New York: Basic Books, 2013).
15. "Former Florida GOP Leaders Say Voter Suppression Was Reason They Pushed New Election Law," *Palm Beach Post*, November 25, 2012, http://www.palmbeachpost.com/news/news/state-regional-govt-politics/early-voting-curbs-called-power-play/nTFDy, accessed September 8, 2015.
16. Jane Mayer, "The Voter Fraud Myth," *New Yorker*, October 29, 2012.
17. Ari Berman, "The GOP War on Voting: In a Campaign Supported by the Koch Brothers, Republicans Are Working to Prevent Millions of Democrats from Voting Next Year," *Rolling Stone*, August 30, 2011.
18. Jim Rutenberg, "This Looks Like a National Strategy: Interview of Ari Berman," *New York Times Magazine*, August 17, 2015.
19. Mayer, "Voter Fraud Myth."
20. Jeremiah Goulka, "Are Voter ID Laws a Form of Racism? A Former Republican Tells It Like It Is: Voter ID Laws Unfairly Burden Minorities," *Mother Jones*, October 15, 2012.
21. "ACORN Accusations: McCain Makes Exaggerated Claims of 'Voter Fraud.' Obama Soft-Pedals His Connections," Factcheck.org, October 18, 2008, http://www.factcheck.org/2008/10/acorn-accusations, accessed August 28, 2015.
22. Katie Connolly, "Poll: Majority of Republicans Believe ACORN Stole the Presidential Election," *Newsweek*, November 9, 2009, http://www.newsweek.com/poll-majority-republicans-believe-acorn-stole-presidential-election-210966, accessed September 5, 2015.
23. "ACORN Accusations," Factcheck.org.
24. Richard L. Hasen, *The Voting Wars: From Florida 2000 to the Next Election Meltdown* (New Haven, CT: Yale University Press, 2012), 54–59.

25. Ibid., 61.
26. Mayer, "The Voter Fraud Myth."
27. Anderson, *Eyes off the Prize*, 64.
28. "Althea Simmons Leads Move to Disqualify Rehnquist," *Jet*, September 15, 1986, 16–17; Tova Andrea Wang, *The Politics of Voter Suppression: Defending and Expanding Americans' Right to Vote* (Ithaca, NY: Cornell University Press, 2012), 46.
29. Jason Stein, "Voter Fraud Convictions in State Don't Match Claims," *Milwaukee Journal Sentinel*, September 25, 2012.
30. Amy Bingham, "Voter Fraud: Non-Existent Problem or Election-Threatening Epidemic? Voter ID Laws Aim to Prevent Fraud but Does Voter Fraud Even Exist?" *ABC News*, September 12, 2012.
31. "Romney Supporter Wears 'Put the White Back in the White House' T-Shirt at Ohio Campaign Event," *Huffington Post*, October 13, 2012, http://www.huffingtonpost.com/2012/10/13/romney-supporter-wears-put-the-white-back-in-the-white-house-campaign-event-ohio_n_1963583.html, accessed November 18, 2015.
32. Max J. Rosenthal, "Texans Allowed to Show Gun Permits But Not Student IDs at Voting Booth," *Huffington Post*, November 16, 2011, http://www.huffingtonpost.com/2011/11/15/texans-gun-permits-student-ids-voting_n_1095530.html, accessed September 5, 2015.
33. NAACP and NAACP-Legal Defense and Educational Fund, "Defending Democracy: Confronting Modern Barriers to Voting Rights in America," 4.
34. Georgia Department of Drivers Services, "Checklist of All Accepted Documents," http://www.dds.ga.gov/secureid/accepteddocs.aspx, accessed September 5, 2015; U.S. State Department, "Fees: U.S. Passports and International Travel," http://travel.state.gov/content/passports/english/passports/information/fees.html, accessed September 6, 2015.
35. Brennan Center, "Citizens Without Proof: A Survey of Americans'

Possession of Documentary Proof of Citizenship and Photo Identification," http://www.brennancenter.org/sites/default/files/legacy/d/download_file_39242.pdf, accessed September 5, 2015.

36. Georgia Department of Drivers Services, "Checklist of All Accepted Documents," http://www.dds.ga.gov/secureid/accepteddocs.aspx, accessed September 5, 2015; "Photos: Black Unemployment Across the U.S.," *BET News*, September 2011, http://www.bet.com/news/national/photos/2011/09/black-unemployment-across-the-u-s.html#!090811-national-job-fair-dc, accessed September 5, 2015.
37. Catherine Rampell, "'Unbanked' America," *New York Times*, December 4, 2009, http://economix.blogs.nytimes.com/2009/12/04/unbanked-america, accessed September 5, 2015.
38. Georgia Department of Drivers Services, "Checklist of All Accepted Documents," http://www.dds.ga.gov/secureid/accepteddocs.aspx, accessed September 5, 2015; Daphne Loquist, "Multi-Generational Households," Working Paper #2013–20, U.S. Census Bureau, https://www.census.gov/hhes/families/files/ASA.Multgen.pdf, accessed September 5, 2015.
39. Goulka, "Are Voter ID Laws a Form of Racism?"; Emma Roller, "State Puts Brakes on Plan to Close DMV Sites," *Milwaukee Journal-Sentinel*, August 4, 2011, http://www.jsonline.com/news/statepolitics/126814653.html, accessed December 25, 2015.
40. Ben Mathis-Lilley, "Alabama, Where ID Is Required to Vote, Closes DMVs in Most 'Black Belt' Counties," *Slate*, October 1, 2015, http://www.slate.com/blogs/the_slatest/2015/10/01/alabama_closes_dmvs_in_majority_of_black_belt_counties_passed_voter_id_law.html, accessed November 20, 2015; Brian Lyman, "Alabama Will Reopen Closed DMV Offices in Black Counties," *Governing*, October 20, 2015, http://www.governing.com/topics/politics/drivers-license-offices-will-reopen-on-limited-basis.html, accessed December 25, 2015.
41. Sari Horwitz, "Pennsylvania Judge Strikes Down Voter ID Law," *Washington Post*, January 17, 2014, https://www.washingtonpost.

com/world/national-security/pennsylvania-judge-strikes-down-voter-id-law/2014/01/17/472d620e-7fa2-11e3-93c1-0e888170b723_story.html, accessed September 5, 2015.

42. Chris Kromm, "Waiting at the Polls: Long Lines and the Right to Vote," *Facing South*, September 17, 2014, http://www.southernstudies.org/2014/09/waiting-at-the-polls-long-lines-and-the-right-to-v.html, accessed September 6, 2015.
43. Amy Sherman, "'Souls to the Polls' Sunday Drew High Numbers of African Americans and Hispanics, Corrine Brown Says," Politifact.com, June 22, 2012, http://www.politifact.com/florida/statements/2012/jun/22/corrine-brown/souls-polls-sunday-drew-more-african-american-and, accessed September 5, 2015; "Florida GOP Leaders Says Voting Law Was Intended to Suppress the Vote," *Examiner*, November 28, 2012, http://www.examiner.com/article/florida-gop-leaders-says-voting-law-was-to-suppress-the-vote, accessed September 6, 2015.
44. Patrik Jonsson, "Court Rules Florida Voter Purge Illegal, but Will It Stop GOP Voting Tweaks?" *Christian Science Monitor*, April 2, 2014, http://www.csmonitor.com/USA/Justice/2014/0402/Court-rules-Florida-voter-purge-illegal-but-will-it-stop-GOP-voting-tweaks, accessed September 5, 2015.
45. Christopher S. Parker and Matt A. Barreto, *Change They Can't Believe In: The Tea Party and Reactionary Politics in America* (Princeton, NJ: Princeton University Press, 2013); True the Vote webpage, https://truethevote.org, accessed September 5, 2015.
46. True the Vote webpage, https://truethevote.org, accessed September 5, 2015; A. J. Vicens and Natasha Khan, "Election Observers True the Vote Accused of Intimidating Minority Voters," *NBC News*, August 25, 2012, http://investigations.nbcnews.com/_news/2012/08/25/13473761-election-observers-true-the-vote-accused-of-intimidating-minority-voters, accessed September 5, 2015; "Voter Harassment, Circa 2012," *New York Times*, September 21, 2012, http://www.nytimes.com/2012/09/22/opinion/voter-harassment-circa-2012.html, accessed September 5, 2015.

47. Leadership Conference on Civil Rights, "The Voting Rights Act at Work in Alabama" video, http://www.civilrights.org/voting-rights/shelby-county-v-holder.html?referrer=https://www.bing.com, accessed November 18, 2015; Debbie Elliott, "Alabama Divided as Court Prepares to Hear Voting Rights Challenge," *NPR*, February 21, 2013, http://www.npr.org/2013/02/25/172603328/alabama-divided-as-court-prepares-to-hear-voting-rights-challenge, accessed September 10, 2013; Calera, Alabama, http://www.city-data.com/city/Calera-Alabama.html, accessed September 5, 2015.
48. Leadership Conference on Civil Rights, "Shelby County v. Holder," http://www.civilrights.org/voting-rights/shelby-county-v-holder.html?referrer=https://www.bing.com, accessed November 18, 2015.
49. *Shelby County v. Holder*, 570 U.S. ___ (2013).
50. Department of Justice, "Section 4 of the Voting Rights Act: Terminating Coverage Under the Act's Special Provisions," http://www.justice.gov/crt/section-4-voting-rights-act#bailout, accessed September 6, 2015; Brief of Amici Curiae Jurisdictions: That Have Bailed Out in Support of Respondents and Urging Affirmance, in *Shelby County v. Holder*, http://moritzlaw.osu.edu/electionlaw/litigation/documents/BriefofAmiciCuriaeJurisdictionsthathavebailedout.pdf, accessed September 6, 2015.
51. Brief of Amici Curiae Jurisdictions: That Have Bailed Out in Support of Respondents and Urging Affirmance, in *Shelby County v. Holder*.
52. NAACP, "Stop the Spread of Voter Suppression," pamphlet.
53. ACLU, "The Battle to Protect the Ballot: Voter Suppression Measures Passed Since 2013," https://www.aclu.org/map/battle-protect-ballot-voter-suppression-measures-passed-2013, accessed September 6, 2015; Wendy R. Weiser and Erik Opsal, "The State of Voting in 2014," *Brennan Center for Justice*, June 17, 2014, http://www.brennancenter.org/analysis/state-voting-2014, accessed September 7, 2015.

54. *Veasey et al. v. Perry et al.*, 2:2013cv00193; "The Real Voter Fraud Is Texas' Voter ID Law," *New York Times*, August 7, 2015, http://nyti.ms/1M9KSbN, accessed August 7, 2015.
55. *In Re: State of Texas, Petitioner*, On Petition for Writ of Mandamus to the United States District Court for the Southern District of Texas, Corpus Christi Division Cases No. 2:13-CV-193 (lead case), 2:13-CV-263 and 2:13-CV-291 (consolidated).
56. *Veasey, et al v. Perry, et al.*, No. 14–41127 (October 14, 2014).
57. *Veasey, et al v. Perry, et al.*, 574 U.S. ____ (2014); Robert Barnes, "Supreme Court Allows Texas to Use Controversial Voter-ID Law" *Washington Post*, October 18, 2014, https://www.washingtonpost.com/politics/courts_law/2014/10/18/0439b116-5623-11e4-892e-602188e70e9c_story.html, accessed November 19, 2015; Brad Friedman, "Supreme Court Allows Texas to Enforce Strict Voter ID Law," *Gawker.com*, October 18, 2014, http://gawker.com/supreme-court-allows-texas-to-enforce-strict-voter-id-l-1647987025, accessed November 19, 2015.
58. *Veasey, et al v. Perry, et al.* No. 14-41127 (August 5, 2015).
59. Erik Eckholm, "Texas ID Law Called Breach of Voting Rights Act," *New York Times*, August 5, 2015, http://www.nytimes.com/2015/08/06/us/appellate-panel-says-texas-id-law-broke-us-voting-rights-act.html, accessed September 6, 2015; "The Real Voter Fraud Is Texas' Voter ID Law," *New York Times*.
60. Mann and Ornstein, *It's Even Worse Than It Looks*, 27, 33, 43, 53, 81–101; Jennifer Newton, "So Much for Hope and Change: Most Americans Don't Believe Government Can Do Anything for Them—or Is Likely to Even Try," *Daily Mail*, July 4, 2014, http://www.dailymail.co.uk/news/article-2680856/So-hope-change-Most-Americans-dont-believe-government-likely-try.html, accessed December 25, 2015.
61. Josh Hicks, "How Much Did the Shutdown Cost the Economy?" *Washington Post*, October 18, 2013, http://www.washingtonpost.com/blogs/federal-eye/wp/2013/10/18/how-much-did-the-shutdown-cost-the-economy, accessed September 7, 2015.

62. Brett LoGiurato, "Boehner: We're on the Path to Default If Obama Doesn't Negotiate on the Debt Ceiling," *Business Insider*, October 6, 2013, http://www.businessinsider.com/boehner-debt-ceiling-default-obama-government-shutdown-2013-10, accessed November 19, 2015; Nick Gillespie, "Let Us Be Clear: Obama Deserves Chief Responsibility for Gov't Shutdown," *Reason.com*, October 1, 2013, https://reason.com/archives/2013/10/01/let-us-be-clear-obama-deserves-chief-res, accessed November 19, 2015.
63. Brenton Smith, "Who Caused the Government Shutdown? Obama and the Democrats Are at Fault," *Mic.com*, October 2, 2013, http://mic.com/articles/65949/who-caused-the-government-shutdown-obama-and-the-democrats-are-at-fault#.EJZupJBNl, accessed November 19, 2015; Andrew O'Hehir, "An Anxious Fox News Blames the Shutdown on Obama," *Salon*, October 1, 2013, http://www.salon.com/2013/10/01/an_anxious_fox_news_blames_the_shutdown_on_obama, accessed November 19, 2015.
64. Mollie Reilly, "Congress Approval Rating Drops to Dismal 5 Percent in Poll," *Huffington Post*, October 9, 2013, http://www.huffingtonpost.com/2013/10/09/congress-approval-rating_n_4069899.html, accessed September 7, 2015; Charlotte Alter, "Voter Turnout in Midterm Elections Hits 72-Year Low: The Last Time Voter Turnout Was This Low the U.S. Was Fighting WWII," *Time*, November 10, 2014, http://time.com/3576090/midterm-elections-turnout-world-war-two, accessed September 7, 2015.
65. Eleazar David Melendez, "Financial Crisis Cost Tops $22 Trillion, GAO Says," *Huffington Post*, February 14, 2013, http://www.huffingtonpost.com/2013/02/14/financial-crisis-cost–gao_n_2687553.html, accessed September 6, 2015; Danielle Kurtzleben, "The Total Iraq and Afghanistan Pricetag: Over $4 Trillion. A New Study Shows That the Cost of Caring for Veterans Will Soar in Coming Decades," *U.S. News and World Report*, March 28, 2013, http://www.usnews.com/news/articles/2013/03/28/the-total-

iraq-and-afghanistan-pricetag-over-4-trillion, accessed September 6, 2015; Department of Health and Human Services, "Number and Percentage of People Without Health Insurance Coverage by State Using 2- and 3-Year Averages: 2006–2007 and 2008–2009, http://www.hhs.gov/healthcare/facts/bystate/statebystate.html, accessed August 28, 2015.

66. "President Obama Job Approval Among Republicans," http://www.realclearpolitics.com/epolls/other/president_obama_job_approval_among_republicans-1047.html, accessed September 7, 2015.
67. Ministry of Truth, "An Open Letter to the People Who Hate Obama More Than They Love America," *Daily Kos*, January 9, 2012, accessed April 27, 2015.
68. "Obama Placed Under Secret Service Protection," CNN, May 3, 2007, http://www.cnn.com/2007/POLITICS/05/03/obama.protection/index.html?eref=weather, accessed September 6, 2015.
69. Rachel Weiner, "Behind the Scenes: Newsweek on McCain in the Dark, Obama Threats, and More," *Huffington Post*, December 6, 2008, http://www.huffingtonpost.com/2008/11/05/obama-we-cant-solve-globa_n_141358.html, accessed September 6, 2015.
70. Tony Hardnen, "Barack Obama Faces 30 Death Threats a Day, Stretching US Secret Service," *Telegraph*, August 3, 2009, http://www.telegraph.co.uk/news/worldnews/barackobama/5967942/Barack-Obama-faces-30-death-threats-a-day-stretching-US-Secret-Service.html, accessed September 6, 2015; "President Bush Job Approval," *Rasmussen Reports*, January 5, 2009, http://www.rasmussenreports.com/public_content/politics/political_updates/president_bush_job_approval, accessed September 6, 2015.
71. Earl Ofari Hutchinson, "Facebook Thinks Praying for President Obama's Assassination Is Okay," *Huffington Post*, June 29, 2010, http://www.huffingtonpost.com/earl-ofari-hutchinson/facebook-thinks-praying-f_b_558044.html, accessed September 6, 2015.
72. Kevin Collier, "What Happens If You Threaten Obama on His

New @POTUS Twitter Account?" *Daily Dot*, May 18, 2015, http://www.dailydot.com/politics/obama-potus-twitter-account-threats, accessed September 6, 2015.

73. John Heilemann and Mark Halperin, *Game Change: Obama and the Clintons, McCain and Palin, and the Race of a Lifetime* (New York: HarperCollins e-books, 2010), location 7364-7385, Kindle.
74. "Rep. Wilson Shouts, 'You Lie' to Obama During Speech," CNN, September 10, 2009, http://www.cnn.com/2009/POLITICS/09/09/joe.wilson, accessed September 6, 2015; Ben Smith, "Joe Wilson's Tally Since 'You Lie' Rises to $2.7 Million," *Politico*, October 8, 2009, http://www.politico.com/blogs/ben-smith/2009/10/joe-wilsons-tally-since-you-lie-rises-to-27-million-021968, accessed September 6, 2015.
75. Eugene Robinson, "Boehner's Invitation to Netanyahu Backfires on Them Both," *Washington Post*, January 29, 2015, https://www.washingtonpost.com/opinions/eugene--robinson-boehners-invitation-to-netanyahu-backfires-on-them-both/2015/01/29/4636fbf0-a7f4-11e4-a06b-9df2002b86a0_story.html, accessed November 20, 2015; Marissa Schultz, "Boehner Admits Keeping Obama in Dark About Netanyahu," *New York Post*, February 15, 2015, http://nypost.com/2015/02/15/boehner-admits-keeping-obama-in-dark-about-netanyahu, accessed November 23, 2015.
76. Ken Taylor, "Obama Hates America and Americans," *Red State*, July 18, 2010, http://www.redstate.com/diary/Ken_Taylor/2010/07/18/obama-hates-america-and-americans, accessed September 6, 2015; Obama's Numbers, Factcheck.org, April 6, 2015, http://www.factcheck.org/2015/04/obamas-numbers-april-2015-update, accessed September 6, 2015.
77. Erin Gloria Ryan, "Secret Service Exhausted by Massive Number of Death Threats Against President Obama," *Jezebel*, November 26, 2012, http://jezebel.com/5963372/massive-number-of-death-threats-against-president-obama-exhausts-the-secret-service, accessed September 6, 2015.

78. Jon Perr, "The Othering of the President," *Daily Kos*, February 22, 2015, accessed August 15, 2015.
79. Rachel Weiner, "John Sununu, the Worst Surrogate?" *Washington Post*, July 17, 2012, http://www.washingtonpost.com/blogs/the-fix/post/john-sununu-mitt-romneys-bestworst-surrogate/2012/07/17/gJQATJXSrW_blog.html, accessed September 6, 2015.
80. Robert Steinback, "Racist E-mails Lead to Resignation of a Florida Police Chief," Southern Poverty Law Center, October 13, 2010, https://www.splcenter.org/hatewatch/2010/10/13/racist-e-mails-lead-resignation-florida-police-chief, accessed September 6, 2015.
81. Katharine Q. Seelye and Jess Bidgood, "Police Official in New Hampshire Resigns Amid Uproar over Slur Against Obama," *New York Times*, May 19, 2014, http://www.nytimes.com/2014/05/20/us/police-official-who-used-slur-against-obama-steps-down.html?_r=0, accessed November 19, 2014; Jessica Glenza, "New Hampshire Police Commissioner Resigns over Obama N-Word Slur," *Guardian*, May 19, 2014, http://www.theguardian.com/world/2014/may/19/new-hampshire-police-commissioner-quits-obama-slur, accessed September 7, 2015.
82. Amanda Terkel, "Ohio Police Dispatcher Passes Along Racist Image of Air Force One," *Think Progress*, August 16, 2009, http://thinkprogress.org/politics/2009/08/16/56320/dispatcher-ohio-pic, September 7, 2015.
83. Casey Harper, "Explosive SF Police Texts: 'Cross Burning Lowers Blood Pressure!'" *Daily Caller*, March 18, 2015, http://readersupportednews.org/news-section2/318-66/29143-focus-explosive-sf-police-texts.html, accessed March 18, 2015.
84. Jon Swain and Oliver Laughland, "Ferguson Officials' Racist Emails Released," *Guardian*, April 3, 2015, http://www.theguardian.com/us-news/2015/apr/03/ferguson-officials-racist-emails-obama, accessed April 4, 2015.
85. William Jelani Cobb, *The Substance of Hope: Barack Obama and the Paradox of Progress* (New York: Walker and Co., 2010).

86. Myisha Cherry, "Why Do I Feel So Vulnerable? Thoughts on Police Brutality Against Black Women," *Huffington Post*, July 17, 2015, http://www.huffingtonpost.com/myisha-cherry/why-do-i-feel-so-vulnerab_b_7819826.html, accessed September 7, 2015; Nikole Hannah-Jones, "Yes, Black America Fears the Police. Here's Why. Shots Were Fired in Long Island, But There Was No Rush to Call 911. It Made Perfect Sense to ProPublica's Nikole Hannah-Jones," ProPublica, March 4, 2015, https://www.propublica.org/article/yes-black-america-fears-the-police-heres-why, accessed September 7, 2015.
87. Ray Sanchez, "Who Was Sandra Bland?" CNN, July 23, 2015, http://www.cnn.com/2015/07/22/us/sandra-bland, accessed September 6, 2015.
88. Christine Hauseraug, "Video Is Released from 2013 North Carolina Police Shooting of Jonathan Ferrell," *New York Times*, August 6, 2015, http://www.nytimes.com/2015/08/07/us/dashboard-camera-video-is-released-from-2013-north-carolina-police-shooting.html, accessed September 6, 2015.
89. Lizette Alvarez and Cara Buckley, "Zimmerman Is Acquitted in Trayvon Martin Killing," *New York Times*, July 13, 2013, http://www.nytimes.com/2013/07/14/us/george-zimmerman-verdict-trayvon-martin.html, accessed September 6, 2015.
90. Ralph Ellis and Melissa Gray, "Tamir Rice Report: No Proof Police Officer Shouted Warning Before Shooting," CNN, June 15, 2015, http://www.cnn.com/2015/06/13/us/tamir-rice-report, accessed September 7, 2015.
91. David A. Graham, "The Mysterious Death of Freddie Gray: When the Baltimore Man Was Arrested, He Was Alive and Well. By the Time He Reached a Police Station, He Couldn't Breathe or Talk. What Happened?" *Atlantic*, April 22, 2015, http://www.theatlantic.com/politics/archive/2015/04/the-mysterious-death-of-freddie-gray/391119, accessed September 7, 2015; Justin Fenton, "Autopsy of Freddie Gray Shows 'High-Energy' Impact," *Baltimore Sun*, June 24, 2015, http://www.baltimoresun.com/

news/maryland/freddie-gray/bs-md-ci-freddie-gray-autopsy-20150623-story.html, accessed September 7, 2015.

92. "Editorial: Rekia Boyd Shooting Was 'Beyond Reckless,' So Cop Got a Pass," *Chicago Tribune*, April 22, 2015, http://www.chicagotribune.com/news/opinion/editorials/ct-cop-verdict-servin-edit-0423-20150422-story.html, accessed September 7, 2015.
93. Abby Goodnough, "Harvard Professor Jailed; Officer Is Accused of Bias," *New York Times*, July 20, 2009, http://www.nytimes.com/2009/07/21/us/21gates.html?_r=0, accessed September 6, 2015.
94. Lawrence Otis Graham, "I Taught My Black Kids That Their Elite Upbringing Would Protect Them from Discrimination. I Was Wrong," *Washington Post*, November 6, 2014, https://www.washingtonpost.com/posteverything/wp/2014/11/06/i-taught-my-black-kids-that-their-elite-upbringing-would-protect-them-from-discrimination-i-was-wrong, accessed September 7, 2015.
95. Dylann Roof, "Manifesto: The Last Rhodesian," lastrhodesian.com/data/documents/rtf88.txt, accessed June 20, 2015; "Charleston Shooting: Dylann Roof Named as Suspect," BBC, June 18, 2015, http://www.bbc.com/news/world-us-canada-33189325, accessed June 19, 2015; Josh Sandburn, "Inside the White Supremacist Group That Influenced Charleston Shooting Suspect," *Time*, June 22, 2015, http://time.com/3930993/dylann-roof-council-of-conservative-citizens-charleston, accessed September 7, 2015; Amber Phillips, "The Political Success of the Council of Conservative Citizens, Explained," *Washington Post*, June 22, 2015, http://www.washingtonpost.com/news/the-fix/wp/2015/06/22/the-odd-political-success-of-the-white-supremacist-council-of-conservative-citizens-explained, accessed September 7, 2015.
96. Phillips, "The Political Success of the Council of Conservative Citizens, Explained"; Sandburn, "Inside the White Supremacist Group That Influenced Charleston Shooting Suspect," *Time*; J.

Richard Cohen, "Dylann Roof, the Charleston Murders and Hate in the Mainstream: The Council of Conservative Citizens, a White Supremacist Group Cited by The Accused Charleston Killer, Has a Long History of Associations with Mainstream Politicians Who've Given the Group Legitimacy," *Southern Poverty Law Center*, https://medium.com/@splcenter/dylann-roof-the-charleston-murders-and-hate-in-the-mainstream-4ce1311bb140, accessed July 25, 2015; Bryan Long, "Group Releases Statement Defending Dylann Roof's 'Legitimate Grievances,'" *Business Insider*, June 22, 2015, http://www.businessinsider.com/council-of-conservative-citizens-defends-dylann-roof-2015-6, accessed September 7, 2015.

97. Tina Nguyen, "Charleston Shooting: Suspected Church Shooter Allegedly Said He Wanted to Start a Race War," *Vanity Fair*, June19,2015,http://www.vanityfair.com/news/2015/06/charleston-church-shooter-confesses-dylan-roof, accessed September 7, 2015.
98. For the respectable version of this, see "Rand Paul Vows to 'Take Our Country Back' in Presidential Candidacy Speech," *NPR*, April 7, 2015, http://www.npr.org/2015/04/07/398123432/rand-paul-vows-to-take-our-country-back-in-presidential-candidacy-speech, accessed September 7, 2015; Elizabeth Chuck, "Donald Trump: 'Don't Worry, We'll Take Our Country Back,'" NBC, July 11, 2015, http://www.nbcnews.com/politics/2016-election/donald-trump-freedomfest-you-cant-be-great-if-you-dont-n390546, accessed September 7, 2015.

Afterword to the Paperback Edition After the Election: Imagining

1 John McCormack, "The Election Came Down to 77,744 Votes in Pennsylvania, Wisconsin, and Michigan: A closer look at the three states that decided the winner in 2016," *Weekly Standard*, November10,2016,http://www.weeklystandard.com/the-election-came-down-to-77744-votes-in-pennsylvania-wisconsin-and-michigan-updated/article/2005323, accessed December 31, 2016.

2 Re-tweet by Leah McElrath on December 11, 2016 of Aleksandr Dugin's November 13, 2016 Facebook entry, https://twitter.com/leahmcelrath/status/808029940520194048?s=03, accessed December 12, 2016; Robert McElvaine, "Where is the Outrage, Where are the Patriots?" ***Huffington Post***, December 12, 2016, http://www.huffingtonpost.com/robert-s-mcelvaine/where-is-the-outrage-wher_b_13569968.html, accessed January 10, 2017.

3 "First Read's Morning Clips: Russian Officials Celebrated Trump Win," NBC, January 6, 2017, http://www.nbcnews.com/politics/first-read/first-read-s-morning-clips-russian-officials-celebrated-trump-win-n703856, accessed January 11, 2017.

4 David Corn, "A Veteran Spy Has Given the FBI Information Alleging a Russian Operation to Cultivate Donald Trump," ***Mother Jones***, October 31, 2016, http://motherjones.com/politics/2016/10/veteran-spy-gave-fbi-info-alleging-russian-operation-cultivate-donald-trump, accessed January 3, 2017; Interview with Kurt Eichenwald, "Is U.S. Foreign Policy for Sale? Behind the Trump Organization's Vast Financial Network," ***Democracy Now!***, September 15, 2016, https://www.democracynow.org/2016/9/15/us_foreign_policy_for_sale_behind, accessed January 11, 2017; "Donald Trump and Hillary Clinton on Putin's 'puppet,'" CBS News, October 19, 2016, http://www.cbsnews.com/videos/donald-trump-and-hillary-clinton-on-putins-puppet/, accessed January 12, 2017.

5 Corn, "A Veteran Spy Has Given the FBI Information Alleging a Russian Operation to Cultivate Donald Trump"; Nick Wadhams and Bradley Saacks, "Trump NATO attack trashes 70 years of foreign policy," ***Detroit News***, July 23, 2016, http://www.detroitnews.com/story/news/politics/2016/07/23/trump-nato-attack-trashes-years-foreign-policy/87487434/, accessed February 5, 2017; "NATO and US foreign policy," ***U.S. Department of State Dispatch*** 4, no. 9 (March 1993): 119. Academic Search Complete, EBSCOhost (accessed February 5, 2017); "Sen. Lindsey Graham: 'We should hit Russia hard' for Election cyberattacks," Fox News, January 13, 2017, http://www.foxnews.com/politics/2017/01/13/

sen-lindsey-graham-should-hit-russia-hard-for-election-cyber attacks.html, accessed February 5, 2017; Nick Hopkins and Luke Harding, "Donald Trump dossier: intelligence sources vouch for author's credibility: Ex-MI6 officer Christopher Steele, named as writer of Donald Trump memo, is 'highly regarded professional,'" ***The Guardian***, January 12, 2017, https://www.theguardian.com/us-news/2017/jan/12/intelligence-sources-vouch-credibility-donald-trump-russia-dossier-author, accessed February 7, 2017.

6 Ed O'Keefe, "Rubio called Trump a dangerous 'con man.' Now he says Trump should be president," ***Washington Post***, May 27, 2016, https://www.washingtonpost.com/politics/rubio-called-trump-a-dangerous-con-man-now-he-says-trump-should-be-president/2016/05/27/b837e16c-2410-11e6-aa84-42391ba52c91_story.html?utm_term=.23fe1048fe0d, accessed January 1, 2017.

7 Noah Bierman and Tracy Wilkinson, "Many GOP Foreign Policy Experts see Donald Trump as Unfit to be President," ***Los Angeles Times***, July 29, 2016, www.latimes.com/politics/la-fg-trump-foreign-policy-20160731-snap-story.html, accessed December 30, 2016.

8 Alexander Burns and Michael Barbaro, "Mitt Romney and John McCain Denounce Donald Trump as a Danger to Democracy," ***New York Times***, March 3, 2016, https://www.nytimes.com/politics/first-draft/2016/03/03/mitt-romney-donald-trump/, accessed January 11, 2017.

9 Thomas Stoddard, "Trump has Republicans Squirming on Russia," ***Real Clear Politics***, December 19, 2016, http://www.realclearpolitics.com/articles/2016/12/19/trump_has_republicans_squirming_on_russia_132596.html, accessed December 20, 2016; Thomas Rid, "How Russia Pulled Off the Biggest Election Hack in U.S. History," ***Esquire***, October 20, 2016, http://www.esquire.com/news-politics/a49791/russian-dnc-emails-hacked/, accessed January 1, 2017; Mark Sumner, "McConnell gave Russia the green light, refused to sign on to protecting election," ***Daily Kos***, December 10, 2016, http://www.dailykos.com/story/2016/12/10/1609468/-McConnell-gave-Russia-the-green-light-refused-to-sign-on-to-protecting-election,

accessed January 1, 2017; Mark Leibovich, "Look Out for the Trump Pivot!" *New York Times*, March 25, 2016, https://www.nytimes.com/2016/03/24/magazine/look-out-for-the-trump-pivot.html, accessed January 11, 2017; Jonah Goldberg, "Waiting for the Pivot at the End of the Universe," *National Review*, August 6, 2016, http://www.nationalreview.com/article/438732/donald-trumps-pivot-isnt-coming, accessed January 11, 2017.

10 Jonathan Mahler and Steve Eder, "'No Vacancies' for Blacks: How Donald Trump Got His Start, and Was First Accused of Bias," *New York Times*, August 27, 2016, https://www.nytimes.com/2016/08/28/us/politics/donald-trump-housing-race.html?_r=0, accessed February 7, 2017; "Ignoring Trump's Record of Racism," *Fair*, May 6, 2011, http://fair.org/take-action/media-advisories/ignoring-trumps-record-of-racism/, accessed February 7, 2017.

11 Morgan Little, "Trump Doubles Down on 'birther' Beliefs Prior to Romney Fundraiser," *Los Angeles Times*, May 29, 2012, http://articles.latimes.com/2012/may/29/news/la-pn-trump-doubles-down-on-birther-beliefs-prior-to-romney-fundraiser-20120529, accessed May 12, 2016; Oliver Laughland, "Donald Trump and the Central Park Five: The Racially-Charged Rise of a Demagogue," *The Guardian*, February 12, 2016, http://www.theguardian.com/us-news/2016/feb/17/central-park-five-donald-trump-jogger-rape-case-new-york, accessed May 12, 2016.

12 Harry Enten, "Trump Is in Fourth Place Among Black Voters," *Five-Thirty-Eight*, August 10, 2016, https://fivethirtyeight.com/features/trump-is-in-fourth-place-among-black-voters/, accessed January 12, 2017.

13 Joan Walsh, "'I don't see Trump as a legitimate president,' Says Rep. John Lewis: The nation's greatest living civil rights hero says what others won't. Will other Democrats follow," *The Nation*, January 14, 2017, https://www.thenation.com/article/i-dont-see-trump-as-a-legitimate-president-says-rep-john-lewis/, accessed January 14, 2017.

14 Amy Walter and David Wasserman, "African American Voters: The Overlooked Key To 2016," ***Cook Political Report***, July 10, 2015, http://cookpolitical.com/story/8666, accessed January 17, 2017; Joy-Ann Reid, "Trump Could Address These Legitimacy Questions—But He Won't," ***The Daily Beast***, January 14, 2017, http://www.thedailybeast.com/articles/2017/01/14/trump-could-address-these-legitimacy-questions-but-he-won-t.html?via=desktop&source=twitter, accessed January 14, 2017; E. J. Dionne Jr., "A Year to Protect Democracy," ***Washington Post***, January 1, 2017, https://www.washingtonpost.com/opinions/a-year-to-protect-democracy/2017/01/01/ec384014-ce98-11e6-a87f-b917067331bb_story.html?postshare=7591483367964313&tid=ss_mail&utm_term=.42f5165a32de, accessed January 1, 2017; Paul Krugman, "America Becomes a Stan," ***New York Times***, January 2, 2017, www.nytimes.com/2017/01/02/opinion/america-beomces-a-stan.html?_r=0, accessed January 2, 2017.

15 David Peppers, "Ohio Democrats Expose New Ohio Voting Laws as Modern-Day Literacy Tests, Voter Suppression," ***Huffington Post***, April 8, 2016, http://www.huffingtonpost.com/david-pepper/ohio-democrats-expose-new_b_9643250.html, accessed June 30, 2016.

16 Andy Sullivan and Grant Smith, "Use it or lose it: Occasional Ohio voters may be shut out in November," Reuters, June 2, 2016, http://www.reuters.com/article/us-usa-votingrights-ohio-insight-idUSKCN0YO19D, accessed January 12, 2017; David Graham, "Ohio's Questionable Voter Purge," ***The Atlantic***, June 3, 2016, http://www.theatlantic.com/politics/archive/2016/06/ohio-voter-purge/485357/, accessed January 12, 2017.

17 Libby Nelson, "There are 4,000 people in a half-mile voting line in Cincinnati today. This isn't okay," ***Vox***, November 6, 2016, http://www.vox.com/presidential-election/2016/11/6/13542680/there-are-4000-people-in-a-half-mile-voting-line-in-cincinnati-today-this-isn-t-okay, accessed January 14, 2017.

18 Todd Beamon, "Kasich: 'Inappropriate' to Attend GOP Convention Without Endorsing Trump," ***Newsmax***, August 5, 2016, http://

www.newsmax.com/Politics/John-Kasich-Inappropriate-Attend-GOP/2016/08/05/id/742377/, accessed January 17, 2017; Todd Beamon, "Kasich: Trump's Rhetoric 'Dangerous and Bad for America,'" *Newsmax*, November 24, 2015, http://www.newsmax.com/Newsfront/john-kasich-donald-trump-tom-moe-campaign-ad/2015/11/24/id/703450/, accessed January 13, 2017.

19 Jim Letizia, "Kasich Won't Attend RNC," WCBE, June 29, 2016, http://wcbe.org/post/kasich-wont-attend-rnc, accessed February 5, 2017; Cassie Spodak, "Kasich on Trump endorsement: 'Why would I?'" CNN, June 9, 2016, http://www.cnn.com/2016/06/09/politics/john-kasich-donald-trump/index.html, accessed January 14, 2017.

20 Sarah Kendzior, "How State Politicians are Quietly Working to Steal the US Presidential Election," *Quartz*, May 20, 2016, http://qz.com/687408/how-local-politicians-are-quietly-working-to-steal-the-us-presidential-election/, accessed December 8, 2016.

21 Martin Dyckman and Darryl Paulson, "Florida's Felon Vote: Destroying Lives and Wasting Taxpayer Dollars," *Tampa Bay Times*, December 29, 2016, http://www.tampabay.com/news/perspective/floridas-felon-vote-destroying-lives-and-wasting-taxpayer-dollars/2307853, accessed December 30, 2016.

22 Martin Dyckman and Darryl Paulson, "Florida's Felon Vote: Destroying Lives and Wasting Taxpayer Dollars," *Tampa Bay Times*, December 29, 2016, http://www.tampabay.com/news/perspective/floridas-felon-vote-destroying-lives-and-wasting-taxpayer-dollars/2307853, accessed December 30, 2016.

23 Eighty percent of those disfranchised are Democrats; once voting rights for convicted felons have been restored, they generally have a 20 percent turnout rate. So, 80 percent of 1.7 million x 20 percent of that figure means that HRC could have picked up more than 272,000 votes. (Hillary Clinton lost FL by 119,770 votes.) Alla Olstein and Kira Lerner, "Republicans were wildly successful at suppressing voters in 2016: Three GOP-controlled states

demonstrate the effectiveness of disenfranchising the opposition," ***Think Progress***, November 15, 2016, https://thinkprogress.org/2016-a-case-study-in-voter-suppression-258b5f90ddcd#.7adruzh1q, accessed November 16, 2016.

24 Ari Berman, "Did Republicans Rig the Election? Voter Suppression was all too Real, and 14 States—Including Important Swing States—had new Voting Restrictions in Place," ***The Nation***, November 15, 2016, www.thenation.com/article/did-republicans-rig-the-election/, accessed December 6, 2016.

25 Tom Kertscher, "Daily Kos official says that, with possible recall looming, Wisconsin Gov. Scott Walker closing DMV offices in poor areas," PolitiFact.com, December 7, 2011, http://www.politifact.com/wisconsin/statements/2011/dec/07/daily-kos/daily-kos-says-possible-recall-looming-wisconsin-g/, accessed January 15, 2017.

26 Berman, "Did Republicans Rig the Election?"; Ari Berman, "A Federal Court Orders Wisconsin to Stop Suppressing the Vote: The state must investigate the DMV's failure to issue voter IDs in time for the November election," ***The Nation***, September 30, 2016, https://www.thenation.com/article/a-federal-court-orders-wisconsin-to-stop-suppressing-the-vote/, accessed January 15, 2017; Lincoln Blades, "We Can't Talk about the Black Vote in the 2016 Election Without Discussing Voter Suppression," ***Teen Vogue***, November 16, 2016, http://www.teenvogue.com/story/black-vote-election-2016-voter-suppression, accessed December 6, 2016; Mary Spicuzza and Keegan Kyle, "Milwaukee elections head says voter ID law hurt city's turnout," ***Milwaukee Journal Sentinel***, November 11, 2016, http://www.jsonline.com/story/news/local/milwaukee/2016/11/10/milwaukee-elections-head-says-voter-id-law-hurt-citys-turnout/93607154/, accessed January 16, 2017.

27 Berman, "Did Republicans Rig the Election?"

28 Brooke Seipel, "North Carolina No Longer a Democracy: Report," ***The Hill***, December 23, 2016, http://www.thehill.com/blogs/

blog-briefing-room/news/311690-north-carolina-is-no-longer-a-democracy-report, accessed December 23, 2016.

29 Jay Michaelson, "North Carolina GOP Brags Racist Voter Suppression is Working – and They're Right," ***The Daily Beast***, November 7, 2016, http://www.thedailybeast.com/articles/2016/11/07/north-carolina-s-racist-voter-suppression-is-working.html, accessed December 6, 2016.

30 Michael Wines and Alan Blinder, "Federal Appeals Court Strikes Down North Carolina Voter ID Requirement," ***New York Times***, July 29, 2016, https://www.nytimes.com/2016/07/30/us/federal-appeals-court-strikes-down-north-carolina-voter-id-provision.html?_r=0, accessed January 15, 2017; Ari Berman, "North Carolina Won't Stop Suppressing the Vote: After courts restored a week of early voting, Republicans are now brazenly cutting early-voting hours," ***The Nation***, August 16, 2016, https://www.thenation.com/article/north-carolina-wont-stop-suppressing-the-vote/, accessed January 15, 2017.

31 Alice Miranda Ollstein, "Republicans were Wildly Successful at Suppressing Voters in 2016," ***Think Progress***, November 15, 2016, https://thinkprogress.org/2016-a-case-study-in-voter-suppression-258b5f90ddcd#.eoolvjzci, accessed December 6, 2017; U.S. Census Bureau, "Quick Facts: Mecklenburg County, North Carolina," http://www.census.gov/quickfacts/table/PST045216/37119,00, accessed February 5, 2017; Lindsey Eaton, "Number of Guilford Co. registered voters increases," Fox News, October 1, 2012, http://myfox8.com/2012/10/01/number-of-guilford-co-registered-voters-increases/, accessed January 15, 2017.

32 Jonathan Lowe, "Last Day of Early Voting Brings Long Lines to NC Polls," Time-Warner Cable News, November 5, 2016, http://www.twcnews.com/nc/charlotte/news/2016/11/5/last-day-of-early-voting-brings-long-lines-to-nc-polls.html, accessed February 5, 2017.

33 Jay Michaelson, "North Carolina GOP Brags Racist Voter Suppression is Working – and They're Right," ***The Daily***

Beast, November 7, 2016, http://www.thedailybeast.com/articles/2016/11/07/north-carolina-s-racist-voter-suppression-is-working.html, accessed December 6, 2016.

34 Max Rosenthal, "North Carolina GOP Brags About How Few Black People Were Able to Vote Early," *Mother Jones*, November 7, 2016, http://www.motherjones.com/politics/2016/11/north-carolina-gop-brags-about-how-few-black-people-were-able-vote-early, accessed January 14, 2017.

35 Ollstein, "Republicans were Wildly Successful at Suppressing Voters in 2016."

36 Michaelson, "North Carolina GOP Brags Racist Voter Suppression is Working."

37 U.S. Census Bureau, "Quick Facts: North Carolina: 2016 est. population," http://www.census.gov/quickfacts/table/RHI225215/37, accessed February 5, 2017.

38 Alice Miranda Ollstein, "Federal court: North Carolina must redraw gerrymandered districts, hold special elections," *Think Progress*, November 30, 2016, https://thinkprogress.org/north-carolina-republicans-ordered-to-redraw-racially-gerrymandered-districts-8b65a35d96e2#.6xj6j1dt0, accessed February 5, 2017; Alice Miranda Ollstein, "North Carolina Republicans sue to preserve racial gerrymandering," *Think Progress*, January 3, 2017, https://thinkprogress.org/north-carolina-republicans-sue-to-preserve-racial-gerrymandering-edbe1cf51c09#.g5mjvwffp, accessed February 5, 2017.

39 Alice Miranda Ollstein, "Alabama Found Guilty of Racial Gerrymandering," *Think Progress*, January 20, 2017, https://thinkprogress.org/alabama-found-guilty-of-racial-gerrymandering-e42f48e19c40#.vmihp68fn, accessed January 21, 2017; Michael Wines, "Judges Find Wisconsin Redistricting Unfairly Favored Republicans," *New York Times*, November 21, 2016, https://www.nytimes.com/2016/11/21/us/wisconsin-redistricting-found-to-unfairly-favor-republicans.html, accessed February 5, 2017.

40 For Kansas see, Hunter Woodall, "Kansas judge rules against Kris Kobach in voter registration case," ***Kansas City Star***, November 4, 2016, http://www.kansascity.com/news/politics-government/article112662668.html, accessed February 7, 2017.

41 Ben Kentish, "Donald Trump Thanks African-Americans for not Voting in US Presidential Election," ***The Independent***, December 11, 2016, http://www.independent.co.uk/news/world/americas/donald-trump-thanks-african-americans-not-voting-us-election-a7467536.html, accessed December 11, 2016.

42 Greg Palast, "The GOP's Stealth War Against Voters," ***Rolling Stone***, August 24, 2016, http://www.rollingstone.com/politics/features/the-gops-stealth-war-against-voters-w435890, accessed February 5, 2017; Thom Hartmann and Richard Greene, "The Massive Election-Rigging Scandal the Media Ignored," ***Salon***, January 10, 2017, http://www.salon.com/2017/01/10/the-massive-election-rigging-scandal-the-media-ignored_partner/, accessed January 22, 2017.

43 Tony Pugh, "Voter Suppression Laws Likely Tipped the Scales for Trump, Civil Rights Groups Say," ***McClatchy***, November 10, 2016, http://www.mcclatchydc.com/news/politics-government/election/article113977353.html, accessed December 6, 2016; Jens Manuel Krogstad, "2016 Electorate Will be the Most Diverse in U.S. History," Pew Research Center, February 3, 2016, http://www.pewresearch.org/fact-tank/2016/02/03/2016-electorate-will-be-the-most-diverse-in-u-s-history/, accessed January 13, 2017.

44 Ollstein, "Republicans were Wildly Successful at Suppressing Voters in 2016."

45 Paul Taylor, "The Growing Electoral Clout of Blacks is Driven by Turnout not Demographics," Pew Research Center, December 12, 2012, http://www.pewsocialtrends.org/2012/12/26/the-growing-electoral-clout-of-blacks-is-driven-by-turnout-not-demographics/, accessed January 13, 2017.

46 Mallory Shelbourne, "GOP Senator: Russian hacking 'hardly news,'" ***The Hill***, December 10, 2016, http://thehill.com/

homenews/campaign/309811-gop-senator-reports-of-russian-interference-hardly-news, accessed January 16, 2017; Hunter, "Sen. Mitch McConnell Needs to Answer for his Role Covering up Russian Election Attacks," ***Daily Kos***, December 11, 2016, http://www.dailykos.com/story/2016/12/11/1609840/-Sen-Mitch-McConnell-needs-to-answer-for-his-role-covering-up-Russian-election-attacks, accessed January 1, 2017; Hayley Miller, "GOP Congressman: Russian Hackers 'Merely Did What The Media Should've Done': What some might call cyberwarfare others apparently consider journalistic best practices," ***Huffington Post***, December 29, 2016, http://www.huffingtonpost.com/entry/trent-franks-russian-hackers_us_58656cb2e4b0eb586488b060, accessed January 16, 2017.

47 "Read the transcript of the conversation among GOP leaders obtained by The Post," ***Washington Post***, https://www.washingtonpost.com/apps/g/page/national/read-the-transcript-of-the-conversation-among-gop-leaders-obtained-by-the-post/2209/?hpid=hp_hp-top-table-main_transcript-6pm%3Ahomepage%2Fstory, accessed May 19, 2017; Adam Entous, "House majority leader to colleagues in 2016: 'I think Putin pays' Trump," ***Washington Post***, May 17, 2017, https://www.washingtonpost.com/world/national-security/house-majority-leader-to-colleagues-in-2016-i-think-putin-pays-trump/2017/05/17/515f6f8a-3aff-11e7-8854-21f359183e8c_story.html?utm_term=.634cc1c36f8d, accessed May 19, 2017.

48 Damon Linker, "The GOP Doesn't have a Donald Trump Problem. It Has an Angry Conservative Base Problem," ***The Week***, July 10, 2015, http://theweek.com/articles/565446/gop-doesnt-have-donald-trump-problem-angry-conservative-base-problem, accessed January 15, 2017; Chauncey DeVega, "The disturbing data on Republicans and racism: Trump backers are the most bigoted within the GOP: Racists are more likely to be Republicans—and the most extreme among them are Donald Trump supporters," ***Salon***, July 6, 2016, http://www.salon.com/2016/07/06/the_

disturbing_data_on_republicans_and_racism_trump_backers_are_the_most_bigoted_within_the_gop/, accessed January 15, 2017; Dan T. Carter, "What Donald Trump Owes George Wallace," *New York Times*, January 8, 2016, https://www.nytimes.com/2016/01/10/opinion/campaign-stops/what-donald-trump-owes-george-wallace.html?_r=0m, accessed February 6, 2017.

49 Scott Eric Kaufman, "Maddow demolishes Donald Trump with horrifying side-by-side comparison to segregationist George Wallace: 'Close your eyes and listen to reports from the '68 election—it's almost like they're talking about Trump,'" *Salon*, January 6, 2016, http://www.salon.com/2016/01/06/maddow_demolishes_donald_trump_with_horrifying_side_by_side_comparison_to_segregationist_george_wallace/, accessed February 6, 2017; Lisa Wade, "White Donald Trump Supporters are More Likely to Oppose Public Polices When They're Made to Think About Black People," *Pacific Standard*, December 26, 2016, https://psmag.com/trump-supporters-are-more-likely-to-oppose-public-policies-when-they-think-about-black-people-b94883884a16#.578oz7mng, accessed December 26, 2016; Michael Tesler, "Trump Voters Think African Americas are Much Less Deserving Than 'Average Americans,'" *Huffington Post*, December 19, 2016, http://www.huffingtonpost.com/michael-tesler/trump-voters-think-africa_b_13732500.html, accessed December 20, 2016.

50 M. J., "Why Republicans hate Obamacare: Why is the Affordable Care Act so despised by so many conservatives?" *The Economist*, December 11, 2016, http://www.economist.com/blogs/economist-explains/2016/12/economist-explains-1, accessed January 15, 2017.

51 Sarah Jones, "A Plurality of Kentuckians Like Obamacare, As Long as It's Called Something Else," *PoliticusUSA*, May 12, 2014, http://www.politicususa.com/2014/05/12/plurality-kentuckians-obamacare-long-called-kynect.html, accessed January 15, 2017.

52 Sarah Kliff, "Why Obamacare Enrolled Voted for Trump: In Whitley County, Kentucky, the Uninsured Rate Decline 60 Percent

under Obamacare. So Why did 82 Percent of Voters there Support Donald Trump?" *Vox*, December 13, 2016, http://www.vox.com/science-and-health/2016/12/13/13848794/kentucky-obamacare-trump, accessed December 13, 2016.

53 Olga Khazan, "If Not Obamacare, Then What? Trump Supporters in Southern Pennsylvania say the Affordable Care Act has been a let down. Here's What They'd Like Instead," ***The Atlantic***, December 20, 2016, https://www.theatlantic.com/health/archive/2016/12/if-not-obamacare-then-what/511130/, accessed December 20, 2016.

54 David Masciotra, "Donald Trump's Winner-Takes-All Wasteland: America Will Never be 'Great' if we Continue to Worship the Hustle," ***Salon***, December 11, 2016, http://www.salon.com/2016/12/11/donald-trumps-winner-takes-all-wasteland-america-will-never-be-great-if-we-continue-to-worship-the-hustle/?utm_source=twitter&utm_medium=socialflow, accessed December 11, 2016.

55 Catherine Woodiwiss, "The Era of White Anxiety is Just Beginning," ***Sojourners***, March 8, 2016, https://sojo.net/articles/era-white-anxiety-just-beginning, accessed December 30, 2016; Steven W. Thrasher, "The Whiteness Project will make you wince. Because white people can be rather awful: You've never seen privilege quite like this: 'You can't even talk about fried chicken or Kool-Aid without wondering if someone's going to get offended,'" ***The Guardian***, October 15, 2014, https://www.theguardian.com/commentisfree/2014/oct/15/whiteness-project-privilege-documentary, accessed February 6, 2017.

56 Jonathan Chait, "Donald Trump Has Proven Liberals Right About the Tea Party," ***New York***, December 7, 2016, http://nymag.com/daily/intelligencer/2016/12/donald-trump-has-proven-liberals-right-about-the-tea-party.html, accessed December 8, 2016.

57 David Edwards, "NPR's Michele Morris: 'Make America Great Again' is Deeply Encoded Promise of 'White Prosperity,'" ***Raw Story***, January 1, 2017, www.rawstory.com/2017/01/nprs-michele-

norris-make-a-america-great-again-is-deeply-encoded-promise-of-white-prosperity/, accessed January 1, 2017.

58 Libby Nelson, "Nearly 20 percent of Trump Supporters Disapprove of Lincoln Freeing the Slaves," *Vox*, February 24, 2016, http://www.vox.com/2016/2/24/11105552/trump-supporters-slavery, accessed January 16, 2017.

59 Derek Thompson, "The Dangerous Myth that Hillary Clinton Ignored the Working Class," *The Atlantic*, December 5, 2016, https://www.theatlantic.com/business/archive/2016/12/hillary-clinton-working-class/509477/, accessed December 6, 2016; David Roberts, "The Most Common Words in Hillary Clinton's Speeches in One Chart: They Weren't About 'Identity Politics,'" *Vox*, December 16, 2016, http://www.vox.com/policy-and-politics/2016/12/16/13972394/most-common-words-hillary-clinton-speech, accessed December 18, 2016.

60 Charles Krauthammer, "The GOP's Ideological Earthquake and its Aftermath," *National Review*, May 5, 2016, http://www.nationalreview.com/article/435045/donald-trump-not-conservative-gop-doesnt-care, accessed January 16, 2017; Derek Thompson, "The Republicans' Attack on the American Dream," *The Atlantic*, November 28, 2016, http://www.theatlantic.com/business/archive/2016/11/conservatives-american-dream/508880/?utm_content=bufferd45b3&utm_medium=social&utm_source=twitter.com&utm_campaign=buffer, accessed January 1, 2017; Bob Herbert, "The War on the Poor is Already Underway," *Bill Moyers*, December 5, 2016, http://billmoyers.com/story/war-poor-already-underway, accessed December 25, 2016; John Cassidy, "Trump's Brazen Dodge to Avoid Dealing With his Conflicts of Interest," *New Yorker*, http://www.newyorker.com/news/john-cassidy/trumps-brazen-dodge-to-avoid-dealing-with-his-conflicts-of-interest, accessed December 14, 2016.

61 Hunter, "Sen. Mitch McConnell Needs to Answer for his Role Covering up Russian Election Attacks," *Daily Kos*, December 11, 2016, http://www.dailykos.com/story/2016/12/11/1609840/-

Sen-Mitch-McConnell-needs-to-answer-for-his-role-covering-up-Russian-election-attacks, accessed January 1, 2017; Katie Bo Williams, "GOP Rep: 'Russia Did What the Media Should Have Done if Info Correct,'" ***The Hill***, December 29, 2016, http://thehill.com/blogs/blog-briefing-room/news/312131-gop-rep-russia-did-what-the-media-shouldve-done-if-info, accessed December 29, 2016; Lawrence Glickman, "Donald Trump and the Anti-New Deal Tradition," ***Process: A Blog for American History***, December 8, 2016, http://www.processhistory.org/trump-anti-new-deal/, accessed December 13, 2016; Josh Zeitz, "The Real Legacy in Jeopardy Under the New Congress? LBJ's," ***Politico***, November 23, 2016, http://www.politico.com/magazine/story/2016/11/new-congress-trump-lbj-214480, accessed December 24, 2016.

62 Gene B. Sperling, "The Quiet War on Medicaid," ***New York Times***, December 25, 2016, http://mobile.nytimes.com/2016/12/25/opinion/the-quiet-war-on-medicaid.html, accessed December 25, 2016; Ryan Cooper, "The Republic Plot to Devour Retirees' Nest Eggs," ***The Week***, December 28, 2016, http://theweek.com/articles/669573/republican-plot-devour-retirees-nest-eggs?utm_source=dlvr.it&utm_medium=twitter, accessed December 28, 2016; David Weigel, "Claiming Mandate, GOP Congress Lays Plans to Propel Sweeping Conservative Agenda," ***Washington Post***, January 1, 2017, https://www.washingtonpost.com/politics/claiming-mandate-gop-congress-lays-plans-to-propel-sweeping-conservative-agenda/2017/01/01/9840338a-ceee-11e6-, accessed January 2, 2017; Joy-Ann Reid, "Hey, White Working Class, Donald Trump Is Already Screwing You Over," ***The Daily Beast***, December 9, 2016, http://www.thedailybeast.com/articles/2016/12/09/hey-white-working-class-donald-trump-is-already-screwing-you-over.html, accessed December 9, 2016.

63 "Jeff Sessions and Martin Luther King: Our view, Nominee's Past Raises Questions About Future Attorney General," ***USA Today***, January 15, 2017, http://www.usatoday.com/story/opinion/

2017/01/15/jeff-sessions-attorney-general-martin-luther-king-editorials-debates/96613378/, accessed January 16, 2017; Ian Millhiser, "Republicans praise Dr. King while plotting to dismantle his legacy: King was a crusader for racial justice and an economic radical," ***Think Progress***, January 16, 2017, https://thinkprogress.org/republicans-praise-dr-king-while-plotting-to-dismantle-his-legacy-3eb90449369d#.5f4871ugq, accessed January 16, 2017; Elizabeth Preza, "National Police Union Expects Trump to Reverse the 'Ban on Racial Profiling,'" ***Raw Story***, December 19, 2016, http://www.rawstory.com/2016/12/national-police-union-calls-on-trump-to-reverse-the-ban-on-racial-profiling/#.WFkCXnbxEAs.twitter, accessed December 20, 2016; Sophia Tesfaye, "John Kasich quietly bans Cleveland voters from raising minimum wage in their city: Republican Ohio Gov. John Kasich worked with Cleveland's city council to block voters' $15-per-hour initiative," ***Salon***, December 22, 2016, http://www.salon.com/2016/12/22/john-kasich-quietly-bans-cleveland-voters-from-raising-minimum-wage-in-their-city/, accessed January 16, 2017; Reid, "Hey, White Working Class, Donald Trump Is Already Screwing You Over"; Zeitz, "The Real Legacy in Jeopardy Under the New Congress? LBJ's"; "The Electoral College: Bill O'Reilly Defends 'The White Establishment," ***National Memo***, December 21, 2016, http://www.nationalmemo.com/bill-oreilly-defends-white-establishment/?utm_campaign=website&utm_source=sd&utm_medium=email, accessed December 22, 2016.

64 Tressie McMillan Cottom, "The Problem with Obama's Faith in White America: The President's Optimism about Race Blinded him to the Pervasiveness and Stubborn Resistance of Racism," ***The Atlantic***, December 13, 2016, https://www.theatlantic.com/politics/archive/2016/12/obamas-faith-in-white-america/510503/, accessed December 14, 2016.

65 Mark Plotkin, "You don't need a flag pin to show patriotism," ***The Hill***, November 13, 2015, http://thehill.com/blogs/pundits-

blog/lawmaker-news/260022-wearing-a-flag-pin-isnt-patriotism-but-opportunism, accessed February 6, 2017; Matthew Nussbaum and Benjamin Oreskes, "More Republicans Viewing Putin Favorably: GOP Sympathies for Putin and His Homeland are Rising," ***Politico***, December 16, 2016, www.politico.com/story/2016/12/gop-russia-putin-support-232714, accessed December 17, 2016.

66 "Clinton and Trump Attributes," http://www.langerresearch.com/wp-content/uploads/1184a152016ElectionTrackingNo15.pdf, accessed January 16, 2017; Mark Schmitt, "What Trump Exposed about the GOP," ***New York Times***, November 11, 2016, http://mobile.nytimes.com/2016/11/11/opinion/identity-over-ideology.html?referer=, accessed December 30, 2016; German Lopez, "Study: Racism and Sexism Predict Support for Trump Much More than Economic Dissatisfaction," ***Vox***, January 4, 2017, http://www.vox.com/identities/2017/1/4/14160956/trump-racism-sexism-economy-study, accessed January 16, 2017; Rupert Neate, "Donald Trump doubles down on Mexico 'rapists' comments despite outrage: Donald Trump, who has already lost business deals with five companies over his remarks, claims statistics show that Latino immigrants are more likely to rape," ***The Guardian***, July 2, 2015, https://www.theguardian.com/us-news/2015/jul/02/donald-trump-racist-claims-mexico-rapes, accessed February 7, 2017; Ben Jacobs, "Trump campaign: 'Nothing wrong' with banning Muslims from entering US," ***The Guardian***, December 7, 2015, https://www.theguardian.com/us-news/2015/dec/07/donald-trump-campaign-defends-muslim-ban-sam-clovis-interview, accessed February 7, 2017; Osamudia James, "Trump sees black America as a dystopian hellhole. So do most white people. Let's not pretend this misconception is found only on the fringe," ***Washington Post***, August 26, 2016, https://www.washingtonpost.com/posteverything/wp/2016/08/26/trump-sees-black-america-as-a-dystopian-hellhole-so-do-most-white-people/?utm_term=.30267b4770a9, accessed February 7, 2017.

67 Kliff, "Why Obamacare Enrollees Voted for Trump."

68 Brooke Seipel, "Obama: Rethink Your Biases if you Take Issue with Government Helping Minorities," ***The Hill***, December 13, 2016, http://thehill.com/blogs/blog-briefing-room/news/310304-obama-if-you-stopped-liking-big-government-once-it-served, accessed December 13, 2016.

69 Corey Brettschneider, "Why Trump's Immigration Rules Are Unconstitutional: Don't pay attention to the administration's spin. The law is clear," ***Politico***, February 01, 2017, http://www.politico.com/magazine/story/2017/02/why-trumps-immigration-rules-are-unconstitutional-214722, accessed February 6, 2017; Trevor Timm, "The Muslim ban has brought the US close to constitutional crisis: A series of troubling events since Friday's order have pushed the country into uncharted territory – and Stephen Bannon was central to the chaos," ***The Guardian***, January 30, 2017, https://www.theguardian.com/commentisfree/2017/jan/30/muslim-ban-consitutional-crisis, accessed February 6, 2017; Ann Wang, "Trump lashes out at 'so-called judge' who temporarily blocked travel ban," ***Washington Post***, February 4, 2017, https://www.washingtonpost.com/news/the-fix/wp/2017/02/04/trump-lashes-out-at-federal-judge-who-temporarily-blocked-travel-ban/?utm_term=.a0bf95559d5d, accessed February 6, 2017; Jon Finer, "Trump Is Attacking Any Institution That Challenges Him: The president has displayed a willingness to go after the press, the intelligence community, and now even the judiciary," ***The Atlantic***, February 5, 2017, https://www.theatlantic.com/politics/archive/2017/02/trump-is-attacking-any-institution-that-challenges-him/515727/, accessed February 6, 2017; Michael M. Grynbaum, "Trump Strategist Stephen Bannon Says Media Should 'Keep Its Mouth Shut,'" ***New York Times***, January 26, 2017, https://www.nytimes.com/2017/01/26/business/media/stephen-bannon-trump-news-media.html, accessed February 6, 2017; Nolan D. McCaskill, "Former NSC member Mullen: Steve Bannon doesn't belong on the National Security Council," ***Politico***, February 6, 2017, http://www.politico.com/story/2017/02/steve-bannon-no-

national-security-council-michael-mullen-234676, accessed February 6, 2017; "Report: Trump not fully briefed on exec order that gave Bannon seat at NSC meetings," Fox News, February 6, 2017, http://www.foxnews.com/politics/2017/02/06/report-trump-not-fully-briefed-on-exec-order-that-gave-bannon-seat-at-nsc-meetings.html, accessed February 6, 2017; Fred Kaplan, "Steve Bannon's Presence on the National Security Council Is Not Just Terrible. It's Illegal," *Slate*, February 1, 2017, http://www.slate.com/articles/news_and_politics/war_stories/2017/02/steve_bannon_doesn_t_belong_on_the_nsc_that_s_what_the_law_says.html, accessed February 6, 2017.

70 Jason Easley, "Trump Has The Highest Unfavorable Rating Of Any President-Elect In The Last 24 Years," *Politicus*, November 17, 2016, http://www.politicususa.com/2016/11/17/trump-highest-unfavorable-rating-president-elect-24-years.html, accessed January 16, 2017.

71 David Wasserman, "2016 Popular Vote," *Cook Political*, January 3, 2017, http://cookpolitical.com/story/10174, accessed January 16, 2017.

72 Barb Darrow, "Turns Out Attendance at Women's March Events Was Bigger Than Estimated," *Fortune*, January 23, 2017, http://fortune.com/2017/01/23/womens-march-crowd-estimates/, accessed February 6, 2017.

73 John Bacon and Alan Gomez, "Protests against Trump's immigration plan rolling in more than 30 cities," *USA Today*, January 29, 2017, http://www.usatoday.com/story/news/nation/2017/01/29/homeland-security-judges-stay-has-little-impact-travel-ban/97211720/, accessed February 6, 2017; Jennifer Peltz and Frank Eltman, "Volunteer Lawyers Have Descended on Major Airports After Trump's Immigration Order," *Time*, February 1, 2017, http://time.com/4656131/trump-immigration-lawyers-airports/, accessed February 7, 2017.

74 Katie Mettler, "The ACLU says it got $24 million in online donations this weekend, six times its yearly average," *Washington Post*,

January30,2017,https://www.washingtonpost.com/news/morning-mix/wp/2017/01/30/the-aclu-says-it-got-24-million-in-donations-this-weekend-six-times-its-yearly-average/?utm_term=.31f7afad4528, accessed February 7, 2017.

75 Lydia Wheeler and Mallory Shelbourne, "Anti-Devos calls jam Senate phone lines," ***The Hill***, January 26, 2017, http://thehill.com/homenews/administration/316321-anti-devos-calls-jam-senate-phone-lines, accessed February 7, 2017; "House GOP lawmakers face backlash in home districts over ObamaCare," Fox News, February 5, 2017, http://www.foxnews.com/politics/2017/02/05/house-gop-lawmakers-face-backlash-in-home-districts-over-obamacare.html, accessed February 7, 2017; Joy Resmovits, "Betsy DeVos 'is unprepared and unqualified' to be Education secretary, charter school booster Eli Broad says," ***Los Angeles Times***, February 1, 2017, http://www.latimes.com/local/education/la-me-eli-broad-opposes-devos-20170201-story.html, accessed February 7, 2017.

76 Donie O'Sullivan, "New Yorkers unite to scrub hateful graffiti from subway," CNN, February 6, 2017, http://www.cnn.com/2017/02/05/us/subway-nazi-graffiti-new-york-trnd/, accessed February 7, 2017.

77 Tina Nguyen, "Donald Trump Picks White-Nationalist Hero as Top White House Adviser: Stephen Bannon, who turned Breitbart News into a haven for racists and anti-Semites, will be Trump's chief strategist and senior counselor," ***Vanity Fair***, November 14, 2016, http://www.vanityfair.com/news/2016/11/steve-bannon-donald-trump-white-house-advisor, accessed February 7, 2017; Paul Krugman, "America Becomes a Stan," ***New York Times***, January 2, 2017, http://www.nytimes.com/2017/01/02/opinion/america-becomes-a-stan.html?_r=0, accessed January 2, 2017; Adam Gopnik, "The Music Donald Trump Can't Hear," ***New Yorker***, January 13, 2017, http://www.newyorker.com/news/daily-comment/the-music-donald-trump-cant-hear, accessed January 16, 2017; Jelani Cobb, "The Return of Civil Disobedience: The sixties

produced a conviction that 'democracy is in the streets,' the Trump era may echo that," *New Yorker*, January 7, 2017, http://www.newyorker.com/magazine/2017/01/09/the-return-of-civil-disobedience, accessed January 17, 2017.

78 Vishal Agraharkar, Wendy Weiser, and Adam Skaggs, ***The Cost of Voter ID Laws: What the Courts Say*** (New York: Brennan Center for Justice, 2011); WALB, "GA Faces Budget Deficit and More Cuts," http://www.walb.com/story/20548798/ga-faces-budget-deficit-and-more-cuts, accessed November 20, 2015; Josh Israel, "Scott Walker's Voter Suppression Plan Would Cost $5.2 Million, Election Board Finds," ***Think Progress***, December 11, 2012, http://thinkprogress.org/justice/2012/12/11/1317681/non-partisan-wisconsin-election-board-scott-walkers-plan-to-end-same-day-voter-registration-would-cost-52-million, accessed November 27, 2015; James Salzer, "More Budget Cuts Ahead for State Health Care, Universities," ***Atlanta Journal Constitution***, August 3, 2012, http://www.ajc.com/news/news/state-regional-govt-politics/more-budget-cuts-ahead-for-state-health-care-unive/nQXjK, accessed November 20, 2015; Tami Luhby, "Gov. Scott Walker Unveils Wisconsin Budget: Plans Major Cuts to Schools and Municipalities," CNN Financial, March 1, 2011, http://money.cnn.com/2011/03/01/news/economy/wisconsin_budget_walker/index.htm, accessed November 27, 2015.

79 Georgia Civil Rights Cold Cases Project at Emory University, https://scholarblogs.emory.edu/emorycoldcases, accessed November 20, 2015.

80 Mathias, "NYPD Stop and Frisks," ***Huffington Post***.

81 Joe Davidson, "Caged Cargo," ***The Best of Emerge Magazine***, ed. George E. Curry (New York: Ballantine Books, 2003), 252–61.

82 Monica Anderson, "Vast Majority of Blacks View the Criminal Justice System as Unfair," Pew Research Center, August 12, 2014, http://www.pewresearch.org/fact-tank/2014/08/12/vast-majority-of-blacks-view-the-criminal-justice-system-as-unfair, accessed November 27, 2015.

83 "Full Coverage: State Budget Crisis," ***Los Angeles Times***, November 20, 2015, http://www.latimes.com/local/la-me-state-budget-sg-storygallery.html, accessed November 20, 2015; "California's Budget Crisis, Overcrowded Prisons Lead to Easier Parole for Convicted Felons," ***New York Daily News***, March 24, 2010, http://www.nydailynews.com/news/national/california-budget-crisis-overcrowded-prisons-lead-easier-parole-convicted-felons-article-1.172320, accessed November 20, 2015; Neil King Jr., "As Prisons Squeeze Budgets, GOP Rethinks Crime Focus," ***Wall Street Journal***, June 21, 2013, http://www.wsj.com/articles/ SB10001424127887323836504578551902602217018, accessed November 27, 2015.

84 Oliver Laughland, Jon Swaine, and Jamiles Lartey, "US Police Killings Headed for 1,100 This Year, with Black Americans Twice as Likely to Die," ***The Guardian***, July 1, 2015, http://www.theguardian.com/us-news/2015/jul/01/us-police-killings-this-year-black-americans, accessed November 27, 2015; Susan Carlson, "City Leaders, Emanuel Hold Emergency Meeting Ahead of Release of Laquan McDonald Video: Community Leaders Have Called on the Mayor to Keep the Peace out of Fear That the Release of the Controversial Footage Could Spark Citywide Riots," November 23, 2015, http://www.nbcchicago.com/news/local/City-Leaders-Call-on-Emanuel-Ahead-of-Release-of-Laquan-McDonald-Video-353009351.html, accessed November 26, 2015; "Tensions Rise in Chicago After Release of Video Showing Police Killing of Laquan McDonald," ***The Guardian***, November 25, 2015, http://www.theguardian.com/us-news/2015/nov/24/laquan-mcdonald-police-killing-chicago-video-released, accessed November 26, 2015; Mark Guarino and Justin Wm. Moyer, "Chicago Protesters Confront Police, Shut Down Interstate After Release of Laquan McDonald Video," ***Washington Post***, November 25, 2015, https://www.washingtonpost.com/news/morning-mix/wp/2015/11/25/chicago-protesters-confront-police-shut-down-interstate-after-release-of-laquan-cdonald-video,

accessed November 26, 2015; "BCA: Video of Jamar Clark Shooting Doesn't Show Everything," November 17, 2015, http://www.kare11.com/story/news/crime/2015/11/17/bca-video-of-jamar-clark-doesnt-show-entire-incident/75947500, accessed November 26, 2015.

Index

White Rage

Carol Anderson

The following questions are intended to enhance your discussion of *White Rage*.

For Discussion

1. Having read this book, how would you define the phrase "white rage" (also consider the definition of "racism")? Does the idea of white rage evolve as the book progresses forward in time? What role would those with white rage prefer African Americans to take on in society?
2. What assumptions about African Americans, U.S. politics/history, and race relations did you have coming into this book? Does Anderson's work contradict or support these assumptions? In what ways does Anderson's writing push against a more mainstream way of talking about these issues, and why does that make this an important text?
3. The book starts with the Reconstruction Era and moves forward mostly chronologically. What other historical eras are discussed? Why did Anderson choose this span of time to examine? How does that scope focus her argument?
4. For some, legality and morality might intersect—but there are many instances in this book where Anderson shows lawmakers, judges, and politicians using the law to serve their

white rage. Discuss some instances in which this occurs. What does this say about our system of government? Are there complications in the system that need to be addressed? In regard to the debate about states' rights, does the divvying of federal powers and state powers hamper the fight for African Americans' equality?

5. How has a legacy of slavery followed African Americans into present day? What other systems have been put into place to mimic the power dynamics of slavery? Consider, for example, the U.S. system of incarceration and voting/voter suppression. How can these systems be altered?
6. What role has the media played in perpetuating violence and inequity against African Africans? Have there been cases in which the media has assisted African Americans in their quest for equality? What does it mean to have media that is predominantly white versus media that includes the voices of people of color?
7. How have African Americans approached ideals of education? How have their rights to education been compromised by white rage? For those African Americans with access to education, how and when do they engage with ideas of "black respectability"? Does "black respectability" undermine African American achievement?
8. Is it possible to discuss racial politics without considering issues of class? How do the two intersect? For African American populations does the idea of the American Dream ever come to fruition?
9. What is the importance of understanding the history of African American suppression in the United States as the country moves deeper into the twenty-first century? How can analyzing this history help promote empathy and better circumstances for African Americans? Are there other ways in which reading this history can be beneficial?

10. Revisit the book cover design. How does it introduce the book and its themes? Think about the image and the color scheme in relation to the broader work. Did the cover affect the way you approached the book? What emotions does the cover evoke in you?

Recommended Reading

Racial Formation in the United States: From the 1960s to the 1990s by Michael Omi and Howard Winant; *Buried in the Bitter Waters: The Hidden History of Racial Cleansing in America* by Elliot Jaspin; *From the War on Poverty to the War on Crime: The Making of Mass Incarceration in America* by Elizabeth Hinton; *The Possessive Investment In Whiteness* by George Lipsitz; *The New Jim Crow: Mass Incarceration in the Age of Colorblindness* by Michelle Alexander; *Stamped from the Beginning: The Definitive History of Racist Ideas in America* by Ibram X. Kendi

A Note on the Author

Carol Anderson is the Charles Howard Candler Professor and Chair of African American Studies at Emory University. She is the author of many books and articles, including *Bourgeois Radicals: The NAACP and the Struggle for Colonial Liberation, 1941–1960*, and *Eyes off the Prize: The United Nations and the African American Struggle for Human Rights: 1944–1955*. She lives in Atlanta, Georgia.